BISECTION

A more or less accurate account of bipolar parenting and twin-wrangling

Kenton Hall

First Published in 2019
This third edition published in 2021 by
Chinbeard Books
www.chinbeardbooks.com

Layout and adaptation by
Andrews UK Limited
www.andrewsuk.com

Contents

Prologue v

1: Baby, Baby 1
2: Toddling Towards Bethlehem. 16
3: Growing Pains 29
4: Sins of the Father. 42
5: Scholasticus Fantasticus. 64
6: A Number of Beasts 77
7: Faith Accompli. 87
8: An Unexpected Inquisition 105
Intermission. 121
9: Future-Proofing 122
10: National Expression 137
11: These Things Will Not Bite You... 157
12: Reel to Real 173
13: Teenage Mutant Ninja Hurdles 192
14: Fifty Ways to Lose Your Marbles 209
16: The Beginning of the Mend 218
16: And What Do You Get? 229

Epilogue 238
Acknowledgments 241
Index. 245
Post-Script. 251
About the Author. 252
By the Same Human 253

AFJ
(love letters)

And to Fathead and Baldy — I swear this is the last thing I'm going to write about you and, yes, I've transferred the money.

Prologue

I have bipolar disorder, two teenaged daughters and a long-term relationship with the Arts that is borderline abusive on both sides.

That's the author's bio out of the way; I should probably attempt to write the rest of the book.

It's not as easy as it sounds. Which is not to say that it necessarily sounds easy. You may, for instance, have an intense fear of paper that would render the entire enterprise a clown-infested nightmare from first word to last. Or, perhaps, you are good at something less hideously insecure than writing and are, therefore, busy installing a cocktail bar into your new yacht.

It is difficult for me, specifically, because, until recently, I had no intention of writing this book at all.

Or anything. Ever again.

A few years ago, I wrote and directed a feature film based on my experiences as a parent, at that time, of two twelve-year-old girls. It was an ambitious project, with a budget that would barely cover the lighting department's sandwiches on any other movie, and it was a labour of love. Then hate. Then love again. Then chiefly hate, with a flicker of lingering affection.

Similar then, to most of my relationships.

If you care to seek it out, I'm not averse to it making its money back in three or four hundred years—I could buy some fresh sandwiches—but, on the advice of multiple mental health professionals, I've drawn a line under it.

Indeed, it is germane to this conversation for one reason and one reason alone.

It broke me.

I'd been broken before, as you will learn. There are periods of my life during which it more-or-less qualified as my profession, but it had never happened quite like this. Maybe it was because I was older and there seemed so much less time to rebuild, or perhaps I was just supremely tired of fighting and failing, rinsing and repeating.

What I do know was that I was, for the first time ever, in serious danger of losing my sense of humour.

Parenting saved both it and me.

After several months of maintaining that I would never again tackle anything longer than a grocery list, I was coaxed into writing again by a suggestion from my doctor that I keep a mood diary. The juxtaposition of those two words made me rightly nauseous, but I was dedicated to my recovery and so, every day, for about a year, I wrote an online journal. I tried to be as honest as I could about how I felt, what I saw and who I was. I also chose to do it for an audience, which should tell you a lot.

Unsurprisingly, it started out as rather depressing reading and I seriously considered covering myself legally by including some hotline numbers in the footer.

Slowly, though, jokes started to creep back in, and the surreal voices in my head that had always ducked and dived through slings and arrows, began to sing once more. Chiefly "The Piña Colada Song" for some reason, but we'll explore that in more detail the next time we walk in the rain.

In the course of rediscovering my muse, I slowly realised that my favourite subject was still my daughters.

Partially out of love and wonder—for and at their intelligence, their sensitivity and their accomplishments—but mostly because I think they are insane.

Honestly, from what I can gather, being sixteen makes bipolar disorder look like an Amish rave.

Now, they will be the first and second to tell you, fiercely and repeatedly, that what I write about them is not always factually accurate.

I have a couple of things to say about that.

Firstly, I have to admit that, due to the nature of my condition, my memory can be a bit of a loose cannon. So, while I am fairly confident that everything between these pages happened, it is entirely possible that some of it didn't happen exactly, or with as many explosions, as I describe. Then again, it's equally likely that I've toned some of it down, for believability.

Secondly, I maintain there is a greater truth to which I am beholden, which is, of course, what I consider to be funnier.

It all has the side effect of removing this volume from the realms of pure autobiography, which is to everyone's benefit. For starters, you have no idea who I am, which would completely stress out the marketing department and they've already got that sick cat to worry about. Also, I once went into a bookstore that had a "Painful Lives" section and however messed up my childhood was, I don't want any part of that.

My parents didn't even have an attic.

Not every word to follow will be about the children—however many notes they write in the margins when they think I'm not looking. Nor will the book entirely concern itself with the ins and outs—or, for that matter, ups and downs—of bipolar disorder.

It is simply the story of one man whose head may have been wired by cowboys but who has found a modicum of joy in wondering why there is a cold cup of tea underneath the sofa.

And if I've learned one thing about life, I'm hoping that I'll remember what it is in the process of telling it.

1: Baby, Baby

My children were born on a January day in 2002. I was twenty-five and they were a fair bit younger, an arrangement which seemed to suit everyone concerned.

Because I am unreasonably fond of understatement, I would classify my mental state at the time as troubled.

I am, you see, the product of a mixed marriage. My father is a psychopath and my mother is a sociopath. They shared, however, a common belief that the other was responsible for most of the world's ills. Despite this, or perhaps because of it, they managed to produce six children over the course of their 21-year marriage, in what can only be described as an arms race.

They also shared a religion, the kind that suited two people with limited funds, undiagnosed mental illnesses and enough repressed rage to power a small industrial town.

It was—and is—one of those faiths that thrive on making ordinary folk feel special, chosen and guaranteed a ringside seat when the Almighty next relapses into an Old Testament fury.

Needless to say, my childhood was challenging.

We'll skirt around the details, for the most part; it's not that kind of book. Besides, I'm never sure how to pitch it. It's not unusual for me to begin what I consider to be a humorous anecdote about my formative years, only to look up and find that my audience is either weeping openly or feverishly starting online petitions.

The key takeaway, for now, is that I was determined to be a better parent than either of my own had been. It was a low bar and I had a decent run-up, so I felt fairly confident that it could be done. However, when the opportunity finally presented itself, I was terrified.

Obviously, most prospective parents have concerns. They worry about money, about the effect a child will have on their relationship, about how pointy the edges of everything they own have suddenly become and, especially, about making mistakes they can't walk back.

I worried because I had always wanted children and I have a terrible history when it comes to getting what I want.

There is a memory to which I often return. I must have been about twelve or thirteen and I was ice-skating. I am Canadian, so this was not uncommon. We try to fit in as many cold weather activities as we can, so we can chuckle politely to ourselves when people from other countries bitch about the weather.

As I slid around the rink, in a not-at-all ungainly or borderline dangerous fashion, I spotted a young couple skating in formation, joined at the mittens by a toddler that I assumed, not wanting to get the police involved, was their own.

My heart thudded in my chest. They looked so happy. So much in love. A *family* and, better still, one that appeared to be the polar opposite of mine, in that no one member was threatening another with the wrath of God.

Also, and this thought I put down to the fact that I was about five years into early onset puberty, I knew that the mother and the father must have done *certain things* in order to have acquired their bundled-up, chubby-faced offspring.

Throw in a couple of critically-acclaimed novels, a hit record or two, Winona Ryder's telephone number and a recurring role on *The Muppet Show* and it was pretty much my ideal life.

A decade later, I had fled to another country, tucked an acrimonious divorce under my belt, chalked up somewhere between two and twelve major nervous breakdowns and was working my way through a series of jobs that, while good, honest labour, taxed my intellect in much the same way as America taxes billionaires.

Things had not gone to plan. Well, not a good plan, anyway.

I hadn't been officially bipolar for long—the application process is long and convoluted—but the signs had been there since early childhood and it had come as a surprise to few. My father, as it happens, had been diagnosed a few years previously, but resisted treatment, finding the side effects unpleasant. Not as unpleasant as we found him, I'd wager, but having subsequently experienced them for myself, I empathise to a degree. At the time, however, I was too busy losing my own mind to think too much about it.

Still, can't say he never gave me anything.

Thankfully, I proved to be far more sensible about my health and had in no way stopped taking my meds because I felt that they were inhibiting my creativity.

No, sir, not me.

I had also developed a theory about breakfast drinking that I wuld still stand by, had it not lead to such an awful lot of lying down. Anything you could successfully mix with fruit, my argument ran, was a perfectly acceptable way to kick-start the day.

All in all, on a scale of one to chiropteran guano, I was quite, quite mad.

The perfect time, therefore, to discover that I had participated in the creation of not one, but two, count them, two additional human beings.

Now, this is where the story becomes difficult to tell in this form, because there are, as you might imagine, other people involved.

The children, for instance, have a mother. She's exceptional at the job and, indeed, currently leads the ex-wife league table, scoring particularly highly in "still speaking to me".

She did not, however, sign up to have her life dissected because I needed an extra thousand words in this chapter.

Nor did their subsequent stepmother, who could not be more supportive of, besotted with, or loving towards children that she inherited through her lamentable choice in men.

I'm a single Dad, in other words, but I'm not suggesting for a moment that I've done any of this parenting on my own.

My life has been enriched and affected by a lot of folk, in fact, but, as I only really have the right to talk about myself, I will keep their cameos to a minimum. Even the children only appear because they are super-vain and would get offended if I left them out.

In any case, it's fewer characters for you to keep track of.

You're welcome.

***

So, let's recap. I'm twenty-five, mentally unwell, recently escaped from a cult and about to become a father.

Clear so far?

Good, because it's time to welcome the true protagonists to the stage.

Enter Fathead and Baldy.

These, obviously, are not their real names, although a quick glance at my CV, which I'm sure I've included somewhere on the cover in an attempt to make myself look interesting, will confirm that I am exactly the type of person who cannot be trusted with nomenclature, but would totally call a child that.

Fathead and Baldy are, however, what I called them when they were small. I still do, on occasion, when I want to annoy them.

Thanks to the wonders of sleep-deprivation there is little room for subtlety

3

during the early days of parenthood, so they gained these nicknames the old-fashioned way. At the time of their birth, one of them had an enormous bloody head and the other looked like the before photo in an ad for minoxidil.

Of course, they changed over the years. Bodies quickly caught up with heads and hairs turned up in droves. Eventually, they would gain other affectionate monikers, more suited to their current development. However, they started out as Fathead and Baldy so, for our purposes, thus they will remain.

It's much better than the first words I applied to them, which were of a more spontaneous nature.

"Fucking hell!"

The twin thing had been, to put it mildly, a surprise, as there had been no indication of the possibility in either lane of the gene pool. When I was younger, I had nursed a suspicion, based on the yawning void I sometimes sensed within myself, that I was actually the surviving member of a pair of twins, but I was probably just hungry.

Regardless, here they were, and there was no denying that there was more than one of them. My sobriety being what it was, I took an opinion poll, just to make sure, until the nurse on the ward asked me to stop.

I did as I was told. I shut my mouth and just stared.

Everyone tells you that the moment you see your child for the first time, your entire life changes. I never really knew what they meant, and, to be honest, at least one of those people swore by the healing power of crystals, so I was reserving judgement.

In this case, however, even Hippie McWhackjob was right on the money. Every trace of the man I'd been—every selfish impulse, every ill-conceived scheme, every artistic indulgence—disappeared as I gazed down on my newly-arrived daughters.

Just kidding. I was still a madman, but I was suddenly and irretrievably *their* madman, from that moment until the end of recorded time.

People talk a good game about unconditional love, but it's usually because they haven't yet encountered the particular set of conditions that form its outer boundaries. In romantic relationships, this may be wilful misconduct in the wet towel arena or it may be the discovery of neatly parcelled human remains in the chest freezer, next to the leftover mince.

The moment, however, my children were born, I knew that they could torch a convent for sport and I would bury the smouldering habits, in the dead of night, before checking if they needed money to buy more petrol.

I'm not suggesting this is healthy, and I still hope their childhood love

4

of Pingu will prevent too much in the way of hot cross nuns, but that's how strong the bond is.

For instance, I have never killed them. Not once. Not even that time when they took apart the TARDIS playset I had spent the best part of a Christmas Day constructing, and refashioned it into a hot tub for Barbie.

That's love.

***

When people find out you have twins, they invariably have questions.

"How did you manage with two babies?"

"Are they identical?"

"Did you dress them the same?"

"Haven't you seen *The Shining*?"

The answers to two, three and four are: "Yes and No", "Did I fuck" and "Not for a very, very long time".

As to how one copes with simultaneous newborns, it's less cut-and-dry.

True, the benefit of infants, especially the fresh ones, is that they're pretty useless at running away, so you can put, like, nine of them on a reasonably flat surface and they'll probably still be there when you get back. It's when they start heading in opposite directions that twins become coronary-inciting.

Nonetheless, looking after any flavour of child is undeniably difficult. It carries with it an enormous, multifactorial responsibility, perhaps best and most simply expressed as "Keep this idiot alive."

My intention is not to insult babies, of course. They are a group with an illustrious past and much to teach us. But, let's be honest, they aren't terribly bright. Their concept of geography is rudimentary at best, their general knowledge is non-existent and their capacity for self-expression lacks detail to a laughable degree.

Imagine if I made the same noise for "I'm hungry" and "I appear to have shat myself" and forced you, under threat of criminal prosecution, to physically explore which I meant.

Exactly. It's not on.

And don't even get me started on their opiate-level addiction to damaging themselves. I'd assume it was deliberate if we hadn't already established that there is a negligible difference, intellectually-speaking, between a baby and a rock with big, googly eyes stuck on it.

This is the real reason why parents continually crow about their children's achievements.

5

"Oh, she's so clever," they hold forth, in a slightly hysterical tone, "She said her first word at nine months. We couldn't believe it. We think she may be gifted."

Now, if you believe that your children are special, I'm not going to argue with you. I won't even take issue with you informing the rest of us, loudly and insistently, of your conviction on that score. I regularly tell people how clever my children are, and I've seen them walk into walls on multiple occasions.

But the obvious translation of such declarations, the dark, subconscious undercurrent, is clearly: "Thank fuck. We thought there was something wrong with it."

You grasp at straws with babies, because you have no idea if you're doing anything right and you're painfully aware you won't know for absolute certain until it's too late and they are either most likely to succeed or most wanted.

So, what was the difference with twins? Basically, "keep this idiot alive" became "keep these idiots alive".

The children's mother had gone directly back to work following her maternity leave, as I was, at the time, a touring musician and therefore had the approximate earning capacity of a shackle manufacturer at an Amnesty International Open Day. It made, therefore, financial—if not actual—sense for me to handle the day-to-day.

I'm grateful for that time, of course, because it was the beginning of the close, honest relationship I have with my daughters, wherein I remind them daily of everything I've ever done and continue to do for them and they reply, hands on hearts, with "It's your own fault for having children".

It's sad to think that, even in this age of increased equality and the breaking down of arbitrary gender barriers, there are some fathers who, willingly or not, miss out on these foundational stages of their child's development.

It is even sadder that, due to continuing pay disparity and long-held societal prejudices, some mothers miss out on the opportunity of more rapidly returning to the land of the living.

I have as much of a fragile ego as anyone, male or otherwise, but being a stay-at-home Dad didn't bother me in the slightest. To be fair, I was still working, either touring with the band or pulling night shifts behind various bars. From time to time, I even ventured boldly into other fields, such as flogging conservatories or attaching bits of metal to other bits of metal for no reason that was ever adequately explained to me.

Nonetheless, I revelled in my day job. Look at me, I said. Verily, I am the very model of a marvellous modern male: secure in my sexuality, willing to sacrifice my career aspirations for the sake of my children and, most importantly, ready and willing to work diligently on my physical and mental health, so as to provide a stable environment in which said children can flourish.

And I wasn't going to let the fact that I was absolutely none of these things get in my way.

Here is a good example of how my brain worked at the time:

Upon discovery that my children were nine months off and marching, I was overcome by a tsunami of good intentions.

"I shall," I proclaimed, "quit smoking."

It is worth noting that, unmedicated, I proclaim a lot of things. It comes with the territory. I have also been known to growl, to hiss, and sometimes, on particularly bad days, to mutter darkly in Latin.

I hadn't been smoking long. One of the tenets of the religion in which I had been raised was that members were only permitted one vice, one thing that was demonstrably bad for them. And, as belonging to the religion in the first place rather neatly fit that description, you were press-ganged into a sort of frenzied clean living.

Thanks to this, I was violently anti-smoking as a child, the kind of self-righteous little bastard who would sidle up to people and start coughing up a lung to make my point. Of course, I realise now that the only reason I survived doing this was because the people in question were blissed out on nicotine

One night, however, about two years before the girls were born, I was handed a cigarette by someone who suggested it might help me to, if I may be forgiven a lapse into medical jargon, "chill the fuck out".

It was like discovering a long-lost friend. Only better, because you didn't have to ask how its day had been or help it move a sofa.

By the following day, I had my own pack of twenty on my hip and a whole new appreciation for life. I wondered, at times aloud, how smoking had failed to make Julie Andrews' list.

The moment I heard I was going to be a father, however, I foreswore those precious tubes of life-giving muck, stuck "Cold Turkey" on repeat and waited for the emotional validation of family and friends to roll gloriously in.

It lasted three-and-a-half days. I came home one night to find a packet of Benson & Hedges taped to the outside of the window, along with a note saying, "Smoke these before you attempt to speak to me again."

So, I started smoking outside instead. Compromise is important.

Years later, I would finally give up when one of my daughters took to phoning me late at night and whispering "you're going to die" in lieu of "hello".

7

Anyway, if I had to sum up my parenting approach at the time, it would sound something like this:

"This is how I am going to do it. I shall brook no argument on the subject. I have considered it carefully, from every conceivable angle, and there is no doubt in my mind that this is the best way to proceed. And, by the way, how awesome am I for being the first person ever to think of it in the entire history of human relations?"

Obviously, that was never going to work, but it didn't stop me from being smug. Little did.

Except, of course, the actual parenting.

Looking after children for any length of time teaches you many things, the foremost of which is that you are a moron.

It's an important lesson to learn. You may think you're hot stuff because you own a guitar and someone once let you see them naked, but the first time you find yourself smeared in another human's faeces, sober, you will be thoroughly disabused of the notion.

The ego heals swiftly, however. Despite having survived by the skin of their teething, our subconscious—to forestall a lifetime of gibbering to itself—represses the sense of utter helplessness and replaces it with a distinct memory of having been splendid from the off. Naturally, having discovered this innate expertise in child-rearing, we feel a deep-seated obligation to pay it forward.

How those who remain in the diaper-strewn foxhole react to this advice is entirely dependent on the proximity of their cutlery.

They aren't the only source of unsolicited counsel, of course. My estrangement from my own parents invariably inspires a condescending look and a rote observation: "They're still your Mum and Dad. They'll have tried their best. When you have your own children, you'll understand."

A greater degree of inaccuracy is difficult to imagine. I understood less. I couldn't contemplate treating my girls the way I had been treated—not without, at least, a severe head injury and a dose of demonic possession. I would certainly never elevate the demands of a short-tempered imaginary friend above the obvious needs of these tiny people placed into my charge.

Nor would I make them pay, if I could help it, for the unique way in which my cerebral cortex had been compiled. I had everyone else in my life for that.

No, I was going to make entirely new mistakes of my own devising. And they were going to be epic.

Here are a few things I accomplished during the first year of my daughters' lives:

8

Once, while changing their nappies, I lost one of them down the side of the bed, where she had decided to roll when my back was turned. Despite this happening within the span of twelve seconds, and her long distance record, to date, being about a centimetre-and-a-half, I nonetheless searched the entire room before finding her.

On another occasion, I was exiting a bus with their pushchair, one of those obscenely wide, double-seated monstrosities designed to enrage childless people who are just trying to get to an overpriced frappuccino before the barista they fancy goes off shift.

If you've ever taken that trip, you'll feel my pain. I have a mental illness and unmanageable hair and I have never felt as judged as I used to when travelling on public transport with infants.

Psychic researchers are missing a trick here. Empirical evidence for the existence of telepathy is theirs for the taking—they need only interview one parent with a buggy, waiting at a bus stop. The passengers' hatred arrives a good ten minutes before they do. You can *taste* it. If it's a busy route, you may also suffer vomiting and nose bleeds.

By the time the bus actually pulls in to pick you up, heads have craned, in concert, towards the window, eyes lit with cold fury. When the doors shush open, the temperature drops by twenty degrees.

If you had a choice, you'd scarper. But you don't. You were four hours behind schedule before you even left the house.

So, you wrestle your precious cargo aboard, as a low incantation begins: "For fuck's sake. For fuck's sake. For fuck's sake."

This is punctuated by a rhythmic tap of watches, a pan-pipe choir of angry sighs and the tap of the driver's foot, temptingly close to the accelerator.

Even when you have finally managed to lift, push, shove and twist into the area set aside for you, dislodging any discontents who have annexed it, your ordeal is not yet complete.

You sit quietly, staring at the floor and willing the children not to start crying. You count stops in your head. If you're feeling particularly bold, you occasionally look up and smile at other passengers, reassuring them that you're aware of the trouble you've caused them and are suitably contrite.

It doesn't help if, at twenty-five, you look twelve, and can, therefore, hear furious and poorly-spelled letters to the *Daily Mail* being composed in at least a dozen outraged heads.

There is no 'k' in scrounger, in case you were wondering.

To prove I'd learned my lesson, I found it useful to keep a selection of leaflets about vasectomies to hand, which I would pretend to read, underlining key passages and making approving noises.

On this particular day, I was already on edge, as the girls had recently decided that, as twins, they needed to explore their individuality, lest they become irreversibly co-dependent.

Their plan involved sleeping in shifts. One would pass out for an hour or so, often face-first into the carpet, while the other seized the opportunity to repeatedly interrogate me about something that was obviously of the utmost urgency, before screaming the house down when I answered incorrectly.

I would attempt to steal a twenty-minute nap during the brief crossovers, but my days and nights largely consisted of staring bleary-eyed into one or the other's face and offering increasingly random rejoinders in the hope of identifying what they were on about and what, exactly, they wanted me to do about it.

"Milk?"

"Nappy?"

"Dummy?"

"Søren Kierkegaard?"

Leaving the house was a Herculean endeavour, complete with furious Hydra.

This time, however, I'd managed to get them on the bus without excessive trauma, we were nearing our destination and I'd soon be able to find somewhere to whimper quietly to myself. Which was good, as I'd already so heavily underscored *vas deferens* that the pen was about to go through the paper.

The bus pulled to the stop and I leapt from my seat to begin the extrication process, lest a riot break out that Ken Loach would feel compelled to immortalise on film.

I succeeded in record time and stood at the open doors, relative freedom tantalisingly close. With a flourish, I pushed the buggy towards the outside world.

And it flipped over.

In time-honoured slow motion, the front wheels fell between the bus and the curb, lodged tight, and propelled the whole shebang head-over-heels. Its handles hit the street opposite and it settled there, upside-down.

For at least fourteen seconds, I was legally dead.

There was a chilling lack of noise. That, or it had been drowned out by the collective gasp from within the bus—sure, *now* they cared—and the single, forceful invocation, by the driver, of his Lord and Saviour.

Somehow, my corpse reanimated for long enough to leap from the bus, fall to its knees, and fearing the worst, look under the buggy.

Fathead and Baldy hung there, on their safety straps, entirely uninjured and giggling to themselves. They glanced over at me and, I swear this is how I remember it, said, in tandem, their joint first word.

"Again!"

I'd like to offer my final example in the form of a warning.

If you ever hang one of those elasticated swings in your home—the kind designed so that your baby can bounce up and down in a convenient doorway while you lie facedown on the couch and desperately try to remember why unprotected sex had seemed like such a good idea at the time—and you fail to fasten one of the straps because you haven't slept for three months and would be hard-pressed to recall your middle name or postcode and the baby, as a result, tips to one side and falls on its head, don't ever tell them.

It might seem like a funny story in retrospect, but I promise you, they will never let you forget it.

∗∗∗

I said I wouldn't delve too deeply into areas of my life that involved others, and I intend to stick to that.

However, this is a story that is as much about my experiences with bipolar disorder as with parenting, and I can't escape the fact that between my illness, my upbringing and my remarkable capacity for dramatic absurdity, my personal life outside of the children has contained a number of Shyamalan-style twists.

In other words, they made no sense and most people who were paying attention saw them coming.

During the first year of the children's lives, while genuinely preoccupied by the sea-change of fatherhood, I was also busy on the blueprints for my latest attempt at self-destruction.

I am nothing if not a multi-tasker.

It involved at least one ill-advised, if sincere, romantic entanglement, a bullish disregard for societal norms, a potent cocktail of self-esteem issues and body dysmorphia and a mercifully brief flirtation with illicit intoxicants that led me to steal all of the spoons from a motorway services as a protest against what I saw as poor customer service.

If humour is, as Mark Twain probably didn't say, tragedy plus time and insanity is, as Einstein probably didn't say, doing the same thing over and over and expecting different results, then I probably didn't say I warned you.

But I might.

By the Bi

So, bipolar disorder.

What can I possibly tell you about it that Stephen Fry hasn't already said better and more charmingly?

Let's start with preconceptions.

I've read many stories by authors who grew up with bipolar parents and there are recurrent themes that give me pause. The foremost being the Jekyll and Hyde concept of the "fun" parent versus the "shockingly abusive crazy-cakes" parent.

I don't doubt any of these accounts because I am also the child of a bipolar parent and I can vouch for the phenomenon. Obviously, in my case, it was complicated by the kind of close, personal relationship with God that historically leads to flambéed French teenagers, but such is the rich tapestry of life.

I'd like to believe that I didn't entirely fit this bill, but I'm sure I had my moments.

I certainly think I was a fun parent when the twins were small. Many were the evenings we would sit on the living room floor, as I wove vast Homeric epics for various Barbies and Their Little Ponies, doing all the voices and wearing out their patience because I kept forgetting to let them have a turn.

On other occasions, I fear, I strayed deep into man-child territory, forcing others, with whom the children may or may not have had a more-or-less maternal relationship, to play the bad guy more often than was fair.

And, equally, there were times when I would become tearful, irritable and, to my shame, fierce. Once, having reached breaking point, I picked up one of the girls by the lapels and shouted at her in a way that, in the moment, distressed her greatly but, thankfully, with the passage of time, only torments me.

But I like to think that the fact that we can now discuss these moments openly means that they were sufficiently rare as to be the exception rather than the rule.

I often ask them now if they had good childhoods and after rolling their eyes and asking if I'm having a mid-life crisis, they always confirm that they were, overall, happy with the service.

It could have been so much worse. More through luck than judgement, my illness never presented as "take them out of school and head to Argentina", for which I'm thankful. And, for all my doubts, I had learned something from my own experiences, and I was never abusive or cruel.

This isn't to say that odd ideas and grandiose schemes did not occur. They did, frequently. At one point, I was thoroughly convinced that I was going to send them both to university on marmot-herding scholarships.

This is, of course, is patently delusional. Marmots are self-starters.

And it is here where my stress levels peak. Much of what is wrong with me—not all, but much—is a direct result of being sold wholesale codswallop by people who had my absolute trust.

These days, I audit myself carefully to ensure that what I tell the children is both factual and useful, and not just something I have convinced myself to be the case through repetition.

My father, with whom I share not just an illness, but a propensity for long-winded storytelling, was a bastard for this. It's taken me years to unpick the difference between what was actually true and what he absolutely, positively believed to be true, but was, in fact, utter bollocks.

Examples of the latter include everything from the existence of government agencies who would, one day, torture the Chosen, to the tale of the stuffed Smurf who, possessed by the Devil, once walked out of a Bible study group in disgust.

He, at least, had the excuse that his brain was predisposed towards accepting anecdotal nonsense as documentary. One can only guess at the motivations of the people who told him this stuff with a straight face.

At this point, I think, it would be a good idea to answer the question which is, even now, flexing its muscles and preparing to leap from your full and well-defined lips.

"But what *is* this bipolar disorder about which you continue to bleat?"

Well, now. There are dictionary definitions and medical delineations that I'm sure you can access without my help. And I'm certainly not going to enable your laziness. It's holding you back and you know it.

But there are a few personal observations that I will offer.

In the simplest terms, I have a mood disorder that means that I suffer from both manic episodes and depressive episodes.

Again, these are terms that are easy to type, but less easy to define. I think that people imagine that bipolar people swing between happy and sad. Whereas, in reality, happy and sad have little or nothing to do with it.

Without many, many pills to level me out, I ping between Sylvia Plath receiving a Ted Hughes anthology for her birthday and Tigger on PCP.

13

The road to Tiggeritude is wonderful, I won't deny it. You feel like nothing can stop you. There is Vaseline smeared on every lens, each significant moment is scored by Rodgers and Hammerstein, and every decision you make is sure to lead to nuclear disarmament and personal wealth.

But it's like being on a runaway train.

"My, what beautiful scenery."

"Wow, what a rush!"

"Who's driving this thing?!"

"Sweet Jesus! Why aren't we stopping?!"

"Is that a wall?"

Your mind speeds up, which means that, at first, you feel quick, sharp and clever. Then quicker, sharper and cleverer. Then you think you're Stephen Hawking. And then you think you're Jesus Christ.

And then you can't think at all and it feels like your head is on fire and you want to cry—you want someone to hold you, to hold you down, but you can't stop laughing and your teeth won't unclench and you don't know why you bought that boat, or got quite so drunk at lunchtime, or copped off with that couple you met outside Primark. And your last remaining cogent thought is: "Please, somebody make it stop. Please, somebody make it stop before I do."

Then the pendulum swings.

And there's no point in you being here. All you've ever done is hurt the people you love and waste the opportunities you've had, and it physically feels like someone has taken a cartoon-sized anvil and placed it on your chest.

This time, you don't want to cry, but you do, huge, racking sobs that render you incomprehensible and utterly inconsolable.

Then, just as abruptly, the tears dry, but it doesn't get better. It just goes away. Everything goes away and you're left cold, numb and slow, every thought assembled by hand by a disgruntled employee who has just been passed over for promotion and never much cared for thoughts in the first place.

Finally, one morning, even they up and quit, a familiar parting shot left on their desk:

"Please, somebody make it stop. Please, somebody make it stop before I do."

Sometimes they manage to, and sometimes they don't. Sometimes it shifts gear before it gets too much and sometimes it doesn't.

And sometimes you end up in hospital, apologising to the people you love for having put them through it again, and no, you don't really want to die, you just wanted some peace and you promise, promise, promise never to do it again, cause the scars on your wrists or your throat, or the ache from your roughly-pumped stomach will serve as reminders of the line that you crossed, at least until your brain learns to side-step the memory and starts the cycle all over again.

Then, for too many, there are times when it all does stop.

For them.

And never, ever stops for everyone left behind.

That's what it is. That's what I have. But it's not who I am.

There are days, in fact, when what keeps the worst of it at bay is the idiocy it seems to inspire in others.

No, eating more nuts will not cure me. No, it isn't the fluoride in my toothpaste. No, it isn't part of a conspiracy by Big Pharma to sell more straitjackets.

Yes, I have tried not having it. Yes, I agree, medication doesn't work for everyone. Yes, I am aware that exercise and meditation and kitten yoga exist, and I'm thrilled they've proved helpful for some.

My aura is fine. Chemtrails aren't real. And, I swear to God, if you say the word "mindfulness" to me one more time, I will resort to fisticuffs.

Also, a polite note to the well-meaning folk who suggest that I should embrace it, as part of who I am:

I would rather embrace a polecat that had recently received bad news and, subsumed in grief, had been neglecting its personal hygiene.

I don't want to embrace it. I want it to pack its things, forget my number and start cruising the bars in search of a rebound.

I want it gone.

Would I take a cure? Hell, yes. It's not a fucking superpower. It's a physically, mentally and emotionally painful disease that has repeatedly robbed me of the people and things I've loved the most, and I'd give it up in a hot second.

But it's not going to get in my way. Not anymore.

And it definitely isn't going to get in my children's way.

Now, let's check back in with our exhausted parent and his growing charges, shall we?

There are probably more jokes over there.

2: Toddling Towards Bethlehem

Cast your mind back to Chapter One.

I know, for some of you, this will actually involve reading it again. You put this book down in a safe place three months ago, and only found it again this morning when you were looking for your keys.

In which case, welcome back.

You may recall, have just re-read, or are, despite your better judgement, prepared to take my word for it that I made mention of a nascent bout of self-destruction during my daughters' first year of life.

I just checked. I did.

Thanks to stupid linear time, year two saw it come to full fruition.

It is therefore, in my memory, divided into two distinct halves. Which is handy thematically but was, at the time, a massive pain in the ass.

Honestly, I already had enough trauma to be going on with. Drama was not in short supply and folly was, emphatically, the coin of the realm.

After a certain point, it's just showing off.

For the first six months, I had assiduously pulled at the dangling threads of my life, trying desperately not to reap what I'd sewn.

By the second half of the year, I was living apart from my children, cooking spaghetti drunk at four o'clock in the morning and writing it all off on my tax return as "research".

Everything in between will have to remain, for the moment, between me and my God-shaped hole.

I shaved off my hair, in a fit of pique, and was, for an uncomfortably long period, completely away with the fairies.

In a fit of Puck.

It was, to put it mildly, not a good time, in a variety of ridiculous and tragic ways. Events ballooned and snowballed as though devised by a soap opera scribe whose dealer had finally returned their calls.

Much of it now seems unlikely. Some of it, clearly impossible. All of it, taking the piss.

In short order, I lost my home life, a close friend, what little was left of my mind, and an enormous amount of weight.

I'm not equating all of these things, obviously, but the bipolar brain is not overly burdened with perspective.

The weight loss, I hoped, would make me look lithe and dangerous, but actually suggested a telethon on my behalf might not be a bad idea.

The bereavement was a punch in the gut, as it would be for anyone. In its wake, however, came a torrent of stupidity, greed and farcicality at which even Kafka might have blanched and which sent me into a spiral of which a crashing helicopter would be proud.

But that's another book. Another much stranger book.

***

In terms of my parenting achievements, these were not my finest hours, days or months. I'm not even convinced I was totally on it for more than ten seconds at a time. I tried to remain present, but, much of the time, I was also trying to remain conscious.

It's hard to explain what it does to you—when you wake every morning and your children are elsewhere. It's the stomach wound of living arrangements.

I was still actively involved and they stayed with me as often as possible, depending on the state of my current accommodation, but I was rapidly becoming a sitcom version of a single Dad, the best of intentions buried so deeply beneath irresponsibility and unpredictability that they would only bob to the surface during very special episodes.

Apparently, they have no recollection of this time, although I suppose they could be lying to spare my feelings. It's not likely though. They lean more towards brutal honesty.

"Father, I appreciate the effort and everything, but this food is disgusting."

I have no doubt, if the memories existed, they would have passed comment by now, or used it as ammunition in an argument about curfews.

If only they knew how effective a play it would be. There are many things that rob me of sleep, but this whole period Clockwork O's my eyes more than any other.

I was angry, I was impatient, I was unreasonable and, worst of all, I was wasting time I could have spent watching them grow.

Fathead and Baldy, you see, were rapidly becoming toddlers, developing enquiring, hilarious and eccentric personalities that were, ahem, poles apart

17

from one another.

Sorry. I could have said something about chalk and cheese, I suppose, but it was more marked than that. They were and are like chalk and, I don't know, the Maldives.

This was evident from the beginning. For supposedly identical twins, they went out of their way to be different. They didn't even have the decency to be born the same size, and one of them insisted on being in an incubator for a while because she hadn't bothered to fully develop her lungs, the lazy git.

By the time they were walking and talking, they were an argument waiting, but not for long, to happen.

I have, periodically, been convinced that they are, in fact, a single complete person that has been inelegantly split into allegorical halves. I have, equally often, been convinced that they are doing it purely to wind me up.

I gradually realised, however, that all toddlers are a law unto themselves. Without Royal Assent, admittedly, but their lobby is persistent and it's only a matter of time.

They are, first and foremost, natural comedians. Partly because their observations are original and acute but predominantly because they are deeply disturbed and constantly on the bottle.

Secondly, they have an unerring ability to make you doubt everything that you have learned or have come to believe. Largely by repeating the word "why?" in a manner that suggests they've seen *Marathon Man* far earlier in their lives than is appropriate.

Finally, they stand at the tops of flights of stairs, holding hands and talking in a synchronised monotone.

Actually, that one may be a twin thing.

People who have little experience with children quite naturally find all of this flummoxing, and tend to ask difficult questions:

"Why the tantrums?"

"Why the crying?"

"Why the insistence on doing precisely the opposite of anything requested?"

Well, I can't speak for everyone, but in my case, I probably need a nap.

As for children, well, just think about the situation in which they find themselves. Every day, they learn a little more about the world, about its pleasures and pitfalls. Quite naturally, they want to explore them, interrogate them, poke them and drool on them.

Who wouldn't?

They have their own likes and dislikes, their own passions and peeves, and their own rapidly evolving conception of how life should be arranged.

Then, every day, someone comes along and contradicts them.

"No."

"Bad."

"You can't do that."

"You mustn't say that."

"You shouldn't touch that."

"Setting fire to your sister is wrong."

If they were adults, we'd be marching for their liberation.

This is how a toddler sees the world:

On the counter, in the kitchen, there is a jar of cookies.

Except that there isn't. What parent has the energy to empty them into a jar? It's a half-eaten packet and you know it.

Anyway, there is a container of some kind with cookies in it. On this occasion, it is in the eye-line of the child, but it wouldn't matter if it wasn't. They can sense sugar.

Now, the child has learned about cookies. The child is very much in favour of cookies. Frankly, cookies have given them faith in a higher power that will remain unshaken until their first romantic disappointment.

Let's follow the child's logic:

"I want cookies. There are cookies present. I will, therefore, eat the fuck out of those cookies."

On the available evidence, without any knowledge of dietary requirements, dental surgery, or the desire to resurrect a partner's rapidly dwindling interest, this is solid thinking.

Then along comes a grumpy, tall person, someone for whom they have great affection but who is often in a mood that suggests that they haven't had a cookie for a good, long while.

"You can't have a cookie," they say.

"Why the fuck not?" their little brains scream.

Actually, it's worse than that, because they don't yet have the benefit of profanity's relief valve and are forced to resort to primal screaming and furniture abuse.

At this point, it is beholden upon said grumpy, tall person to explain why they can't have a cookie in a way that makes sense to them.

This is an obscenely difficult task, rendered impossible if you've forgotten, as appears to be the case with most people, what it was actually like to be their age.

The problem is that both of you have valid points, you're just working from different information sets.

19

And, let's be honest, sometimes we say they can't have a cookie because we're stressed, the cookies are *far*, or the little shits woke us up at five o'clock because they were bored and we haven't properly forgiven them yet.

I'm not for a moment pretending that I have a perfect record on this score, but I tried hard to see things from the girls' point-of-view when they were small. We did, after all, share an approximate maturity level.

Put it this way—as far as I understood myself, I understood them. Take from that what you will.

I certainly enjoyed the blank slate nature of instructing them in the subjects I considered most important. It was, perhaps, not the most rounded of educations, but it was eclectic and contained a larger than average number of costume changes.

We didn't ignore the classics, of course. I was a dab hand at "why is the sky blue?" and "where do babies come from?" The answers to which are, obviously and respectively, "something something atmosphere" and "Norway".

I also gave them an intensive primer in what boys think and why it's wrong, an introduction to the collected works of Elvis Costello and some entertaining lectures on why owning hundreds of books you've already read is not a waste of time, despite what they might have heard elsewhere.

On the whole, I'm confident that I passed on many things they would not have learned otherwise, for which I am assured, although not by them, that they will one day be grateful.

In turn, they taught me that it's really funny when little kids swear, but you're supposed to pretend it's not, that you should never be too busy to play because, eventually, they will stop asking, and that you shouldn't be too petulant when they can colour inside the lines better than you can.

***

I know it's dangerous to live through your children, but they also, in that second year, managed to redress one of the great shames of my life.

Oh, god. This is even harder to admit than I imagined.

Try not to judge me too harshly. I was young. The world was a different place.

Okay. Deep breath.

I cannot tie my shoelaces for shit.

Shut up. I mean it. It's really bad. Worryingly bad, like a misanthropic doctor might pop through the door at any minute and tell me it's not lupus.

I put it down to being a left-handed person from a family of right-handed people. And, of course, an idiot. I mean, it's not as if I haven't tried. I've tucked a herd of rabbits into holes and under bridges, and looped all the loops known to science, but I still end up trailing laces behind me like streamers from a bicycle wheel.

I am also clumsy to a near slapstick degree, so, if it weren't for loafers and the work of the good people at Velcro, I would be dead.

But, goddamn it, I could tie the hell out of their shoes. Securely, quickly and, though I say it myself, with no small amount of flair.

I mean, the first time, sweat was dripping off me like a bomb squad rookie, but I held my nerve. I took a lace in either hand, uttered a wildly hypocritical prayer, and went to work.

The rest is a bit of a blur, but moments later, there they were: Two pairs of efficiently fastened footwear and two small children wondering, for neither the first nor last time, why their father was laughing quite so hysterically.

It was like a Biblical miracle, but even less plausible.

It sounds a small thing, perhaps, but the threat of them stumbling into traffic, with anything like the frequency that I do, was a tremendous motivator.

And, more importantly, it was one item off the long list of things I feared I wouldn't be able to do for my children.

But then, being thankful for small mercies is something you learn early on.

Not to mention the mercies of the small.

One of my daughters, the possessor of the aforementioned *bonce grosse*, has always been an openly affectionate and emotionally demonstrative sort.

More on her later.

The other, she of the threadbare pate, is less so. By which I mean, she actively protests physical contact of any kind. Which is her right, but it was unsettling when she was small. If you attempted to put your arm around her, she would bat it away, giving you a look both accusatory and pitying.

This isn't to say that she is without emotion. She just expresses it in her own unique manner.

Furiously.

"Goodnight! I love you!" she barks, as she stomps off to bed.

"Are you okay?!" she demands, in a tone that suggests that you'd better be, or it's going to kick off.

"I love you all so much!" she says, with narrowed eyes, outraged that you have caused her to form such an onerous bond.

When I'm depressed, or, for that matter, manic, you might imagine that their reactions would vary wildly. And in some ways, you would be right.

Well done you.

21

In a lot of other ways, and these are the ways on which I wish to concentrate, you are so pathetically wrong that, to be candid, I feel a little sorry for you.

I think you ought to take a moment to think about what you've done. Right. Are you ready to re-join the class?

Very well. But we'll have no more of your nonsense.

There is a temptation, when you suffer from mental illness, at least during those rare moments when it's still up to you, to conceal your symptoms from other people.

You don't want to be a burden; you don't want to be thought weak, incapable or generally *less*.

Experience has also taught you that some of your more outré behaviour, while making perfect sense to you, alarms others. Whether that's pouring whisky on your cornflakes or staging a light operetta during your great-aunt's funeral, the general feeling is that the more comprehensively you can hide those neon lights under that lead-lined bushel, the better.

With children, it cannot be done. No matter how hard you try to hide the tears, they always know something is up.

In fact, they can be frighteningly perceptive, especially for people who have to be reminded on a semi-regular basis that fire is hot. By the age of two, they've definitely worked out what "sad" is and are firmly against it.

So, you try to put on a happy face. You pretend that everything is hunky dory or, at least, the second side of Ziggy Stardust.

Why? Because you want them to feel secure. You want to spare them pain. And, more selfishly, you want them to think of you as superhuman and infallible, until the fateful day when you forget to clear your browser history and those feet of clay come into sharp relief.

I was no exception. When with my children, I essayed a sane, level, grown-up version of myself that, honestly, should have led to the revocation of my Equity card.

Oh, on the right rung of the ladder of crazy, we could have a fine old time, joyous and sepia-tinted. But, if I continued to rocket upwards, my increasing irritability and lack of focus meant that even being in the same room as a pair of two-year-olds could feel like someone was scraping a razor blade up and down each of my nerves, individually and simultaneously.

If I was on my way down, I would often just stare at them, going about their mysterious business, and wonder how the universe could possibly think they deserved such a flawed creature as their protector and sage.

But then they'd crawl up next to me, even the grouchy one, look me straight in the eye and repeat the words I'd said to them more often than any others:

22

"It's okay. It's going to be okay."

And they were right. It was. And it would be.

Then their heads would fold on to my shoulder, they'd snuggle in close, and they'd whisper, sleepily and sweetly:

"Can I have a cookie?"

All Bi Myself

I know what you're thinking. How on earth did such a fine, upstanding young gentleman—with big eyes, interesting hair and a geek's gratitude for any form of intimate attention—end up as a single Dad?

Actually, if you've been paying attention, that's probably the last question that you're asking.

More likely is: "How did anyone put up with you long enough for you to procreate?"

They are both exceptional questions and I will try to answer them as honestly as I can, while sparing the blushes and digestive systems of all concerned.

Former partners, you may now breathe out. I know you only bought this book because you worry about my finances—bless your hearts—so there will be neither kissing nor telling here.

Also, it would be an incredibly short chapter. I'm no Don Juan.

Hell, I'm barely Don Knotts.

There have, however, been a handful of amazing people in my life, all of whom I have let down in ways as specific to them as they were special to me.

But I have known love. I know it still.

I have been taught to love, though I was a slow and unruly pupil.

I have been lost in love, and found myself in its absence.

I have been a colossal dick.

Look, I'm not going to come out of this section particularly well. I've accepted that. Frankly, I'd have cut it altogether if it weren't so key to the story.

Besides, it's as close as this book is likely to get to a sexy bit. You'll have to read rather hard between the lines, and for full effect, have the free range, ethically-produced pornography of your choice on in the background, but, with a little luck and a prevailing wind, it may help the airport sales.

So, without going into specifics, here are some of the ways in which bipolar disorder, aided and abetted by more generic jackassery, has fucked up my relationships.

But, first, a caveat.

I'm going to use broad brush strokes here, both to protect the innocent and to insulate myself against accusations of "speaking for all bipolar people".

I wouldn't dare speak for another bipolar person.

I have no idea how they'd take it.

Boom. Et cetera.

I'm allowed to tell that joke, by the way. I'm also allowed to use the following words and phrases with impunity: crazy, mad, looney, bonkers-nutso, insane (both intra and extra-membrane), "not playing with a full deck and, for some reason, using a flock of geese as cards", "two airline employees short of a Penthouse letter", and "Sir Denis Thatcher".

Now, other people, with their own mental health conditions, may, for whatever reason, take issue with how I choose to describe mine, so let me be clear:

It's my doolally tap and I'll cry if I want to.

We will discuss overcoming stigma, I promise. We will probe stereotypes, positive and negative reinforcement, the role of language in the definition of self and why it's important for you to accept that we are not all serial killers. These are huge issues that demand serious consideration, and they will receive their due.

For now, I've got a bunch of self-deprecating material about relationships that I've been working up and I'd hate to see it go to waste.

Because I have, after much thought, usually late at night and often drunk, identified several key ways in which love has, in my experience, been most often thwarted by crazy.

Feeling literary, I have chosen to personify them.

Not only does this allow me to cloak some of the more personal elements of the story, but I can also refer to them to as the Nine Bruises, which makes me extremely happy, and not a little aroused.

I told you that this was the sexy bit.

We first turn our attention to Perceptiona. The daughter of Paranoia, God of Bad Weed, and Hallucina, Goddess of Weed That Has Clearly Been Laced with Something, Perceptiona has the power to alter her devotee's reality, in ways that never start being fun.

When Perceptiona comes out to play, you may believe that your partner is about to leave, is having an affair, or is in league with a cabal of sinister veterinarians. At the same time, you may become convinced that the song you've just written will solve all of your financial problems, bring about world peace and cure leprosy.

Deceptinor is Perceptiona's older brother, and specialises in justification. Everything you do, he whispers in your ear, is so obviously for the best, that there must be something seriously wrong with anyone who demurs. Can't they see that if you didn't spend the grocery money on studio time and absinthe, it would be a gross dereliction of your duty as an artist?

Of course you haven't slept for three days. Yes, the ghost of Ulysses S. Grant suggested that chord change in the middle eight. No, you don't think that's a problem.

It's an opportunity.

Duh.

Cantankerachore is in charge of irritability. The offspring of two minor deities, Ed and Nancy, Cantankerachore has spent her entire existence having to spell her name for strangers and is, therefore, done with people.

Mnemofiend is a more complicated case. The Bruise of Memory, she has been observing the activities of her siblings since the dawn of time. She sees every poor decision they have inspired, every atom of damage they have wreaked, but, whenever presented with an opportunity to course correct, conveniently forgets the lot.

She often works alongside Argumenta, the Bruise of Pointless Shouting. Her sole purpose is to be right. Indisputably, at all times and with a deep-seated contempt for such trivial irritants as facts or sense. In most versions of the story, she is finally killed when she attempts to prove that a crocodile is a vat of frozen yogurt by attacking it with a spoon.

The Bruise of Workaholics is Neglectia. She assigns importance to the aspects of her supplicants' lives by use of an enchanted tombola.

No matter how often it spins, however, work will always emerge in the top three, alongside personal validation and unfocused outrage. Paying attention to the emotional and physical needs of other people always comes last and is often misspelt.

If the moon is in the second house and Aquarius is in the guest bedroom, Neglectia melds with Perceptiona, Deceptinor and Cantankerachore to form a dreadful gestalt that can only be defeated by Interventia, the Goddess of Smacks Up the Back of the Head.

Neglectia is the second most dangerous Bruise of them all and is historically represented by an hourglass containing a single grain of sand and bearing the Latin inscription *Non tempus hoc modo* (Translation: I don't have time for this right now).

Callioopsyadaisy is the Bruise of Epic Fuck-Ups. She's kept pretty busy.

The Bruise of Libido, Sexual Decision Making, Jealousy and Body Issues is called Steve, and the less said about him the better.

The most vicious, the most feared, and the cruellest of the lot, however, is Lucidia.

The Lifter of Veils. The Speaker of Truths. The Bringer of Flop Sweat. These are just a few of things that people would call her if they weren't busy imploring her to fuck right off.

Lucidia is a trickster, you see. She leaves her mark, raw, jagged and bleeding, in the most savage manner possible.

By making you well.

Briefly, unexpectedly and almost always immediately after the other eight have been kicking your life around like a sentient soccer ball.

You would think that this would be a relief, a boon, a consummation most devoutly to be wished.

Bollocks is it.

We are afraid of losing our minds. It haunts us, a fate considered worse than death or being made to discuss poetry with teenage boys.

We attend self-help seminars in attempts to avoid it, donating vast sums of money to the dentists of our chosen gurus. We sit cross-legged, muttering mantras. We run marathons, take vitamins, quit drinking, start book clubs.

We even fly to Switzerland when the choice is taken out of our hands.

We pursue any and every opportunity to lower our stress levels, find our work-life balance, improve our relationships, hone our bodies—whatever we can do to keep that pesky mind where we can bloody well see it.

But we rarely talk about the pain of having lost it and then finding the damned thing again. The sheer horror of realising what you've done, what you've said, how much you've broken, and neither remembering nor understanding why.

There is a reason why there is such a thing as an insanity defence. There is also a reason why so many people regard it as a cop-out.

It was you, but it wasn't you. Your voice said those hurtful words. Your body did those terrible things. Your mind told you those outrageous lies.

But when you come to, knee-deep in the carnage, it just doesn't make any sense. You're not the type of person who would say those things, do those things, believe those things.

That's not who you are.

But you still have to shoulder the burden, you still have to make the amends. Because it happened. It all happened. And even if blame is mitigated by understanding, reality is less pliant.

The sensible response is to thank your lucky stars that you are loved enough and wanted enough to be forgiven, that your struggle has not gone unobserved and that your true self has not been entirely obscured by your shadow.

27

If you are deranged, and let's go out on a limb and say that you are, you will, instead, resent the way in which people act as though the things you did and didn't do, said or forgot to say, actually occurred or failed to occur. You will convince yourself that you are misunderstood, that you are above the need to explain yourself and that you will be proved right, in the end.

You will say "Fuck you" when you meant to say "Thank you". You will start an argument while "I love you" watches aghast from the back of your tongue. You will stand in the sun and shiver for effect.

If you are me, and at least one of us is, you will make every mistake on the above list, staging a decade-long Grand Guignol that would agitate the stomach of the most jaded trauma surgeon. And then, as an encore, you will commit the ultimate act of insanity.

For along will come a person who wants everything you need but have deemed jejune. They will be someone who speaks directly to the version of you that has always lurked beneath your own brain's malice. They will not have time for any of your bullshit.

And you will fall so hard that you will tell yourself that you're all better now. But, of course, you're not.

And you will assure yourself that you will stop pushing them away the second you've proved yourself to the entire world and are able to provide them with everything they don't need, and for which they never asked.

You will forget that they are just as complex as you, because who could be? You won't imagine that their struggles are as titanic as yours, because how could they be? You won't realise how unhappy you are making them, because you love them so much.

Then, in a courageous and necessary act of self-preservation, they will leave. And immediately rocket to the top of the long list of regrets which wake you in the middle of the night, all the more brutal because you'd hoped your heart was less addled than your head.

But it will shock you into action, too late, and help you find your way out of the fog, too slowly, and you will come out the other side, both as heartbroken and as sane as you have ever been.

Forever bereft, but forever indebted, because the universe's latest cruelty has woken you to its greatest gift:

Throughout it all, miraculously, the two hearts you could not have survived breaking have remained, somehow, insulated from the flames.

And while it may never be quite right for you, you can make it right for them. And that, truly, will be enough.

Most days.

3: Growing Pains

Although it is undoubtedly to the benefit of its length, the trouble with writing this book is that I keep remembering things.

For someone who has probably only spent about a sixteenth of his life as the person he would like to be, this is an issue.

On the other hand, it turns out there are a greater number of halfway useful insights locked away in my noggin than I had imagined. Until now, I thought it was primarily comprised of suspicion of the Oxford comma, the rhythm guitar part to Billy Bragg's *The Saturday Boy* and vivid fantasies about punching various world leaders in the throat.

Much of this acumen is hindsight-assisted, of course, but looking back on Fathead and Baldy at three, I realise how quickly the cores of our beings are locked into place.

This is comforting, in a way, because there is a dark truth that only parents truly understand.

Let me make it clear, I'm not one of those people who thinks that you're not a whole person until you've had children, or that your life is somehow less fulfilling for not bringing life into the world. There's a fucktonne of things that people without children know that I don't know. For instance, what it's like to know where all your things are, or what food that isn't reformed turkey tastes like.

There are also many ways to become a parent, not all of which involve vodka or vengeful latex manufacturers. I particularly salute all those who choose to take a child into their family, especially those who do so after reading this book.

However, there is one thing that you only experience while raising a child—or being child-adjacent for any length of time—and it's not something any of us like to talk about. Or even consciously acknowledge.

When children arrive, by whatever means, it is an invitation to love in a completely different way. Most of us accept gladly, even if we occasionally forget to RSVP.

They become our world. We sacrifice parts of ourselves to their happiness and well-being that would set off alarm bells in any other relationship and inspire a sternly worded questionnaire in *Cosmopolitan.*

And then, every year or so, those people disappear and are replaced. They have the same names, the same ambivalent reactions to vegetables, the same predilection for property damage, but they aren't the same.

So far, so science fiction mini-series.

Now, you may say that this is the natural order of things, but that's just the *nom de guerre* of anything that sucks ass but about which there isn't much you can do.

It's a perpetual grieving process. You come home for three hundred and sixty-five consecutive days to adorable three-year-olds whose primary ambition is to get away with shaving the cat. That's your life. You're a parent to three-year-olds. That is who you are.

Flash-forward thirteen years, and several generations of doppelgänger, and you'll find yourself in the middle of an uncomfortably graphic conversation about Idris Elba's muscle tone and what you won't do is wonder where the time has gone.

You'll wonder where they have gone.

I loved having three-year-olds. I was pretty good at it. It made me happy, so far as I knew how.

I don't have three-year-olds anymore. Writing about that time is writing about something I've lost. Loved ones I've lost.

I'm undoubtedly overthinking it—and it doesn't compare to the abyss of more permanent grief—but sorrow is seldom diminished by logic.

Never mind the more practical consideration that just as you reach basic competence in one type of parenting, you're forced to start again from scratch.

This is the real reason people have multiple children, which would, otherwise, seem like gluttony for poverty. After all, why waste a perfectly good skill set? And who else is going to wear all those rompers?

Please don't answer that.

The one saving grace of the whole shit-show is when you can see the progression, when you can connect the dots between the child you remember and the adult that is barrelling towards you at an unseemly pace.

With my two, that lies in their relationship to each other.

I'm a natural sceptic, but there is something ineffable about the bond between twins. They appear to be joined at a quantum level, in a way that can leave the rest of us bewildered and envious.

We poor slobs, with our singular births and our unique combinations of upbringing and genetics, are, in the final analysis, alone. We can make all the connections we like, we can share lives and fluids, we can brand our souls with the marks of others, but when the twilight descends, it's just us. A star turn, propped up by a rotating cast of supporting players.

But they've always had each other and they always will. That is, if one of them doesn't finally snap and murder the other, which is a real possibility. Even then, a haunting is all but inevitable.

You look at twins and you start to fathom some of the zanier ideas with which theology has burdened us. They aren't quite two people, at least in the sense that you and I understand it, and they cost far too much to be one.

Having said that, there is a definite pecking order within their sorority. I'm just not entirely sure who is pecking whom.

What it boils down to is that, despite there being a gap of only eight minutes between their births, Fathead is the big sister and Baldy is the little sister.

Don't ask me. It's *their* subconscious adherence to societal structures.

In practical terms, as far as I can work out, this means that Baldy does not have to carry cash, remember appointments, plan social engagements or take responsibility for joint transgressions. She is, in other words, the Queen.

Fathead, by way of recompense, gets to choose the events they attend, with whom they hang and the level to which they are annoyed with Molly or Polly or Holly, or whoever is the current *bête noire* of their friendship circle.

For a long time, this seemed to work for both of them. They knew their roles; they had both traded off in favour of power or convenience. Fathead was duly protective of her often distracted sister, while, at the same time, wanting to put her head through a wall at regular intervals. Baldy, in turn, spent most of her time in a beautiful, make-believe world where humans were less needy and emotional, but which nevertheless annoyed her.

This isn't to insinuate that the looking after didn't flow both ways. It did then and it certainly does now. It was just that, in the beginning, Baldy wasn't always aware that there was any looking after to be done. She saved her energy for the large-scale stuff, like plotting elaborate revenge if someone was mean.

This may seem like a recipe for disaster—and it absolutely is—but it has made them a force with which to be reckoned.

They certainly employed a tag-team approach when it came to tackling obstacles. Where one child might eventually work out how to clamber over the side of a crib, twins will, by way of reconnaissance, launch their sibling

31

over and then, having established the lay of the land, use them to break their own fall.

Where one toddler might be kept indoors by the daunting distance between their grubby little mitts and the door handle, two will work out a system whereby one lifts the other, the door is opened and they are halfway to a nearby Chinese restaurant before you're back from the kitchen.

The latter, alas, is not a hypothetical situation.

They were also intensely verbal. If you've read this far, and aren't just skimming this in a bookshop like a cheap bastard, then you might have some idea where they picked that up. Needless to say, they were surrounded by words from birth, some of which were, from time to time, fruitier than was prudent.

But it was having each other to talk to—or communicate telepathically with, which I'm not ruling out—that truly accelerated their skills. By three, you could have a fairly decent conversation with them. Certainly a more sophisticated one than you might have with your average ski instructor or *Daily Mail* reader.

I don't know why I'm picking on ski instructors, but I'm thinking constant cold and habitual collisions with foliage aren't going to result, organically, in a treatise on memory as a theme in *À la recherche du temps perdu*. (Translation: "*How* many pages?")

There are, however, several downsides to bright, talkative children.

One, they rat you out, constantly:

"Daddy said we could have a cookie before dinner, if we didn't tell you."

"Daddy had a long nap this afternoon. We didn't mind; we had all this fire to play with."

"Daddy smokes a special pipe with diamonds in."

Of course, I'm exaggerating for comic effect. I would never let them have a cookie before dinner. Balanced diets are important.

They are also more readily able to express the strongly held opinions on which they have been fulminating since birth, in a way that is humorous, moving and dicey in the presence of police officers.

I remember one afternoon in particular.

Don't worry. I'm as surprised as you are.

Anyway, I was sitting on the living room floor, listening to a copy of the band's latest album and attempting to learn the lyrics while sober, on the off-chance it ever came up.

Baldy tottered in and sidled up. She stood in silence for a long minute, lips pursed, like a record executive listening for the single.

I watched sympathetically, realising how unsettling it must have been for her. Her father's voice, blasting from the stereo, instead of demanding to know why his wallet was covered in shampoo.

Or perhaps, I thought, the confusion would come later, when she realised that not every Dad wrote songs, or stories, or pretended to be other people for money.

Either way, I knew this was going to be one of those teachable moments that always fuck up the last five minutes of American comedies.

Sure enough, after a suitable period of contemplation, she turned to me, a serious look on her sweet little brow. Mentally, I ran through potential answers to the questions that were about to burst forth from her lips.

"Don't play that one when you go to work, Daddy. It's crap," she said.

And left the room.

We make such a fuss about the fact that children can swim instinctively, but seldom marvel sufficiently at their innate ability to drop a mic.

The worst part was that my immediate response was not, as would have been sensible, a quick internal monologue:

"Don't worry about it. She's three. Her favourite song is the theme to that terrifying nocturnal horticulture programme; she may not be your target audience."

Nor did I attempt to engage her in a conversation about what she didn't like about it, by way of developing her critical faculties.

"No, it isn't!" I shouted, instead, to an empty room.

Then I sulked for a bit.

Because here's the other thing that, on reflection, I've recognised about myself. I enjoyed raising three-year-olds because I was a three-year-old. Sure, I fed them and made them have a bath and read stories to them and kept their blood, for the most part, on the inside of their bodies. But my strength as a parent was exactly the same as my weakness as a human being.

I hadn't forgotten what it is was like to be three.

When I was actually a child, I was forced to grow up too quickly. It was the only way to survive. I had to deal with an endless array of operatically adult emotions and attempt to make sense of them through an inadequate combination of my limited life experience and the several hundred books I had read to escape from it.

As an adult, perhaps understandably, I went in heavily for overcompensation. For so many years, I had been told, "This is how it is. Accept it or face the consequences." Having finally made my escape, therefore, my worldview immediately regressed to that of a toddler:

It wasn't fair. And I was going to shout at it until it was.

I'm still not entirely convinced that I was wrong, but I eventually grasped the concept that this was about as effective and attractive in a grown person as you'd think.

Now, I don't think people should necessarily grow out of this immediately or completely; the world needs some outrage. Just because something is inefficient or ill-advised does not mean that it is incorrect.

It's all about balance.

Young people, for example, are often savaged by their natural predators—elderly newspaper columnists—for complaining that things aren't fair, as though it was ludicrous to expect them to be.

But that's not the problem. Things should be fair. They just aren't. And no amount of shouting is going to change that.

The trick, then, is to somehow teach your children what fairness looks like, explain why it's rapidly becoming extinct, and suggest how they might make the best of it, should they ever stumble upon any.

Unfortunately, this doesn't make for the kind of inspiring speeches on which my personality is founded.

I look back on the twins at three, therefore, and realise with a heart-thump that if they end up with any forbearance, any flexibility or any talent for navigating the illiterate echo chamber that is modern discourse, then it won't have anything to do with how I was then.

On the other hand, due to the same penchant for fevered ranting, they will never stand for racism, sexism, homophobia, animal cruelty, religious extremism or child abuse. My concern is that they might not stand for forgiveness or redemption either. And they'll definitely think it's perfectly acceptable to slag off bands you don't like.

I've changed, but the past hasn't.

And it's not just that I've mellowed in my old age—and before you start, I had my first mid-life crisis at twelve, I'm absolutely on borrowed time—or that I've matured, finally.

Both those things are true, I hope, but as most people get there without psychotic breaks or artistic overreach, I'm wary of positioning them as ordinary emotional development. I had to be dragged into adulthood, shit-fitting all the way.

No, my current approach is largely driven by terror, nature's adrenaline suppository. Their first childhood intersected with my second, and while most of us acknowledge, in vague terms, that we will fuck up our kids in one way or another, when the reality of what that means sets in, the tenor of your panic is almost entirely governed by the precision of your self-awareness.

We're making people, and, frankly, we're often more focused when we're making breakfast.

That's not to cast aspersions on your parenting style, should you have one. I'm sure you're batting a thousand, every time you step up to the plate, and nary a one of your faults, prejudices or less salubrious partialities have been inadvertently transmitted to the next generation.

Your mum's a sarcastic bastard.

However, this is one of the few occasions where there are genuine benefits to being mentally ill. I am *so* obsessively worried about having messed them up, via madness or method, that, sometimes, I catch perfectly normal missteps that would, otherwise, have passed without remark.

For everything else, I take comfort in the fact that, one day, the world's therapists will raise jeroboams of champagne to my eccentric legacy.

But we're getting ahead of ourselves.

For the moment, a father is sleeping fitfully on the couch, watched over by two three-year-olds who are a little worried about what he's going to be when he grows up.

Bi-lateral Disarmament

I cannot overestimate the importance of this section, and not just because I don't think I'm going to better that sub-heading.

Rather, I think you should pay particular attention to this bit because it concerns a thorny subject—fraught with controversy—and I've no hope whatsoever of it not driving at least one person into an enraged and rabid froth.

And you seem like the type that might get off on that.

See, now you're worried. You've laughed, at minimum, at four-and-a-half jokes so far, and if I turn out to be racist, or anti-vaccine, or convinced the Earth is an isosceles triangle built by ferrets, then you are going to have to face some hard truths about yourself.

Relax. It's nothing like that.

I promise.

Now, Israel and Palestine…

Come back.

I want to talk about an entirely different hot potato.

Medication.

I should make it clear that I am in no way advising the use of potatoes as a replacement for professional medical advice, and, moreover, I'm sure none of you actually thought that I was.

But it's as well to make sure in this litigious age.

Are you sure you wouldn't prefer to talk about the Middle East?

Absolutely sure?

What if we just discuss whether the term "Middle East" is inappropriately Eurocentric in the context of post-imperialist cultural identity?

Fine. Try not to set fire to me all at once.

I am pro-medication. I couldn't function properly without it, and I think there are a great many people in the same shoddily-constructed boat. It wasn't until, in a spasm of desperation, I forced myself to start taking it again that I realised quite how ill I had become.

In fact, without the veritable cocktail of chemical chicanery that I swallow every day, I wouldn't have survived the last couple of years. Of that I have no doubt. Whether I'd have succumbed to the disease physically or mentally, my self had fractured to the point that, without some kind of intervention, I wasn't coming back.

This would, of course, have been unacceptable and, worse, tonally all over the place. My life works best as a surrealist fable, not a kitchen-sink drama.

You may have noticed, however, that I refer to it as "chicanery". Actually, I *know* you will have noticed because the alliteration surrounding it will have made you throw up in your mouth a little.

I meant it though. Medication is a lie. It's a useful lie, a well-meant lie, but a lie nonetheless.

There is no cure for what I have, so it can only ever be a feint. If I miss even a single dose, I can feel the shadow version of myself stir itself from slumber and coil itself to strike, pissed at having fallen for the misdirection. It murmurs and hisses and coos, trying to convince me that missing another dose would be the best idea ever. It's crazed and it's cruel, but it's warm and familiar, and feels so much more like the real me than I do.

Its voice is so seductive, Eve would have eaten from the Tree of Rusty Nails and Gangrene.

"Didn't we have more fun before?" it purrs.

"Haven't you felt so much less since we parted? Don't you feel slower? Less inspired?"

"Don't you miss it?"

The answer to all of the above is, of course, yes, which is exactly the fear that prompted me to resist medication for so many years. I thought I would lose myself to torpor and—shudders—normalcy.

Instead, I lost everyone else.

It didn't help that, the first time I was prescribed medication, things did not go terribly well, in much the same way as the Battle of Stalingrad did not go terribly smoothly.

Unbeknownst to me, there was, at the time, a new drug on the market that doctors were ever so excited about. They giggled behind their hands, whenever two or more would gather. There were lipstick-mottled posters on walls and hands slipping slyly under the covers when they thought of it at night. That sort of thing.

Unfortunately, one of the side effects of this blunder drug was to lower inhibitions. Which, for someone with suicidal impulses, was not necessarily, in the strictest sense, helpful.

I was unsurprised, some years later, to see a television exposé on the drug and its victims. It seems they had been handing this particular pill out like candy.

37

To diabetics.

In many ways, I was one of the lucky ones. I survived. I did, however, end up with two scarred wrists and, one time, I threw myself into a moat.

Long story.

The experience put me off medication, as well it might. It felt like I was wading through treacle, wearing a balaclava made of bees. I couldn't think. I couldn't write. And I couldn't stay out of moats, which had never previously been an issue. It was all stick and no carrot.

I tried various alternatives, for a while, but soon convinced myself that I was becoming psychologically dependent on them and flushed the lot.

From that point onwards, I decided, I was going to battle this *au naturel*. I was eventually persuaded to put my clothes back on, but I still maintained that I could manage my condition using a homemade brew, equal parts cigarettes, coffee, whisky and theatrical biographies.

That I thought it was working only reinforces how much it was not.

All I had done was shift the goalposts. Only a complete breakdown counted as ill. Everything else was "managing". And every remission was an absolute victory, an excuse to nip over to Versailles and sign treaties.

With similar knock-on effects.

It would be fifteen years before I tried again. Fifteen years of stumbling from crisis to crisis, yelling "Coping strategies!" at anyone who dared question the success of my approach.

Before I went back on meds, I would have sworn that I only suffered two or three major setbacks during that time.

Now, I count twenty-six.

At this point, I wouldn't blame you for wondering how the topic of medication has become as divisive as it has. If you're sick, you take the medicine, you feel better. Outside of specialist groups who would prefer you not to ingest anything that wasn't, at some point in its existence, bark, most people wouldn't see anything wrong with this.

Yet, somehow, when it comes to matters of the mind, everyone starts muttering about a second gunman.

So, why the disparity?

Well, part of it, as far I can tell, is that corporations make money from drugs. Which is true. And some of those corporations, in a truly shocking turn of events, care more about that money than about the welfare of the people who scoff their wares.

Also, water has a distinct dryness deficiency. (Don't worry. We've got something for that.)

This spurs some people to raise Verve songs to the level of holy writ.

The other, knottier problem is the completely valid question of whether everyone who has been prescribed medication actually needs it, or whether it is simply a crutch, a mask or some other context-specific accessory.

It's a legitimate concern. A lot of people don't need pills shoved down their throats. They need other help. They need to talk; they need to be supported to address trauma or reassured that they are not alone.

For instance, I've always been cagey about therapy, largely because I fear that I'm not very good at it, but I know for a fact it can help. Likewise, any number of other approaches—be they rigorously practical or marinated in new age wackiness—can be beneficial, depending on the needs of the individual.

But someone once told me that they had made their son's bipolar disorder *go away* by changing their diet and, while I try to avoid judging other people's parenting, it was to everyone's advantage that I wasn't armed.

In the end, it's the same old saw. People are afraid of what they don't understand, and even more afraid of it sneaking up on them from behind. Accepting the need for medication means accepting that something is wrong and, more than that, accepting that you, or your partner, or your child, or your friend, might be—pause for foreboding musical sting—one of *them*.

We'll circle back to that thought later.

For now, here are a few facts for even the most contrary amongst you to ponder:

Not everyone who is depressed suffers from depression. Not everyone who is sad is depressed. Not everyone who is different is mentally ill. And not everyone who is mentally ill is incapable, dangerous or, indeed, a savant.

It's a welter of individuality and complication. Just like every other thing ever.

The crux of the matter, however, as in so many things, is this:

It's none of your fucking business.

If I listed all of the social issues to which the above maxim applies, this book would make *The Lord of the Rings* look like a vegan delicatessen menu. So, I won't even attempt it. Take note of it though; you'll be surprised how much grief it will save you.

I need medication to be okay. I believe this to be an objective fact, and not a blind faith in science or a failure of lateral thinking. Trust me, I'm perfectly capable of believing all sorts of nonsense, but this is not one of those times.

You may not. Your sister may not. Your chiropodist may not. To which I say, huzzah. Having to take medication for the rest of your life is vile. For two to three months after I started taking mine, I felt like I was being rewritten from the inside out. It didn't feel like a crutch so much as being beaten to death with one.

But, eventually, it got better. And so did I. It's never going to be less than unpleasant and I'm never going to feel one hundred percent right.

I can still feel, however, and, for the first time in a long time, I can survive doing so. Also, moat-free since 2003. So, I'm going to call that a win.

I'm not a poster boy for medication as a cure-all, by any stretch of the imagination. My medication *cures* fuck-all. But it does enable me to sit and write this book, rather than write four blazingly inspired pages of it and then sit on a wall for three days, singing John Denver songs to myself and cackling.

That's never actually happened, by the way. But, by now, you wouldn't be surprised if it had. And neither would I.

Of course, this is only one person's opinion and should be treated as such. However, for those of you at the back who disagree and think that I'd be better off going for a nice walk, a quick thought experiment:

You are in a bar, talking to friends. For the sake of tradition, they were born, respectively, in England, Scotland and Ireland and they diverge religiously across three of the better-funded faiths.

This will have no further impact on the story.

Anyway, the door bursts open and in strolls a mutual acquaintance. You're not sure where he's from and to the best of your knowledge, he's an agnostic.

As you watch him make his way across the room, you get the unnerving feeling that something isn't quite right. His movements are oddly jittery, his salutations a little too passionate and there is a sheen on his forehead in which you can see reflected the dust-encrusted chandelier above.

But what do you know? You're into your second bottle of something to which wine was once described. You're probably emitting a faint glow yourself.

You're about to raise your hand in greeting, when Rabbi O'Malley lays a warning hand on your shoulder and whispers in your ear:

"He's off his meds."

Okay, answer the next question honestly.

Is your first impulse to immediately go out and buy him a sturdy pair of brogues?

I didn't think so. No, you cast your eyes down, lest you catch those of the med-less chap in question and he, in turn, stabs you in yours. Then you walk backwards, slowly, tapping your watch and commenting on the sheer amount of weather we've been having lately.

Most importantly of all, you wish he *had* taken his meds and saved you this embarrassing display.

I guess what I'm saying is:

Make up your fucking mind.

4: Sins of the Father

Where was I?

That's a question I've often asked myself, and for which I have yet to receive a satisfying answer. I've led the kind of life in which looking back is something best avoided. As in a horror film, my safest bet has always been to keep running, not craning to check if the killer is still on my heels.

That way lies running into trees or falling over my boyfriend's dead body.

Also, they definitely are. And despite the woodland setting, they've somehow acquired a ride-on lawnmower, a tuning fork and a battery-operated air pump and it will do me no good whatsoever to brood over what they intend to do with them.

That said, learning from our mistakes does, unfortunately, rely heavily on knowing what they were. That's not always pleasant. By which I mean, it's always awful. But you can't make an omelette without breaking, as every parent knows, every fucking thing.

Most people, as I'm sure you've surmised, don't bother learning from their mistakes, but rather work hard to refine them into über-mistakes that they can replicate on demand, like a party trick.

It's endlessly frustrating, but easy to understand. No one likes to admit they were wrong. Certainly not sober, and definitely not to anyone who might appreciate it.

Sorry, as a great philosopher once said, seems to be the hardest word.

With anemone a close second.

Being, as a species, so infrequently right, this might seem counterintuitive. If we're honest, most of us could throw a rock in the air and, nine times out of eight, hit an amend that needs making. But we should never underestimate the desire of every human to be considered square-jawed and bulletproof— or the equivalent thereof, according to taste. Even, and often especially, the worst of them.

Us. I meant us. Of course I did.

What antennae?

Plus, owning up leads to consequences, and, like the friend of a friend who tags along to parties and scoffs the good crackers, no one is fond of them.

One day, hopefully, we'll discover a method of self-improvement that involves less cringing and day drinking, but for the moment, we dance with the one what brought us.

***

The twins' birthday is conveniently located at the beginning of the year, so it's fairly easy to date most of what I remember.

Far easier to date than I am, at any rate.

If you had asked me, in 2006, whether I thought I was a good Dad, I would have said, "yes".

I would, however, have pronounced it "yesh" and then immediately fallen over.

On the other hand, if you had asked me if I thought I was a good *person*, I might have hesitated briefly on my way down, which is a good trick if you can pull it off.

Self-medication was the order of the day.

Bipolar memories, as I may already have intimated, are hellish to navigate. If I stick to the headlines and tell you that I was perpetually drunk, habitually choleric, regularly delusional and nursing a Christ complex that would make Mel Gibson look like Mel Tormé, then you might conclude that I was a thoroughly obnoxious person who had no business shaping young minds.

And you'd be right. But the beauty and the tragedy of human beings is that we are rarely one thing or the other.

Under the wrong circumstances, such as being awake, I was a terrible partner, an inconstant friend and a distracted father. And for the same reasons: No matter how much I cared, no matter how thoroughly I catalogued the changes I needed to make, no matter how high-minded my principles, no matter how kind and loving I like to believe I was under the surface, I could not get out of my own head.

I doubt I could even have found the door.

I prioritised my career, which is not unusual, but with the chemically-assisted spin that I truly, in my heart, believed that if I did, it would make everything better.

And not just the normal things, like money or security.

I mean *everything*. Art, music, science, human relationships, gender disparity, soup, the percentage of people able to spell Luxembourg and the length of time a pear will remain ripe before rotting.

Simultaneously, the backgrounded, rational version of me was flicking through pictures of the children, clock-watching and muttering like the White Rabbit.

The latter, at least, was something that my shadow could get behind. Unfortunately, his White Rabbit was more Jefferson Airplane than Lewis Carroll.

"Oh my beers and whiskies!" was his battle cry.

I drank for two reasons. To drown the sorrow and to drown the joy. Instinctively, I knew neither could be trusted, so I liquored them up in the hopes that they'd talk.

Now, I'm aware that I've tossed a tabloid's worth of shady backstory your way, but, in truth, I've been lucky. Just not in the boring, obvious way of good things happening to me with any frequency.

This is auspicious in its own right, as when good things have happened to me, I've invariably contrived to fuck them up.

Besides, I have a gambling problem.

No, my good fortune is that whenever I've staggered into a situation which, by anyone's measure, would be considered appalling, I've usually managed to do so by weaving past two others that were positively tragic.

In other words, I've been getting away with it.

Drinking is a classic example. I was a drunk, but not an alcoholic. I'm not saying that in an "I can stop any time I want to!" kind of way, but, rather, to respect the struggle of those whose disease is actually alcoholism.

My disease was bipolar disorder. I was, however, treating it with alcohol, which is like treating a broken leg with hammers. When I eventually started treating it with other things, I stopped getting drunk. To put it in context, a bottle of scotch, gifted at Christmas, will now last me until the following June, whereas it wouldn't previously have made it through this sentence.

Also, the only thing more powerful than my low self-esteem is my exceedingly low tolerance for nausea. I was fine with the pink elephants, but I couldn't take all the twirling.

The children never suffered directly from my drinking, but they were in constant danger of doing so, emotionally if not physically. That's what I find difficult to forgive.

On the whole, I was pretty high functioning. Alcohol took the edge off of the gathering dread and it freed me to be what I thought of as my best self.

a literate buffoon, pushing the envelope, saying the unsayable, conjuring the improbable and lending an air of fevered romance to the most mundane of situations. Byron by way of the Marx Brothers.

It is certainly true that I had a remarkable capacity for it, at least in terms of intake without actual death. With the exception of certain friends of a Celtic disposition, I could not only drink most people under the table, I could build a serviceable table while doing so.

Having come from such a suffocating background, this delighted me. I let my hair down like Rapunzel on smack.

And it made me miserable.

Because what I hadn't yet worked out was that the line between being interesting and being a curiosity is perilously thin.

***

The girls were four years old. After two years of trial by ordeal, not to mention ordure, I'd somehow managed to put my home life back together.

New start, same me. I'm sure we can see where that's headed.

At the time, I was an office administrator by day and a musician by night. Which I realise, having typed it, sounds like the worst straight-to-streaming movie of all time. Probably called *Heartstrings*.

Nonetheless, I was trying to be more responsible, less frantic, more attentive, less destructive.

Trouble was, I was also trying to take over the world, which, I'll stress again, seemed completely reasonable at the time. My sea-faring vessel was due any second, my moment was rushing, ill-chosen shoes in hand, to meet me at the next corner, and stardom was calling late at night to ask if I wanted to come over, watch a movie and see what happened.

Meanwhile, parenting had thrown some new curveballs into the mix. The girls now spent their days with a childminder, ahead of starting school the following year. Like all working parents, I now had to *make* time for them. As with most self-assembly tasks, it was soon clear that there were a number of important parts missing, damaged, or actually dried-up liquorice allsorts.

I was struggling to keep up. They needed more attention than I felt I was able to give. Worse, they needed more attention than I felt was sufficient to give.

I mistook the fact that I was thinking about them constantly for being there. This was a technique that I would perfect over the years, in many important relationships, before learning that, unlike one's children, grown-ups have a choice as to whether to put up with it or not.

45

So, yes, Fathead and Baldy were always on my mind, but if Willie Nelson has taught us anything, other than the importance of a good accountant, it's that this, in the final reckoning, doesn't count for much. Also, almost every thought of them was tethered to remorse—over my varied and increasingly obvious failings as a person and, especially, my inability to focus more on them and less on the domination of all that I surveyed.

That's partially what the alcohol was for.

I lived in constant fear, too, that now that they were walking, talking and pontificating, I would start to see signs of having passed my disorder on, like a really shitty hand-me-down sweater.

It started with Baldy.

As we've established, the marginally younger of my two daughters was a particular child. She also had a temper that reminded me uneasily of my own. It flared frequently and spectacularly, most commonly if things were not exactly to her specifications.

Things were never exactly to her specifications.

Also, none of us were completely clear on what, exactly, her specifications were.

Here's an example which occurred regularly:

If you gave her food she didn't like, even if she'd liked it just fine the previous day or minute, a faint but ominous ticking sound would fade in, emanating from somewhere behind her eyes.

This would usually give you between three and three-and-a-half seconds to take cover or procure a human shield. If any part of that food, however, inadvertently touched a different bit of food that she would, otherwise, have deemed acceptable, this would be shortened to milliseconds.

The resultant explosion could be seen from space, which was, ironically, where you wished either, but not both, of you were instead.

Other things that could set her off: Talking to her, looking at her, not talking to her or looking at her, being in the same room, being in a different room, describing a room to her in which either of you had once been, feeding her, failing to feed her, feeding someone else before or after her, waking her up, putting her to bed, singing, writing, breathing and generally being alive in an annoying way.

Regular attempts were made to address the issue. Colourful charts were constructed, reminding her to count to ten before she spoke, to consider the feelings of others and not to attack anything with a pulse. Quiet time was encouraged. Therapy was considered.

But, primarily, teeth were gritted and waves were ridden.

46

She had become a "mummy's girl" as she'd grown older, and, by this point, considered her mother leaving the house as tantamount to treason. As a result, she considered being left with me as an unacceptably cruel and unusual punishment. And the feeling, to my mortification, was rapidly becoming mutual.

Before you make disapproving noises, let's remember that loving your children does not mean liking them all the time. It pretty much precludes it. Growth is a painful, messy process and children, in common with all living things, are sometimes assholes.

In fact, a huge part of loving them is picking them up on this, so they don't take it out on society by becoming religious extremists or telemarketers.

You shouldn't, therefore, beat yourself up too much when the odd unworthy thought crosses your mind.

You will, obviously, but the point stands.

I was more in favour with the fatheaded one, although she had the good taste to be combative with her mother, for the sake of balance.

It's clear now that the reason for all of this was simple enough. Baldy and I were incredibly similar, neither of us liked that side of ourselves and certainly didn't want to be reminded of it by the other.

She was the child though and I was the adult. This, apparently, means that I should suck it up, but I'm having my lawyer look into it.

It all came to a head, literally, when Baldy's brain decided that being angry while awake was not sufficient for her purposes, and developed the sleep disorder that you know as "night terrors" and I know as "What the fuck was that?"

It is still the single most terrifying thing I have ever witnessed and I've seen the pool scene from *Showgirls*.

Putting it into words may be tricky, as I'm not sure anything short of a prolonged death rattle would do it justice, but I'll give it my best shot.

First, you need to imagine a sleepwalking child.

I'll set the scene.

You are in the living room. The lights are off, the television on, and you are flicking through the channels in the hope of nudity and strong language— anything to reassure you that you are still a functioning adult.

If you are part of a couple, you may even be edging closer to one another in cautious increments, praying that the house will remain silent enough, for long enough, to make physical contact both possible and relatively guilt-free.

Then out of the corner of your eye, a child suddenly appears.

47

And it is always suddenly. Children are basically walking jump scares, which is why there are so many creepy films devoted to them. Birth is the last time any child appears gradually and that's only because that's more of a psychological horror.

Upon clocking their arrival, you travel a startled two feet upwards and a shame-faced six inches sideways—if you'd had your hand anywhere interesting—and, laws of physics be damned, momentarily hover.

A preternatural hush descends until, at last, you return to *terra firma* and locate your voice.

"You okay, honey?" you ask the child.

They do not respond.

"Honey?" you repeat, with the feigned good humour of a political prisoner.

Nothing. Their eyes are blank and staring, mirroring the light from the television—which is now showing an infomercial for needlessly sharp knives that you switched to in panic.

"Is everything alright?"

Silence.

Then they start to lurch towards you and, though you wouldn't even admit it with a wet washcloth over your mouth, your first thought is "Please don't eat my face."

Now, picture all of that, but instead of zombie-ing in your direction, the child is running around in circles and screaming. And not screaming like a baby that wants a bottle, or even a toddler that's been taught a crushing life lesson by an errant balloon.

That would be enchanting, by comparison.

No, they are screaming like a banshee in search of the blood of the innocent, or a born again Christian that wants gay people to pack it in with all the gayness.

In desperation, I researched the condition. Apparently, only somewhere between one and six percent of children experience night terrors and the most common symptom is, wait for it, "inconsolability".

"Bloody typical" and "No shit" were my considered responses to this information.

Your initial instinct, when your child is multi-tasking fight and flight, is to grab them and hold them in place until they calm down. That or adopt the foetal position and cry.

I favoured a combined approach.

Professional advice, however, suggests that you should not intervene or interact with them until the episode has ended. Which only proves that people who write professional advice have no children. As does the fact that their professional advice largely consists of complete sentences and doesn't have any jam on it.

Another sentence, which was no doubt intended to be reassuring, leapt out at me:

"Night terrors cause no long term damage to the child."

I'm sure this is true. You will note, however, that it makes no mention of the long-term damage done to parents, which is acute.

It's been about a decade since the last incident and a chill still runs down my spine whenever she leaves her room to go to the bathroom during the night.

At the time, however, the fallout took other forms. As part of my research, I also learned that the chances of a child experiencing night terrors were exponentially increased by having a parent with a sleep condition.

Guess what.

My father, in addition to his myriad other charms, was a sleepwalker.

Once, when I was little, he was in the middle of a job-mandated course on the safe handling of rodenticides and other fun poisons, the completion of which would allow him to legally arm farmers.

I lived on the prairie, okay?

No, I wouldn't say it was a big house, as such.

Why do you ask?

Anyhow, late one night, after he had spent a long day learning how to creep up on stoats or something, we awoke, en bloc, to a metallic banging from somewhere in the house.

It sounded as though we were being burgled by a Trinidadian steel band.

We gathered in the hallway, my mother and I, and crept towards the noise. To this day, I'm not sure why I was involved in this. I was five. I can only assume that she intended for me to appear suddenly at the intruder and frighten them off.

Eventually, we found my father in the living room. He had systematically removed every floor vent, and was making his way around them, broomstick in hand, whacking determinedly away at the rats he could clearly hear scuttling within.

I can only imagine that, even if it's technically unconnected, bipolar disorder enriches and invigorates these nocturnal perambulations.

My sister used to sleepwalk too and, as she was the most like my father, I breathed a premature sigh of relief that this quirk, at least, had passed me over.

No such luck.

As I got older, my sleep became more and more erratic. Insomnia plagued me most nights, my mind flat-out refusing to shut down, like HAL 9000 after ten lines of coke. And even if I did, eventually, succumb to slumber, my subconscious would immediately hoist me back onto my feet again, to ply the family trade.

But, in keeping with my nature, I added a twist.

I sleep*eat*.

It's exactly what it sounds like. I often wake to find myself with an impressively elaborate sandwich in my hand or four half-eaten apples under my pillow. One night, there was an episode involving a mug of gravy and a broken toe, but I'd prefer not to talk about it.

I have, once or twice, tried to pass it off as a sort of pre-emptive breakfast-in-bed, but, unfortunately, I am not attracted to stupid people.

So, yeah, I had a horrible feeling I knew exactly where Baldy had picked up her night terrors.

This freaked me out almost as much as the piercing shrieks and frenzied wailing. I had concrete evidence of having passed a condition down to my child.

With what else had I lumbered the poor little sod?

We're all smug when someone says they have our eyes or our cheekbones, but it's less biologically satisfying to have given them our glitches.

And to have given them our *pain*? It doesn't bear thinking about.

I, therefore, immediately thought about it. And as, in my brain, worry and obsession are basically synonymous, I tormented myself about it.

Of course, there is something far more wrong with the above state of affairs than might seem apparent at first glance.

Think it through.

A parent has two children.

One of these children is more difficult than the other and needs specialised attention.

With me so far?

Right, then. What is the mark of a good parent in this situation?

Take your time. It's a tricky one.

Is it, perhaps, that they work hard to find creative solutions to the problem, never, not even for a moment, losing faith that their child will come through this difficult period better, stronger and more qualified to, one day, deliver a motivational speech about their journey?

Or is it that they treat their child no differently than any other, allowing them to find their own path, in their own time?

50

Maybe it's teaching the child to embrace difference, to celebrate diversity of mind and spirit, and channel their ferocious energy into something more positive.

Wrong. Wrong. And wrong.

Well, not wrong exactly. Those are fine things to do and should be given a whirl, but they are none of them the answer to the question.

Let's start again.

A parent has *two* children.

Yep. Right there in front of you.

It was right there in front of me too.

Usually asking for juice.

Of all the missteps I've made as a parent, the one that most often comes back to bite me in the ass is the assumption I made that because one of my children had specific and visible—not to mention audible—challenges, the other was just fine and dandy and should be left to get on with it.

I am hopeful that I figured this out before it left permanent scarring. The jury will remain out until the teen pregnancy window closes.

My parents created a rebel by holding me down. I created a rebel by holding her up.

In the animated lion cub sense, not the understaffed petrol station sense, although that would be one way of getting my money back.

Fathead was the good child. The sweet child. The calm child. The one who spontaneously hugged your leg as you covered the tears with claims of hay fever. The one who smiled when you came home, instead of raising a disappointed eyebrow. The one who was easy to deal with.

The one who, because of this, had been carrying a weight on her shoulders since birth.

A weight that looked just like her, but shouted louder.

And this is what I mean about being distracted. I was so caught up in watching one child for signs that she'd inherited my disorder, I was absentmindedly gifting my damage to the other.

She was expected to look after her sister. She was expected to placate her sister. She was expected to give up what she wanted for the sake of an easy life.

Because of her sister.

"Can you just let her have the toy?"

"Is it alright if we have something else for dinner?"

"Could you just make sure she doesn't punch her teacher?"

There's no other way of saying it—this was a total dick move on my part. I didn't see it; I couldn't see it. I told myself I was just trying to get through the day. I told myself that I was doing the best that I could. I sold myself an industrial vat's worth of other piss-poor excuses.

Which were all about me, and therein lay the problem.

She deserved better and I truly hope that she feels she's getting it now.

If she doesn't, or it's all too little, too late, then I'm sorry.

And I'd like the baby to call me "Pops".

Bi Me A River

I said we'd talk about the stigma surrounding mental illness, and that time has come.

Sort of.

This may not unfold as you'd expect. I have complicated views on the subject. I think they are nuanced and I think that I've earned them, but maturity and medicine have taught me to be circumspect when mouthing off about sensitive issues.

Obviously, it would have been better if they had taught me *not* to mouth off about sensitive issues, but even science has its limits.

So, be assured, if I say something with which you violently take issue, its not a deliberate attempt to provoke.

It would have been once. I used to say a lot of things. Primarily things I wish I could take back. There were endless rooms I couldn't read; there were lines I couldn't bear to towtoe. I enjoyed shocking people. I thrilled at being inappropriate. Rarely with malice, but unquestionably driven by rage.

I understand why now, and I think those closest to me do too, which is why I've largely been forgiven. But it won't be forgotten. You can't erase the impression you've made. To some, I will always be an arrogant, unreliable lunatic.

Mostly, I don't blame them. But, also, I do.

I wasn't trying to be arrogant, I was lashing out because I felt constrained—because I'd been bullied. I thought I was fighting the battle of brain over brawn. I thought I was speaking on behalf of every misfit, every nerd, every broken soul. I thought I was simply suffering fools unhappily.

I also thought so little of myself that I imagined conceit to be beyond my grasp.

Yet, somewhere along the way, I *became* arrogant. I just couldn't see it, because I'd convinced myself that I was justified. That I was right. And if there is a more dangerous headspace to be in than that, history has yet to record it.

We're all prepared to imagine that we are, objectively, better than at least *some* people. Murderers, for instance. Or people who walk slowly in pairs. But the moment you truly believe you're better than anybody, you're automatically not.

In my head, I am a shy person. A retiring person. Someone who is most at home when curled up in an armchair with a good book. I think of myself as a good listener. A feminist. Open-minded. On the side of the angels. Only not angels, because made up.

See? I still can't help myself.

In other people's heads, I am a loudmouthed, attention-seeking blowhard with delusions of grandeur.

Are those people's opinions worth worrying about? If you can learn from them, I say yes. If they can't be changed, regardless of how you have, then I say no.

But I have to allow for the possibility that I am wrong.

I didn't want to be unreliable either, but the fact is that I would so regularly push myself beyond my limits—trying to do everything, including things that were distinctly none of my nevermind—that I'd just as frequently burn out and disappear into the dark for a spell, incapable of even the simplest tasks.

Do the reasons matter when the end result was I couldn't be counted upon? It's hard to convince myself that they do.

And, finally, I *was* a lunatic. According to any dictionary you care to consult, be it Oxford or Urban, I have exhibited behaviour that fits, so I'll wear it.

But here's the thing.

It's one thing to call myself crazy. I've owned it, and it reminds me not to take everything I think at face value. Besides, for better or worse, I have the ability to articulate what I'm feeling and how it has affected my life. Many people don't. That being the case, I feel I have a responsibility to stand up and say, "I'm mad as hell but I'm going to keep taking it."

That sounded better in my head.

When other people think of you as "crazy", however, it's a different story. They build Bedlam around you and brick up the door.

So, as above, you take your revenge by describing it melodramatically. Then they roll their eyes and question your sexual history. You, in turn, completely lose your shit and bring up Hitler. At which point, they shrug infuriatingly and say, "See? Crazy."

It's a never-ending cycle—like an all-steroid *Tour de France*.

The foulest wound you can inflict on a person, outside of anything requiring a leather apron, is to discount them. When someone uses "crazy" as their conversational endgame, they are basically saying that, due to your condition, your opinions are suspect and your reactions without merit.

And the reason this hits so hard, whether it causes you to bite back or slink away, is because you aren't convinced that they're wrong.

54

There is one cold, hard fact that I face every day:

Even the people who love me the most, who know me the best and have stood by me the longest do not trust me.

Not completely.

That's hard. I *understand*, but to pretend it didn't wound me, I'd have to be a much better actor than I am.

And, at risk of seeming immodest, that's saying something. My Hamlet, in the parking lot of that Denny's, the night I discovered tequila, is still spoken of with awe.

Don't mistake me. These are people on whom I can rely and into whose hands I would unblinkingly place everything I consider of value. They'll defend me to the hilt. Vehemently. They'd do just about anything for me and I never doubt for a moment that they truly love me, or, at least, have done.

But they can't say the same thing in return. Because I'm mentally ill, my words, my feelings, my intentions will always fall short of a sure thing.

"Is it you speaking?" they ask themselves "Or is it the illness?"

"Do you want *me*, or do you just need someone?"

"Is that a weasel dressed as Nelson in your pocket or are you just happy to see me?"

"Yep. I thought so. Weasel."

The frustration for those of us on this side of the fence is that there absolutely is a real us in here, beneath the layers of wayward chemistry, and the things we feel are genuine. We love you. We do. Often more than we can express. And though we know our actions don't always line up with that, we are trying. And, heartbreakingly, we do understand that this isn't necessarily good enough.

Of course, stigma isn't just an individual hurdle, it's a global one. And, donning my most diplomatic of hats, it could be handled better.

It comes down to personhood and our seeming obsession with limiting its parameters. Every form of prejudice stems from some variation on this theme:

"People like me are normal. Our day-to-day lives are similar. We react in similar ways and we believe similar things. I am still mildly afraid of them, but purely on the basis that they are not actually me, which would be for the best, but I guess you can't have everything."

How this is put into practice varies according to the nature of the individual. For some, it never rises above slight suspicion and cautious bemusement. For others, straight in with the poorly-spelled banners and arson.

We're all guilty of it, to one degree or another. Even when we make a concerted effort to walk a mile in someone else's shoes, we do it in a way that marginalises them.

"Look at these weird, uncomfortable shoes that I'm wearing!" we cry, as though that's helping anybody.

It also doesn't help that the mentally ill, in the media, are presented as either vicious killers with a raft of cinematically-interesting fetishes, or match-counting, vision-having, near-mystical creatures with something *very important* to teach us about humanity.

True empathy, I think, means being able to imagine that you could *be* them, had the universe been nudged by passing wait staff while rolling your particular die. Which means that unless you keep a bag of left-footed stilettos under your mattress or have an imaginary friend who explains physics to you, you're going to have to assume more mundane things in common.

It's almost impossible. I have no idea what it is like not to be mentally ill. It takes colossal leaps of the imagination for me to even work out what life *feels* like for people who aren't.

Is it nice?

It's nice, isn't it?

I mean, you piece together what you can from films and books and music, but most of those are made by people like me trying to figure it out for themselves, so the waters couldn't be muddier if they recorded for Chess.

Making things more complicated is that, contrary to popular opinion, there are, at last count, 7.6 billion universes, each contained within a single head. This was never going to be a recipe for harmony and hugging. When neighbouring cosmoses start chiming in on the worth of your own, the weight of history favours insurrection.

If someone labels you as "abnormal", in other words, it's difficult not to, rather than expend energy on trying to change their minds, turn around and rebrand "normal" in your own image.

I've been down that road. I felt less judgement from people who had suffered similarly, so I began to actively resent and dislike those who hadn't (see also, every human interaction ever).

It starts with anger at the individuals who have made you feel small or worthless, which is logical enough, but then rapidly expands to include everyone else. Before long, your definition of a person is you, maybe your kids and three-quarters of whoever you're in love with, provided things are going well.

So while the people who care about you are, to their credit, trying to make sense of how best to reach out, you're often more interested in how quickly they can fuck off.

That's no way to spend a life.

I should know. I did.

I've met many kind, thoughtful people who have done everything within their power to support me when I've needed it. And I've met many blinkered, callous assholes who think that people in pain and crisis are fit subjects for derision and abuse.

Neither group understood mental illness better than the other, they simply made different choices.

In simplistic terms, people with mental health issues want the same things as everyone else, they just face a different set of obstacles. None of us get everything we want—there have been epic songs on the subject, I believe— but the percentages increase exponentially when we're not doing it on our own.

If you want to help someone with a mental illness—I'm presuming that you didn't buy this book to work out how to burn them at the stake (the secret is good kindling)—just being there is the best place to start. You have to do it with your eyes open though. It's never easy. It does take a toll. If it was all fun and frolic, it would be called a mental carnival.

Actually, a mental carnival sounds great. I'd go to that.

What you should not do, however, is pretend that you know what they're feeling. Because you can't. If you haven't been through it, you can't.

This is why, as hard you try to be compassionate, you secretly think suicide is selfish.

This next bit was hard to write, so I'm going to go ahead and assume it's also hard to read. I think you should attempt it, but I'll understand if you want to skip ahead to the next funny bit about the kids.

I'm far from the only person to have pointed this out, but suicidal feelings, generally, stem from desperation, not laziness or self-interest. And in the case of those who are mentally ill, it is a late-stage and too-often-final symptom of a chronic disease, like pneumonia when your immune system has flaked out.

It is certainly not an "easy way out", any more than a flesh-eating disease is an excellent weight loss programme.

However, I can imagine why that's difficult to wrap your head around. If nothing has ever caused your survival instinct, one of the most basic traits of all life, to go off-line, then how could you understand? The concept of no longer wanting to be is so alien to most people that they are reduced to focussing on the pain the act itself causes.

57

After all, it's hard to miss. It leaves devastation in its wake, forever changing those it touches. It leaves behind questions that will never be answered. Most especially: "Why?"

I have tried to kill myself on multiple occasions. Tried and, thankfully, failed. It hasn't happened since the children were born and, when the idea flits across my mind, as it still does, I tell myself it is not an option because they exist, and I could not, under any circumstances, put them through that.

But I know that's not true. There are circumstances. I've skated dangerously close to some of them. My daily task is to identify them and run, as fast as my stumpy little legs will carry me, in the opposite direction. Sometimes metaphorically, sometimes literally.

I go through a lot of shoes.

Because I don't want to die, not really. I'm still curious about what happens next. It's been utterly ridiculous thus far, so, realistically, anything could happen.

I've my fingers crossed for unicorns.

But sometimes, I just want it to stop. It's too much. Or too little. And never just right.

Ironically, though, the thing that wears down your resistance most is that the risk of it happening—a prospect that you must acknowledge to have any chance of preventing it—tears a bloody great strip from the self-worth of anyone who loves you.

How can they not be enough?

The hard and unpopular answer is—unless their bodies contain a miracle drug of some kind that can be painlessly extracted and widely synthesised— they just can't.

I want to beat it. I want to live. But I also, deep in my soul, need that to be easier; I need living to be something I can deal with more readily. Because my shadow, always planning his coup, still thinks going out in a blaze of sorry is a brilliant plan. And that bastard feeds on struggle; the weaker I get, the stronger he grows.

All of that back and forth, however, occurs in the depths. The weakness is the first thing to break the surface, the first sign that others witness. And we belittle the weak.

I know I do. I don't mean to, but I do.

For example, I *hate* the word "trigger". On a gut-level. I'm as liberal a snowflake as ever melted pathetically on this battlefield we call existence, but when I hear someone complain that they've been "triggered", my first instinct is to slap them and tell them to grow up.

Intellectually, I think shying away from difficult subjects because someone's feelings may get hurt is nonsensical. Dangerous, even.

However, I know from experience that words and events can set me off down the wrong path. When Robin Williams passed away, for instance, I crashed like a rephrased Oedipal case. Not because he was a celebrity or a figure from my childhood, but because, for so long, I thought I recognised something familiar behind his public face, and it had made me feel less isolated. So, when he died, it truly rattled me. I thought, "If he can't make it, how can I?" I became convinced that, eventually, no matter how hard I fought it, one day the choice would be taken out of my hands and I'd make that terrible decision.

So I was triggered; I know it's a thing. But I would never have *said* I was triggered, because it feels like a dodge. It feels like a buzz-word. It feels glib.

And yet, only a few paragraphs ago, I felt the need to flag up that we'd be going to a dark place.

I said this would be complicated.

What's more, my first instinct is probably right. There are undoubtedly people who piggy-back on to movements and taxonomy for attention, for self-aggrandisement, even to let themselves off the hook for deliberate wrongdoing.

My question, upon reflection, is this:

"So?"

We must never mistake matters of principle for licence to be a tool.

If even one person is harmed, in any way, because we felt a burning need to prove a point, then that is a failure on *our* part. There will be times, I'm sure, when it cannot be avoided but this should still be cause for regret and should never be undertaken without consideration.

Saying they *shouldn't* have been harmed by it is not much of a defence.

"Did you or did you not, on the evening of August 8th, stab the plaintiff here represented, in the chest?"

"I did, your honour. Yes."

"Have you anything to say, by way of mitigation?"

"Yes, your honour. I'll think you'll find that if the plaintiff had been wearing a thicker jacket, as would have been sensible, considering the inclemency of the weather, then my knife—which, by the way, I have a perfect right to carry—wouldn't even have broken the skin."

"You have a right to carry a knife, you say?"

"Yes, your honour."

"On what grounds?"

"That there are an awful lot of stabbable people about, your honour."

"I see. And is it your habit to stab these people, when you encounter them?"

"Yes, but most of them think it's funny."

"Funny?"

"That I should try to stab them when they're wearing such thick jackets, your honour. We have a right good laugh about it."

"Interesting. Anything else?"

"Yes, your honour. I would like it entered into evidence that many of the people that I've stabbed have stabbed me right back."

"Including the plaintiff?"

"No, they just sort of lay there and bled a bit. But the option was there."

My head tells me that people need to stop bitching so much and just get on with it. My heart reminds me that this is never as easy as it sounds.

And that I will never know for sure which bit applies to which person.

So, these days, I try to err on the side of kindness, as wishy-washy and fence-straddling as this sometimes appears in a low light.

As with so many things, this shift began with the children. We have a lot of late night conversations these days, especially now that bedtimes cannot be enforced with as much authority. And it was during one of these far-ranging, tangent-baiting tête-à-têtes that Fathead told me that, more than anything else, she wanted to be remembered as kind. Obviously, I wept for a good ten minutes, then looked into finance options on a pony.

I used to think that the world was full of idiots, except for me. But I've grown as a person and am now utterly convinced that the world is full of idiots, including me.

It's an important distinction.

Surely though, this is kiddie stuff. Being nice? That's what you've got? Who would argue against being nice?

First off, I said kind, not nice. There's a world of difference.

Also, we do. Constantly.

"Sure," we say, "Kindness is great in *theory*. But Frank over there doesn't deserve it, so, obviously, we'll need to make an exception for him."

Then someone asks what Frank did. And we tell them, with a shade too much glee. Mind you, what Frank did *is* horrible and, as the graphic details pile up, everyone is soon in agreement that the milk of human kindness would only curdle on his fetid lips. Better to save it for worthier mouths.

"Any more like Frank?" someone then asks, not wanting to get caught out again.

"Well, Beatrice isn't great."

"What did she do?"

What Beatrice did was not cool—not quite as bad as what Frank did, but still well out of order—and we wouldn't want to be seen to be drawing arbitrary lines, so we cut her off from the kindness as well.

You see where this is going?

Good. You may now skip to the next chapter.

For the rest of you, my point is that if we start putting conditions on kindness, we will soon warm to our task.

That may seem less like a logical extension of my argument and more of a transparent attempt to get a quote printed on a mug, but when you consider how people often view the mentally ill, I think it's worth keeping in mind. Or in the cupboard with the tea things.

We're often told to judge people by their actions. But when it comes to those suffering from mental illness, how they act and what they say can be the furthest thing from an accurate representation of who they are as a person. But knowing that doesn't make it any less disconcerting to watch them navigate their distorted universe. It can be alarming.

You will often have no idea what to do.

So I say, having a default reaction is going to save a lot of time and heartache. And, as baseline responses go, kindness will hit the spot far more consistently than, for instance, flapping your arms about and squawking. There is a reason why kindness and humanity are considered synonyms, despite how far apart they appear to have been drifted.

I'm not naïve. There are times when you must protect yourself. We are none of us saints and few of us martyrs.

There are periods when even I struggle to be around my comrades-in-harm. It has a knock-on effect on my own well-being and I owe my children my least compromised self. So, I do comprehend how hard it is, for anyone, to tackle something so intrinsically private—not to mention arcane—from the outside.

And, yes, some people with mental illnesses have done terrible things. There's no point pretending that isn't so. But so have people with Volvos or dandruff.

Judge as you find. That's the basis of real parity. No one is asking you to condone or excuse anything with which you disagree. Or, for that matter, fix anything.

Just take a moment and really try to understand.

We can do that, can't we?

Even if we can't do anything about it, or can't quite get there completely, we can do that.

I sincerely believe that, if we do, each of those moments, those attempts, will eventually accrue into greater comprehension of each other.

But I'm crazy, so what do I know?

Things are slowly getting better. Conversations are being had. Awareness is being raised. There's even an official week dedicated to it. I mean, I have fifty-two of them, but, hey, it's not a competition.

But we do have a long way to go. And it will continue to be challenging, because it requires letting go of ourselves, something for which, so far, we've shown little aptitude. We need to accept that all of the beliefs and values and policies and strictures by which we steer our ships are meaningless by comparison to the severely frayed threads that should and could connect us to each other.

Yes, that sounds right.

Now, a word to my fellow afflicted. If all of the above is true, then we also have some obligations.

Such as learning the difference between stigma and stigmata.

No, I'm not about to trot out the old "there is always someone worse off than you" argument, as true as that is. Our pain is our pain. Other people's pain doesn't enter into it. But few things make me angrier than someone deliberately using their illness as an excuse.

Seriously, how dare you? Do you realise how many of us fight till we're bloody, every moment of our lives, to keep the demons at bay? How can you possibly justify setting an extra place for them and then complaining about the mess?

It's a reason for a lot of things. It is never an excuse.

Keep your high horse stabled; I know perfectly well that's not fair. But it is true. We aren't always in control of our feelings, or our speech, or our actions. But we still have to face the consequences.

Sometimes, we don't even remember the cause of the effect that's kicking our ass round the town. But our buttocks are still bruised and the area is still circumnavigated.

If we hope for forgiveness, we must take responsibility. You can't lay claim to clemency, you can only accept it with gratitude.

It's a rubbish hand, but you still have to play it.

And I have no right to say any of the above, even if you agree with it. Which I do.

Because there are times, despite knowing *all* the better, where I still assess people on the tiniest sliver of the whole, make assumptions based on who I am, rather than who they are. And, as I've thoroughly demonstrated, I can be incredibly didactic, particularly if I've built up a head of steam.

I know this may come as a shock, but, even heavily medicated, I still love a good, old-fashioned tirade. They're just not delivered at 100 miles per hour anymore. And there's a greater chance that I actually know what I'm talking about.

Also, despite having nominated kindness as my lodestone, there remain windmills at which I feel compelled to tilt, calling out what *I* decree to be unkindness, what feels to *me* to be cruelty, what strikes *me* as to the detriment of me, mine, you, yours, even Frank's and Beatrice's.

And that's fine. It's to be expected—we all have things that we perceive to be obvious, despite nothing ever having been obvious ever. It's within working parameters. But I have to keep examining everything, from as many different angles as my rapidly deteriorating knees will allow, if I'm going to avoid stumbling into the same traps I feel compelled to decry.

Not because I'm mentally ill, but because I'm human.

Same as you.

Wow. This whole chapter would have been so much shorter if I'd led with that.

5: Scholasticus Fantasticus

Rites of passage used to mean something when I was younger. You'd get a bunch of your friends together, ideally from different socioeconomic backgrounds, grab some sleeping bags and some poorly constructed flashlights and go in search of a dead body, which would often double as a metaphor for something.

I know it sounds a little cornball, but I'll tell you this: You would always learn something about yourself along the way, whether you wanted to or not. And by the time you got home, you'd be a little older, a little wiser and totally ready to ace your Starfleet Academy entrance exam.

You try telling kids today that and see what they say.

If they're anything like mine, they'll drone on about being forced to watch old movies.

They have their own rites of passage, of course, but they are drawn from much more recent films, and usually have elaborate dance sequences attached.

I wonder, however, if they comprehend that for every milestone that they reach, I gain a millstone.

Actually, I don't wonder that at all. They don't. Not yet, anyway. When we're children, we assume that adults are fully-formed creatures—a sneak peek of what's to come.

And, at first, we want to get there as quickly as humanly possible. We want to grow up, gain control of the television remote and the refrigerator, and be on our merry way. We want to be allowed to do stuff. Plus, there's this thing called "sex" that some of the older kids seem quite keen on, and while it sounds absolutely mental, it's causing a distant bell to chime, somewhere inside, and we're prepared to give it a chance to explain itself.

Of course, the nearer we get to adulthood, the more of the downside we see. Not only are the grown-ups not finished, they appear to be falling apart. Their waists are expanding, their hair is greying, their getting-out-of-chairs is

64

suddenly an aural experience, and, from what we can tell, they aren't allowed to do half as many things as we imagined.

We tell ourselves, however, that they're just doing it wrong, and when we become grown-ups we're going to sidestep all of that unpleasantness and live lives of deep contentment and ice cream for dinner.

But we can't see the stopwatch running in the corner of their screen. The word "obsolescence" has yet to enter our vocabulary.

As adults, conversely, we're fond of saying that we're exactly the same person on the inside, regardless of our age.

"I still feel eighteen!" we proclaim.

Which is true, if what we mean by that is that we live in a state of constant terror about what comes next, and crippling doubt over whether we're prepared for it.

Besides, when your kids stand next to you, older and taller than the last time you looked, the passage of time is all too apparent.

And you can't help but question whether you are still that child on a journey of self-discovery, or two steps from being the corpse in the woods.

***

When your children start school, there are two major changes that occur in short order.

One, your entire schedule shifts. For the next thirteen years or so, everything will be built around getting them to and from their education, rather than simply ferrying them frantically between all the things they're determined to smash, consume or cover in lipstick.

And if you were imagining that it would lead to increased freedom, with a fresh crop of state-sanctioned adults to whom you can turn them over between nine and three every day, forget it. Your responsibilities do not end at the school gates.

Secondly, the number of children you have will increase exponentially and without recourse to any of the fun things that resulted in the initial batch.

Basically, prepare yourself for something I like to think of as shotgun adoption.

But that's all to come. First, you must brave the school run. And brave is exactly the right word, because it requires nerves of steel.

For starters, getting children up for school is one of the most torturous activities ever invented. For years, you have perfected the art of "letting them sleep" in the mornings, so that you could tackle important tasks like laundry, or sitting quietly with your head in your hands.

65

True, the twins had been with a childminder for a year or two—and during that time had attended nursery, which is basically a euphemism for napping around—but you could deliver them half-asleep to her. In fact, it was easier if they weren't completely awake, as anyone who has tried to put a coat on a child will tell you.

But with school, apparently, you have to send them bright-eyed and bushy-tailed, ready to learn, or at least, ready to alternately play the recorder and recite the alphabet.

The first year of school is one of only two periods in a person's life during which combining these two activities is considered a worthwhile use of time, and experiencing the other depends on your feelings about recreational drugs.

You've garnered a little information about my children's avatars so far. So, you tell me:

How much fun was it getting them up in the morning?

The answer is, of course, fuck you.

Perhaps needless to say at this juncture, Baldy was the more difficult of the two. Fathead could be gently persuaded to rise, by waving bits of breakfast under her nose. Baldy first had to be persuaded not to murder everyone in the house.

She does not wake up happy, even now, but she used to wake up hazardous. At some point during her childhood, she had, probably to score a free holiday, signed up for a timeshare demon—the other half of which, I assume, was purchased by an equally irate Australian child. This creature took control for the first half-an-hour or so, swooping through the house, demanding sacrifices, in the form of adults' tears.

Honestly, it made *The Exorcist* look like *Bear in the Big Blue House*. Although, typing that, I'm aware that, to non-parents, that probably doesn't sound any more comforting.

Nor should it. If we really wanted to take care of overpopulation, Durex ads would consist entirely of clips from children's television.

Once the beast had taken its pound of flesh, things would begin to settle down. From this point on, you'd think the job would be comparatively simple. Get them—now dressed, largely groomed and dwarfed beneath totemic Disney rucksacks—out of the house.

But, no, for this is where hilarity truly fails to ensue. I don't know why I expected differently—being a man of extremes—but excitable children do not calm to the point of trouble-free handling, but rather into a state of paralysis.

"Come on, we have to go!"

"I *am* going."

"Sorry. My fault. It just looked like you were sitting on the couch, watching TV and eating the good bits out of your lunch. It must be my eyes."

"I *am* going!"

"That's not even what I said. But we do have to get a move on or you're going to be late for school."

Okay, that last one is on me, but demonstrates how steeply your IQ can dip when speaking to children. "Late for school" is not a threat. You might as well say, "If we don't leave now, you're going to have to go and live in a house made of candy and dreams."

I'm not entirely sure how children's sense of time works—I'm sure there are some theoretical physicists burning through a hefty grant as we speak—but it appears to be endlessly elastic, dependent on the circumstances.

If you extend their bedtime by half-an-hour, to allow them to finish the mural they've started on their bedroom wall—a startling work in crayon, leftover marmalade and their mother's eye-shadow—they will complain loudly of its transience to all who will listen.

By way of contrast, the seven-and-a-half minutes between them asking for a snack and receiving it is apparently the equivalent of a five to ten stretch for manslaughter.

Tell them that you have to leave the house in fifteen minutes, therefore, and they will immediately start building a scale model of the Sagrada Família, feeling themselves to have plenty of time to spare.

You, of course, will begin to get tense.

They do not like it when you get tense. And they will tell you so, in no uncertain terms.

"Don't put on your angry face!"

"This is not my angry face."

"It *looks* like your angry face."

"Well, you'd know."

"Mummy! Daddy's being mean!"

"I'm not being… Just put your shoes on."

"I am."

"Those are not your shoes. *That* is a tennis racket and *that* is a drawing of an otter."

"It's not my fault that I don't know where my shoes are."

And because they are small and cute, and you have spent most of the previous evening trying to convince them that calm and collected is the path to all that is good and shiny, you bite your tongue. Hard. You will be tasting copper for the rest of the day.

Eventually though, by some miracle, all three of you leave the house. Except now, they're the ones in a hurry.

"Daddy! We're going to be late!"

"Are you kidding me?"

"Don't swear, Daddy!"

"I didn't swear!"

"You *did*. You've just cut it out, so you don't look like a bad parent."

"Shut up."

Of course, they're not in a hurry because they want to get to school on time. They have other appointments to keep. With, namely, every child of their approximate age that lives between their house and the school.

This is the walk of the Pied Piper.

I would start every morning with two children, a mild headache and a broken spirit. By the time I reached the school, I would be surrounded by upwards of fifteen five and six-year-olds, my headache would have blossomed into a full-blown migraine and my spirit would be limping painfully in the direction of the astral plane.

They seemed to appear quite randomly, as if in answer to a call that only they could hear. They'd stream from houses, leap from behind bus stops and parachute in from above. For the sake of efficiency, they would already be talking on arrival, folding into the general hubbub as though they'd been there the entire time.

I have spent a large part of my professional life standing directly in front of the loudest drummer in the universe, a person who, when he hits a snare drum, causes women to spontaneously give birth, whether or not they are pregnant at the time.

He is not to blame for any hearing loss that I have suffered over the years.

The sound made by a crowd of children, on their way to school, is difficult to describe. It's not quite deafening, as that would almost be a mercy. It is, instead, somehow both thunderous and shrill. It would certainly fall under most people's definition of noise pollution, or possibly terrorism.

My two, being twins, have never had a problem starting conversations. It's like a built-in ice-breaker. So, they would hold court at the centre of the group, explaining the various pros and cons of being a pair, as I trudged along beside them, trying to blink away the spots from in front of my eyes.

I couldn't zone out completely, however, as, now they had been introduced into the general populace, their genetic predisposition for saying whatever popped into their heads needed careful monitoring.

Picture the scene, if you will.

68

It is an obscenely bright morning. I am leading my children and their entourage up a preposterously steep hill towards the school gates. They are many and I am tired. The young are chattering amongst themselves, discussing the major issues of the day.

"I had porridge for breakfast," says one girl, by way of opening remarks.

The group nods as one. They've had porridge for breakfast; this feels relatable.

A boy to her left, however, dissents.

"I hate porridge," he opines, "It's horrid."

A low rumbling starts up. The group is now split into ideological factions. Conflict is imminent.

Another of their number steps up to the plate, appeasement on their mind.

"I like apples," they say. Firmly, but I think with an open heart.

This seems to strike a more universal chord and fences are quickly mended. Are they not all human? If you skin their knees, do they not want a colourful plaster?

It's Fathead's turn to contribute to the conversation. She mulls her next words carefully. In the current climate, the wrong response could wreck literal seconds of delicate negotiation.

"My Dad's half-gay," she says.

I stop walking.

A dozen or so heads turn and look up at me and I become aware that they are waiting for me to comment.

Now, I do actually have a sensible answer to this, the one I would give to an adult: Everyone exists on a sliding scale of sexuality and while I have largely been attracted to women, I've kissed a few boys and I'm not entirely averse. I'm not totally sold on the scratchiness of beards, but you have to take the rough with the smooth. As it were. Plus, Jon Hamm exists in the world, and I'd happily get to know him better over a romantic meal.

A considerably expurgated version of this answer has been passed down to the twins over the years, by way of insulating them against the casual homophobia that thrives in a playground environment.

They have evidently translated this into "half-gay". I suppose an eighty-twenty split is harder to quantify at their age. I am proud to see that they have accepted this interpretation without confusion or outrage; I just don't want to feel like I'm coat-tailing an identity for which so many people have fought so bravely.

The problem I face, however, is how to clarify this for a group of children— whose parents I don't know—in a way that will satisfy my principles and contain no denials, but not lead to accusations of impropriety.

"Hell yes, half-gay as the day is half-long!" is obviously not going to cut it.

Nor can I countenance anything that to a child's ears will sound like: "What? No! I never said that. Who's gay? What's gay? Why's gay? *How's* gay?"

So, I shrug.

Fathead shrugs.

Baldy rolls her eyes, but I'm not sure whether it's connected to the conversation or she just hasn't for a while and is trying to meet a quota.

The rest of the kids blink, one or two giggle a little, and then they all go back to what they'd been talking about previously ("I like cereal!") without a second thought

I drop them off at school and accept the cheek kisses that are not yet too embarrassing for words—but only from my own children, because otherwise it would be weird—then head off to sit on a bench for half-an-hour while listening to mournful oboe music.

The above scene, which is entirely true, other than the fact that it was actually a bassoon, just goes to reinforce that prejudice is learned, not inborn and there might be some hope for the future if *some* adults learn to keep their ignorant mouths shut.

This is not to say that children are innocent. They really are not. At least, not in the sense of being without guile or savagery. They're waist-deep in those.

They are natural, yes, but that's a different state of being altogether.

Because Nature is not harmless. Far from it. Nature made things that bite you, sting you, drown you and generally fuck with your sense of well-being.

For instance, the next time you begin to think that the phrase "all-natural" is a harbinger of happy healthy fun times, consider the humble alligator.

Alligators are as natural as the day is half-gay. I don't think that's up for debate. But they are also sick and sneaky bastards, my only genuine phobia and one of two reasons I will never go to Florida. I will jump off a cliff, lick a spider, eat at a restaurant with a misspelt food in its name, even endure the odd episode of reality television, but show me a picture of an alligator, and I will set a new land-speed record for the Canadian male.

Just no.

I don't feel the same need to hit children with the nearest oar as I do with alligators—which is for the best—but they are, in many ways, no less frightening.

If two adults fight, they can stoop pretty low, although it usually revolves around having enjoyed the sexual favours of the other's mother. And this, in a way, is nice, as it builds a familial connection.

Kids though. They get dark.

"Could I have a go on the swings, please?"

"I hope your mother gets cancer."

It's pretty fucked up. And this is before they cotton on to the concept of mortality or the idea that their parents aren't as on top of things as they like to pretend.

It's not evil, exactly—I think a lot of them are just feeling out their boundaries—but having a bottle of holy water to hand isn't a bad idea either.

Children *en masse* can be particularly deadly, rendering school a minefield. Not literally, not yet, but if modern America is any indication of what's to come, we're not far off.

As a parent, your first job is to protect your children. And your second job is to enable them to protect themselves. These two jobs often get in one another's way, but no more so than being a vampire and a detective, and that usually works out okay.

The first challenge that you will likely encounter during your child's school life is bullying. Up until that point, they may have been bitten once or twice by another child, or had a toy snatched from their grasp, but they're as likely to have been the perpetrator as the victim. It's not about cruelty at that age, it's just an extension of the cookie metaphor we discussed earlier. Want it? Have it. Annoyed by it? Bite it.

School bullying is different. It's the beginning of true nastiness, and the first addictive taste of how much easier it can be to get what you want by force. It's the birth of active selfishness, rather than just underdeveloped empathy.

It's not a new phenomenon, but it does seem to have reached a sort of golden age. The effects are certainly unmistakable and in desperate need of being addressed. Not because we're softer now—if we were softer now, we'd have less bullies—and not because our precious little angels should be sheltered from anything challenging. I mean, the world is full of bullies, and we have to prepare our children for them.

Of course, I'd argue that we should also be propagating the idea that it's not a rewarding way to behave, despite what they see on the news, but I know that, to some of you, this reeks of both namby-ness and pamby-ness.

No, the reason why it is a *such* an important issue, one that is incredibly close to my heart, is because I am not allowed to punch children in the face.

And, more disastrously, they know it.

I want to be clear. I would take no pleasure from punching children in the face. In principle, I'm against it and I don't mind who knows. But I do think

71

that there are some children that might benefit from *thinking* that I might punch them very hard indeed, in the face, and without warning.

I was bullied myself as a child, due to my bookish demeanour and the many ways in which my parents' religion conspired to draw unwanted attention to me. Like the time they rounded on me after a parent-teacher conference because I'd coloured in a Thanksgiving turkey that a kindly teacher, hoping to help me acclimate, had assured me was simply your common-or-garden-non-pagan-gluttony-festival turkey. Or how I was made to leave school assemblies whenever anyone started singing the Canadian National Anthem. Even if it was only under their breath.

Bullies didn't get far with me, oddly enough, due to both my chemical imbalance—useful for the first and only time—and my rapidly developing, and deeply ironic, capacity for self-preservation. I had quickly worked out that because most people thought of me as, basically, Oscar Wilde without the dress sense, I might not get away with starting fights but I could finish them without a stain on my character or, most of the time, my shirt.

One day, as I waited at a bus stop with my sister, a young Cro-Magnon, who went by the unlikely name of Shane, started throwing rocks at us. They missed—I assume inbreeding dulls the eyesight—but my temper revved nonetheless. Shane had been a nemesis of mine for the entire school year and had, indeed, once spat on my head.

Enough was enough.

Before I even knew I was considering it, I had picked up a much larger rock and, with a force and accuracy that flatly disproved the scandalous things my P.E. teacher had written about me, bounced it satisfyingly off the side of his thick skull.

He, of course, immediately began to cry. And, unfortunately, bleed.

Later, in the principal's office, I was prepared to be read both the riot act and a few of its more controversial amendments. I didn't often get into trouble—at least, not at school, where the rules made some kind of logical sense—but if it was ever going to happen, it was now.

Shane blubbed out the story of what had happened, snivelling in the way that all bullies do when their supremacy is challenged. I sat with my arms crossed, seething and silent, and wracked my brain for some kind of defence.

The principal thought carefully for a moment, looking for all the world like King Solomon about to propose one of his creative custody arrangements.

To my eternal surprise, he turned not to me, but to the Nephilim at my side.

"Why on Earth would he do that?" the principal asked Shane. "All he does is read books."

And something deep inside me clicked into place that I've been trying to dislodge ever since.

If my parents had spent a little more time wishing they could punch Shane in the face and a little less making it impossible for me not to drop Biblical references into my writing at weird moments, then perhaps I wouldn't have had to become quite as manipulative and scrappy to survive.

After all, this is one of the key attributes of being a parent. You can fill your bucket to the brim with Utopian values, but when it comes down to it, if someone is mean to your kid, you're not much further up the evolutionary ladder than any other animal.

It's like one of those bleak moral dilemmas that drunk friends like to proffer at four o'clock in the morning.

"If you had to sacrifice your child to save a million people, would you?"

To which the only correct response, to my mind, is to roll up your sleeves and demand to be taken to these million so-called people so that you can kill them with your bare hands.

Call me old-fashioned, if you will.

This is also one of the biggest strains that children put on the relationship between parents. Before their arrival, you can both declare undying devotion until the herd rocks up, but, afterwards, you both know you'd shoot the other without hesitation if it meant saving the kids.

And should your life happen to veer that way, this is also an excellent method of vetting anyone for a potential step-parenting position. If they've any qualms about smothering you with your own pyjamas to keep the children from harm, they are not the person for you.

I am well-served on both fronts.

You know how, in a movie, one lover will often turn to the other and say, "If I am captured/turned into a Nazi Death Robot/convinced to cast my vote based on what I read on the sides of buses, you must promise to kill me!" and the other lover sheds a single tear, but swears blind that they will, especially if it's the bit about the buses?

I bet most of you sit there and think, "They'll never do it. Their love is too strong."

I think: "Shit, they're going to die."

Because I know, if I ever went crazy enough to be a danger to my children, there are two bullets out there with my name on them.

I could have done without the photographic evidence, to be honest, but I suppose it keeps me vigilant.

It's a perfectly sound system of checks and balances, but, alas, the school years are the beginning of allowing the children out of your immediate orbit, of *not* being there at all times to maim on their behalf. And their primary antagonists will not be monsters, human or otherwise, but other children who, let me remind you, I am not allowed to punch in the face.

It's all vastly discombobulating.

Yes, I know it's an unnecessarily big word, but read it out loud.

Feels good, doesn't it?

Just me, then.

To cap it all off, as a reward for your restraint, you will get the pleasure of many of those children living in your house on a semi-permanent basis, eating your food, sniggering at your sci-fi collectables and making poor life choices over which you have no direct jurisdiction.

Saying that, mine never seem to be at anybody else's house, so it's possible I just got screwed.

The kicker is, you'll eventually get attached to them too. And they to you— which is less surprising, as you've been paying for their birthday presents for the previous decade.

Of course, the other people who will be introduced into your life, whether you like it or not, are your children's teachers. This is a lottery. Sometimes, you and your child will be entrusted to the care of an inspirational, saintly creature whose entire life revolves around the instruction and edification of their class—someone who refuses to buckle beneath a needlessly bureaucratic system that wants nothing more than to carve the idealism out of them, one pointless piece of paperwork at a time.

When this happens, you will find it difficult, come parents' evening, not to stand on a desk and invoke Whitman. Even after the cease-and-desist.

On other occasions, the person in charge will have been written by Roald Dahl, the day after his dog died. They will have taken their understandable fury at not being allowed to punch children in the face and transformed it into a deep and abiding resentment of anything or anyone under six feet tall.

These are the teachers who think shouting is the purest form of communication and that children should be neither seen, nor heard, nor conceived. Thankfully, they are few and far between, but I would be much happier if they were fewer and further between. If there were, say, two, and one was in Auckland and the other in a hitherto uncharted region of space, I could probably come to terms with it.

Once again, I try to make fewer assumptions of late and I have seen first-hand the benefit of teaching the children to respect all of their teachers regardless of perceived ogre-osity. I hope the person who brought me round to this way of thinking is reading this and sees that I *am* capable of change, even if I'm still less accomplished at cleaning than I'd like. Especially as she has one of the bullets.

That said, as a general statement, I believe that teaching is one of the most important jobs in the world and that anyone who doesn't treat it as a sacred duty should be fired out of a cannon into the side of a truck.

Other opinions are available.

In the main, though, we've been lucky and my children have had a comprehensive enough education over the years to enable them to ask me for money in multiple languages. Yes, I have taken issue with the system on a number of topics, in my unique, unmedicated way, but I'm trying to tell this in some kind of order, so you'll have to bait your breath.

Of course, the true moral of the story is that the children loved every minute of it, and look back on the early days of their education with fondness.

Just not the mornings.

Never the mornings.

Can't Bi Me Love

Let's talk about love.

I know. It feels like we've done this bit already, but we've barely even scratched the surface. We've circled around it, yes. We've dug into my romantic failures and we've celebrated the deep, spiritual and, frankly, exhausting connection between a father and his children.

And I'm sure we all agree that they were good for a chuckle or two.

What we haven't done is talk about how, living with this disorder, I feel about love.

And we should.

Because I can't escape the feeling that some of this reads as if it has always been me against the world.

It really hasn't.

I'll keep it brief, though, because, on this subject, I believe a few well-chosen words are much more fitting than my usual linguistic gymnastics.

So, here goes.

Thank you.

You know who you are and I hope you know why.

And if there is one thing I am grateful for, one thing that I actually gained from this disease that I wouldn't give back, it is that my love for you exploded in my head and my heart with an intensity so far beyond the clichés that we're sold that, to my ears, love songs on the radio sound like little more than jingles for off-brand protein bars.

I couldn't always show it. I couldn't always live up to it. And I couldn't always focus on what was right in front of me. But somewhere along the way—aided rather than hampered by the disconnect in my head—I saw you. Really saw you. And you were glorious.

You *are* glorious. And, now, though my light has, of necessity, dimmed somewhat, yours never will.

It is burned into my memory.

And I'm glad of it.

I just wanted to say that.

And, you know what?

It's my book. So I can.

6: A Number of Beasts

Flashforward warning.

I'm writing this on the night that Fathead and Baldy completed their final GCSE papers. For the benefit of international readers, these are a series of exams taken at the age of sixteen, to prove that you can still write coherently through bitter, besieged tears.

There will be more on this later.

There is an air of relief about the house, slightly offset, for me at least, by the fact that they have invited friends round to celebrate and they are all singing karaoke in the room below mine. At this precise moment, a teenage boy is essaying the female part to "Barbie Girl" in a quavering falsetto.

It also means that I'm having to write wearing trousers, which is against what little religion I have.

Outside my window, a road rage incident is unfolding, with one woman having a decent stab at the record for the largest number of racist, homophobic and generally repulsive remarks employed during a single argument about rights of way.

So, in one ear, I have a screeching voice assuring everyone who might have been wondering that its owner is, indeed, a girl by Mattel in a world by Mattel. In the other, an increasingly incandescent motorist is attempting to disprove the inverse-square law by remaining at the same elevated volume no matter how far down the street she's stomped.

"Because your girlfriend can't fucking drive, you muppet!" is her decidedly less catchy refrain—though I imagine it might make for a decent techno track.

It is, therefore, a joy to cast my mind back to simpler times, when the girls were only six and I was worried less about the poor state of my mental health and more about mining it for three-minute pop numbers.

Oh, Jesus. He's doing "Uptown Girl" now.

Anyway, back in those heady days of 2008, I was enjoying what I considered to be a rare remission of symptoms, which basically meant that I was prepared to let my propensity for self-harm find its own way, rather than actively encouraging it.

My band had been touring pretty hard for the previous three years, coming off the back of a record about which nice things had been said, raising our celebrity alphabet status from a wobbly W to a fairly solid Q.

Looking back now, I can see that I hadn't escaped from mania at all, it had just been anchored to something tangible and so wasn't as readily apparent. People *did* like what we did—other than the ones who didn't and whose names I kept in a regularly updated notebook, in a strongbox, in the shed—and we had actual achievements to which I could point and say "Hah!" whenever I felt in need of reassurance.

Also, most of my friends were musicians. We were all just as dedicated; we were all putting in the hours. So, it was appallingly easy to convince myself that this was an artist thing, not a mental thing.

What I didn't realise is that most of them switched it off when they went home—not all, but most. And even if it wasn't as straightforward as that—musician sanity being graded on a curve—they were not regularly walking the streets at three o'clock in the morning, half-cut, writing lyrics, agonising over reviews—good or bad, didn't matter, still worth an agonise—or convincing themselves that every minor fracture was, in fact, the big break.

The word "all-consuming" gets thrown around a lot, but most of the time is taken to mean that someone is really rather fond of something and spends a lot of their time—arguably an excessive amount—in activities surrounding it.

It ain't that. Not with me, anyway.

You can dig right into a chicken, but if there are still bones left at the end, you didn't consume it all.

I eat the plate.

And so, the music was never my hobby. It wasn't even my job or my career. It was my *life*.

All musicians say this at some point, but it usually translates as, "I don't understand why you're upset, but isn't this guitar pretty?"

I meant it quite literally. Music, or rather the fact that I made music, had become my identity. In some ways, this was useful, as I'd never really had one of my own before. They'd always been sort of draped, second-hand, over my shoulders by people with agendas. Or by me, dressing hastily.

But, as was its way, bipolar disorder had helped me take an already questionable set of behaviours and push them to their extremes.

It wasn't drugs—they had never really taken hold for me. I was, admittedly, still putting away an extraordinary amount of alcohol, but, for the moment, its effects were more insidious than instant. And, yes, the old standbys of financial profligacy and poor impulse control did put in occasional appearances, but I had both a slightly better handle on them than usual and a circle of friends prepared to bail me out.

Mostly, it was just severe tunnel vision. Where the tunnel was actually a straw, and the vision a badly translated audiobook.

Unfortunately, this also coincided with the girls becoming aware enough to pass judgement.

"You're *always* working!" made its first appearance somewhere around this time. As did the often, but not always, related: "You're *always* tired!" Of course, I didn't hear them for what they were: perfectly reasonable requests for attention. I heard them as complaints about my parenting—a sore subject, particularly as I knew the grievances were valid.

So, I ended up giving a lot of impassioned speeches about how Mummies and Daddies had to work so children such as themselves could have houses to live in and food to eat and zeitgeist-y Christmas presents to have tired of by Boxing Day and really they should appreciate it all a little more.

To their credit, at no point did they point out that I was a manic depressive musician and, therefore, lectures on lifestyle management weren't exactly my purview.

A quick aside:

I just popped downstairs—following the closing bars of "Livin' On A Prayer"—to ask Fathead if she remembered any of this and she informed me that neither of them had any idea of what was actually going on at the time.

This was briefly comforting. I couldn't have done too much damage. Not if they hadn't even noticed. But, obviously, she wasn't finished.

"We just thought that Daddy was crazy."

Out of the mouths of babes, and so on.

I nodded quietly. I may even have tightened my mouth a smidge. Then I noticed the other party guests were starting to stare and came back to my room, leaving the twins to their hosting duties.

They have never been under any illusion about the fact that I was not like other fathers. Neither have their friends, who, from the start, divided into two groups—the ones who thought I was "cool" and the ones who thought I was "weird". I didn't mind; I was used to people splitting along those lines. Well, except for the "cool" bit.

From time to time though, I'd overhear them bragging about me. I'd be in the kitchen, over-caffeinating, when from the next room, I'd hear their chirpy little voices nattering away.

"My Daddy is a musician," Fathead would be telling a friend, with just enough pride in her voice to be moving, but not so much that she couldn't disavow it later.

"No, he isn't."

Flat-out denials are a six-year-old's default response when confronted with information that they can't process.

"He is. e's been on the ro."

"He hasn't."

Politicians have a similar problem.

"He HAS."

"Well, he's probably not very good."

I'd restrain myself from leaping out from behind the kitchen door and shouting, "Oh, like you're the expert? What's your favourite Beatles song? Huh? Huh? I bet it's '"Yellow Submarine". '. Of *course* it is. Cause you're *so* musical. Take your stuffed whatever that is—a beaver?—and your *Janet and John* books and get the hell out of my house."

After all, some of them thought I was cool, and I didn't want to risk throwing off the percentages.

"Yeah. Well, I don't think you even have a Dad."

"I do so."

"Prove it."

"He dropped me off. You saw him."

"I saw NOTHING."

At this point, Baldy—who I didn't even realise had been in there with them—would usually wander into the kitchen, having become bored with a conversation that clearly wasn't going anywhere fast. Having caught me eavesdropping, she'd shake her head sadly, point silently at an apple on the countertop and cock her head to one side.

I'd sigh, then cut it up into the meticulously precise slices she liked—an unspoken bargain to keep the whole sorry business between us.

We were starting to come to an understanding.

But I felt guilty, all the time. I was pretending to be this normal guy, looking after his kids, when I was around. When I was elsewhere, I played the decadent, bohemian rock star, nothing but gravity holding him down. I was in serious conflict with myself. And we were both losing.

What I really wanted, deep down, was an ordinary life run by an ordinary head, but as the latter wasn't a possibility, I had convinced myself that the former was likewise out of reach. I would have to Frankenstein something together and hope for the best.

I had all the right ingredients to make a life, it seemed, but, unfortunately, the chef was on fire. And when that happens, there's usually a refund in the offing.

It wasn't fair on the people around me, for which I continually beat myself up—until the next distraction hove into view. But neither was it fair on me, a vital chunk of information that I was too consumed with self-loathing to acknowledge.

And, of course, my loved ones had their own problems, as is their wont, and deserved the kind of unyielding support they'd always dished out. As my issues were louder and had a science-y name, however, they were plumb out of luck.

I still think that diagnosis is essential to confronting a condition, but sometimes the accompanying labels concern me. We already know that when diagnoses become biographies, prejudice starts swinging its dick about. But it can be equally detrimental to the sufferer's self-image. You become your burden. So, maybe we should keep it simple: a laundry list of potential challenges, alongside a few handy tips and tricks. You'd still know there was a reason for why you felt the way you did; you'd still be able to take the appropriate steps or medication. But you could avoid these kind of exchanges:

"Actually, I'm struggling myself right now."

"*I'm* bipolar."

"Daddy, can you take us to the park?"

"I'm *bipolar.*"

"Sir, we don't allow horses in the dining room."

"I'm bipolar?"

I'm not saying everyone uses their condition as a get-out-of-jail-free card, but it is awfully tempting. Without a catchy title, though, it would take so long to explain our particular impairment that we might as well just attempt the thing being requested of us.

I'm an idealist, I know.

My other major concern, back then, was that for all that I'd worried that the children were too much like me, in a great many ways they were turning out to be confusingly different.

They were popular, for one thing. When I started kindergarten, my teacher told my mother that I was the only eccentric five-year-old she'd ever met. And she was not wrong. Whereas, while I don't think that they've ever been entirely mainstream, or even *compos mentis*, my two have always seemed to fit in just fine.

At six, they enjoyed the music and films and television programmes that their friends liked. They were current. They weren't at constant war with the world around them.

And they didn't like books.

You have no idea how much this pained me. I had long dreamed of sharing my adoration of books with my children, not to mention introducing them to the vast and varied library I had accumulated. Books had always been my comfort food, my lifeline to the wider world, and my ticket out of the hot mess that was my mind.

Books were my friends.

Ah, don't look at me like that. I had people friends too.

When I moved to England, I came with three suitcases. Two of these contained nothing but books, with the other divided equally between clothing and boxes of Kraft Dinner, which I'd heard they didn't have on these shores.

For those of you who haven't experienced the life-altering wonders of Kraft Dinner, it is a packaged macaroni and cheese dish, distinguished by a powdered cheese sauce of luminous orange. It tastes and feels like a lingering hug from a feverish friend. Unfortunately, I'm pretty sure this is because the sauce is radioactive, which would explain why only weak-ass imposters appear under the Kraft banner overseas.

But it was my books with which I truly couldn't part, no matter how uncomfortable it was to lug them across a brand new country, especially one already predisposed to pass judgement on foreigners.

They were to form the foundation of a truly magnificent—or as others would have it, gratuitously large—collection, which I built over the following years, despite my poverty, by walking into charity shops, waving my hand in the vague direction of the shelves, like a demented socialite in an art gallery, and declaring, "I'll take the lot."

If I had been presented with such a cornucopia when I was a child, instead of a selection of horribly written Bible tracts and a dog-eared copy of *When Bears Attack*, my sexual awakening would have come even sooner than it did. Although, I suppose it saved me some particularly nasty paper cuts.

But my kids. Oh, my kids would be able to read whatever they wanted, whenever they wanted.

And they did. They read nothing. Ever.

Oh, I'd read to them when they were little. A full-on performance piece, every night, to polite, if restrained, applause.

And, of course, they *could* read. But, as far as they were concerned, reading was a school thing. As soon as their homework was done, their eyes yearned for more visual pleasures.

They liked films. Which was something at least. I had a similarly long list of classics that I was desperate to share with them.

A small piece of advice for people who are anything like me:

No one enjoys you watching them watch something. Not children, not significant others. And especially not after you've just finished telling them that it's the best film ever, it changed your life and you just *know* they're going to love it. It's too much pressure and it will only lead to arguments that neither party can actually believe are happening but both are unwilling to lose.

Besides, no one is going to clock the line of dialogue that transformed the way you saw the world if they're busy thinking, "If he doesn't stop staring at the side of my head, I am going to impale him on this shrimp fork."

Anyway, the children did not want to watch any of the films that I suggested. They only wanted to watch one film: whichever was their current favourite, on a loop, *ad infinitum.*

The year they were six, I saw *Matilda,* from beginning to end, 512 times and portions of it upwards of 4,000.

The next year it would be *Charlie's Angels* and I would miss *Matilda* very much.

That's how it's been all along though. Over the years, I've been witness to a cavalcade of their obsessions, fascinations and passions. Some of these have been fleeting, others have taken more enduring root. And many have, in the moment, made me want to chew through the side of my own face. Yet sometimes, in the quiet hours, I find myself returning to them of my own accord, nostalgic for a time that I wish I could remember with more clarity.

And I have to believe that, if I've done my job properly, this will eventually be mutual.

Years from now, two sisters—perhaps long separated by busy lives, or the occasional lawsuit—may gather in front of those bookshelves and consider the vast array of words that helped to make their father the man he was. The man that raised them, that taught them right from wrong, real fruit from plastic fruit, and music from Bieber.

And they will turn to each other and smile one of those secret twin smiles that make people check that their wallets are still there. They'll both reach out for the other's hand and, as one, their eyes will scan across the titles, the authors—all those stories that must once have been so familiar to their dear old Dad. That he spoke about, and wrote about, and nagged them like such a little bitch to read.

Then, one of them will reach up and, carefully, almost reverently, slide a volume from its perch and turn it over in their hands, feeling the weight of it, the texture of it.

They won't remember them being so heavy. So solid. Like they'd been carved into their space in the world.

So much like him.

Oh, that man, they'll think. So contrary, yet so kind. So angry, yet so easily manipulated.

It will almost be like I'm there with them. Instead of in the home where they've put me.

And then, as if on cue, the sisters will turn and look each other in the eye, the way they used to, when they were children. A lifetime of shared experiences will flood their minds, from the womb to the second in which they stand. The shared joys, the far more grudgingly shared bedrooms, even the accidentally shared romantic partners about which they've vowed never to speak.

They'll think about their own children—Moustache and Wonky Eye, Monobrow and little Sausage Fingers—and the incredible gift that they now have the opportunity to pass down to them.

Four words will occur. Suddenly, simultaneously and with an intensity that almost robs them of breath, although that might be because no one's dusted in ages.

And, without consultation, they'll speak them aloud, together, as in sync as they have ever been.

"Think they're worth anything?"

Bi the Rivers of Babylon

Before we proceed, there are few *mea culpas* that I'd like to get out of the way.

I've talked a little about how being bipolar can make you say things that, upon medicated reflection, turn out to be ill-advised, factually incorrect, unkind, unfair, contrary to the laws of physics or just plain rude.

But it's not just about what you say. *How* you say it can be equally devastating. And you definitely have a preferred way of saying it. The polite word for it is "zealously". The impolite word is unprintable. There is no debate, no quarter given. You stand by every utterance, or, at least, jump belligerently up and down. Clarification, correction, even the gentlest of follow-up questions are all treated as unprovoked acts of aggression.

So, while we're all here, I'd like to officially retract, in print, some of my more egregious errors of speech and thought.

Many of them were a direct result of what was going on in my brain. Others were just me being an ass. I shall let you decide which was which, because I can't tell the difference anymore.

In no particular order:

Because I did not like something, it did not make it shit. You were not wrong for liking it, and however "educated" I thought my tastes were, it neither meant that I knew better, nor that it mattered.

Any issues that were inexplicably thrown up for me by the ordinary human past to which you had every right, were entirely my problem and, unequivocally, not yours. Which shouldn't need saying, but clearly does, because, for some reason, I blamed you.

When I said I was "doing my best", it often meant I was "doing whatever made me feel better in the short term" but I didn't want to deal with the ramifications of coming to terms with that.

Your opinion was not only as valid as mine, but usually made more sense and was less frequently based on a dream I'd had the previous evening.

If I ever complained that you didn't understand me, it was because you understood me better than I did, which was worrying.

I was not always the smartest person in the room. I think it's clear, however, that I was often the biggest idiot.

No one was out to get me. Well, that one guy, but I should have learned to let that go.

The universe owed me sod all.

Wanting a home and security were not—and are not—bourgeois desires. I was projecting, due to my own lack of success in this area.

Artists are not better than other people.

You weren't being overly demanding. A toilet should be cleaner than that.

Often, it *was* my fault.

If you'd really loved me, you'd have done exactly what you did. I have absolutely no idea why this was ever in doubt.

Cigarettes were not a suitable replacement for medication.

Therapy is not a con.

That band that everybody likes is not just "music for virgins to dry hump to"—they seem to mean a lot to folk and, let's face it, that's all that's important.

Being poor did not make me more authentic.

Nor did being sick.

I didn't know what I was doing. Not even a little bit.

I didn't have it all under control.

I wasn't fine.

And, perhaps most importantly, it would be in no one's best interest if I ruled the world. In fact, it would be a nightmare.

Just imagine the toilets.

7: Faith Accompli

2009 was a banner year.

And then, a Hulk year.

I'm here all week. Try the soy-based veal substitute.

Stop groaning. My geekdom is a matter of public record; I think you've got off lightly.

Besides, it's accurate—there was a severe transformation looming. It wouldn't be as green, nor, alas, as musclebound, but would certainly be as marked. And I did rip a lot of trousers along the way, but I'm pretty sure that was unrelated.

In short, I was about to reach the end of more ropes than a hangman's test dummy.

Gallows humour is my other favourite.

I'm not even sorry.

I don't know if you can tell, but, at the moment of writing this, I'm a tiny bit tweaked. It's probably not as obvious on the page, because you can read the words at your own speed, and not the one at which they are currently tumbling from my brain to my fingers.

Also, I just came back and edited out most of the conspiracy theories.

Apparently, the Illuminati have nothing to do with my electricity bill.

But, in all seriousness, I'm going to let this chapter ride, unvarnished, because I think it's important to acknowledge that I am mitigated, not mended.

There will always be days like this, when I have more ideas than craft and my attention span is not my friend.

Still, it's not a particularly bad episode. The meds are still working, they just seem tired and in need of a couple of couch days. My jaw hurts from clenching, my left eye keeps twitching and I feel like someone is trying to administer electroshock from the inside, but I'm still in the driver's seat.

Truth is, I've been working too hard, relaxing too badly and trying to cram too much in, a combination that has always legged me up. Plus, every so often, the chemicals that I ingest decide that they've had it up to here with the chemicals that I create and cease to be on speaking terms.

The end result of all of the above is usually a mini-relapse—a tinny echo of the bad old days.

It also happens whenever I get a cold, or anything else with a fever attached. My theory is that 100 degrees, or thereabouts, is the boiling point of brains. I have no scientific evidence whatsoever for this, but that doesn't stop anyone else from making wild claims, so I feel like I'm within my rights.

Don't get me wrong, I'm okay. I'm not great, but I'm not yet crying over videos of babies hugging either. Yes, I can feel the other guy straining at his leash, but he can wind his neck in. It's not happening.

Nonetheless, it's a timely, if tiresome, reminder to keep my eye on the ball. Sometimes, I'm daft enough to forget. I was in constant pain for so many years, that it's become dangerously easy to treat the drop in intensity as absence. It's like when you have the flu. You feel diabolical for days on end, then you wake up one morning and you only feel wretched.

Hurrah! You're well!

But you're not. If you don't believe me, try eating something.

Told you.

So, no matter how balanced I feel, if I ever kid myself into thinking that my altered ego has upped stakes and moseyed on, then all the work I've done so far will be for naught and this book will not have a happy ending.

Or any ending at all. I'd be too busy finishing the first one-and-a-half chapters of fourteen other books. Four of which would be about the life cycle of the avocado.

It would be tempting to consider it happenstance—were the link not so nasally plain—that I should reach this particular chapter during a period when the barbarians are once more at the gate.

I'm overstating. One barbarian. Two at a push. And I think the other one is there to carry the luggage.

Regardless, the year under discussion was one during which, after muddling through—emphasis firmly on the mud—for yonks, I really started to lose it. Not my mind, although that did go walkabout for a stretch, but something I needed even more desperately.

Faith.

***

I have a predictably complicated history with faith. I was brought up to consider it chief amongst the virtues, provided, of course, that its eyesight was dodgy. And I heard the word every day of my life, usually as a feckless reply to any enquiry that adults wished to deflect.

But, for all of my supposed piety, I don't think I ever had faith as a child. I was a good little boy—on the outside—and I believed God was in his heavens, being cross, because I had no reason to think otherwise. It didn't require faith, in my household, to accept that you were being watched and judged and punished for your sins. It was bloody well beheld. Mine was a religion of extrapolation.

Lest we forget, these were people whose idea of a bedtime story was to teach you what to do if a demon visited you in the night.

So not faith, then, but fear.

As a child, I was constantly afraid. Of my parents, of God—both backed by armies of self-appointed moral arbiters—and, equally, of what would happen if I ever escaped either. I existed in a state of perpetual unease, with a side order of righteous indignation, like a rabbit writing a book report about *Watership Down*.

Above all else, I was terrified that everything that I had been taught was true and thus, ironically, prayed nightly that I was wrong. That my perfectly natural thoughts and desires were not evil. That the world was closer to the one I'd read about in my books than the one I'd read in about in *His* book. That I could, one day, be free—to do what I wanted, any old time—without consigning my eternal prospects to a fiery dustbin.

Concentrate on the next bit, or you might get lost. I had to read it a couple of times myself.

I implored God not to be listening. And my prayer, in a roundabout way, was answered.

And that's when I started to have faith.

Friends have often theorised that my upbringing—while abysmal—was an excellent boot camp for what I would go on to do. As a performer, I take their point. I was preaching from the age of three; audiences don't phase me. In terms of being a writer, again, it's quite easy to appear erudite if you can quote a holy book at will. Especially if you do it sardonically.

But the biggest problem with growing up in a cult is that, at your most impressionable age, you're trapped inside a fantasy novel. The people around you hold no truck with metaphor. Nor any other large vehicle. It's all as literal and as tangible as anything you can lay your hands upon—which may explain why so many of the tenets involve keeping your hands to yourself.

I also think this is why their followers are encouraged to renounce stories of witchcraft and sorcery, or anything else remotely magical. They've been conditioned to believe any old tat; if they found out there was less boring gibberish to be had, you'd never keep them in line.

That kind of heightened existence isn't like a shirt that you can put on and take off; it worms its way into your bones. The religion you can leave behind, but it's harder to shift the religiosity. You continue to see the universe in grand terms—and your place in it as significant. If you are, say, medically prone to delusion, this is all turned up to eleven.

You convince yourself that there has to be a reason for everything. There's no way you could possibly have been made to suffer so much, if there wasn't a pay-off in the works. Success against the odds—what else could you possibly have been built for?

And so, you end up living less of a life and more of an autobiography. Always waiting for the chapter when it all falls into place—and never doubting that will it come.

And never stopping to count the pages you've skipped trying to reach it faster.

***

It's not entirely without its benefits, that kind of unyielding self-belief. When I told Fathead and Baldy, now seven, that they could be anything they wanted to be when they grew up, I meant it.

Take me as an example, I'd say.

I came from nothing. I had no support. I moved to a new country, at the age of nineteen, with nothing but the pasta and the books on my back.

And, yet, look at me now—about to achieve power and fame beyond the dreams of ambitious people with healthy sleep patterns.

They believed me, of course, as I'd believed my parents when they told me that one day, we'd live forever on a paradisiacal New Earth, cleansed by holy fire of modern aberrations such as rock music and feminism.

And, crucially, *I* believed me—despite my entire life to date having consisted of evidence to the contrary. So many almosts littering the frame. So many missteps contaminating the crime scene. So many signs that the opponent to whom I was squaring up was not a mountain that would, however stubbornly, erode under sufficient pressure, but an out-of-control whirligig of dumb luck.

90

Still, I gave short shrift to that kind of negative thinking. Common sense was all very well—a fine way to approach crossing the street or using an oven glove—but when it came to more esoteric pursuits, it only got in the way.

Besides, my mama didn't raise no quitter.

She did, on the other hand, raise a deeply disturbed, emotionally needy, control freak with little or no sense of perspective. And he was raring to take the show on the road.

And so, that year, despite my exhaustion—and already reeling from serial knockbacks—I dug in and worked harder than I had ever done in my life. I pulled out all of the stops. I put myself on the line like never before.

This was going to be it. All in. Do or die.

And, at first, it felt like it might actually work. Doors started to open a crack. Opportunities raised their heads, bashfully, over the parapet. My musical compatriots and I were talking the talk, walking the walk, dancing the dance and, vitally, exerting the exertion.

This was our moment. All we had to do was seize it.

And we did. Artistically. We made something great. Something of which to be proud. Something that, I'm still confident, will stand the test of time, in its own humble way.

Nobody cared.

Of course, that was not a result I could accept. So, I pushed harder. I worked twenty hours a day, into the night and back out again, growing shorter of fuse with every siesta-free minute that passed.

And, still, nobody gave a good goddamn.

I made rash decisions, trying to keep the boat afloat. I burned through money. I risked friendships. I broke promises. I tarnished memories.

Then, when I felt I'd warmed up sufficiently, I really went for it.

I dragged other people along for the ride. Friends put their money where my mouth was—cheerleading like their own lives depended on it. Others saw the big flashing "vacancy" sign over my head and tried to pull me back from the brink.

But I'd gone too far to stop, I told myself. There would be time to fix all I'd broken once the dust had settled, but, for now, I had a Goliath to topple.

It had to work this time. It *had* to.

There were two seven-year-old girls patiently waiting for Daddy to be back in the room and I couldn't bear to face them defeated.

What more noble cause could there be? I would give my children a brighter future. I could offer them the security that I had always lacked. And

I would gift to them a certainty that any foe can be vanquished, if you remain unbroken and unbowed.

And, hopefully, that would make up for the fact that my actual motivations were far murkier.

Either way, failure was unthinkable.

Impossible.

Inevitable.

It took a while for it to sink in—adrenalised to the gills as I was. For a few months, I kept going through the motions, however stiff and ungainly they had become.

And then, one day, almost as an afterthought, it hit me.

It was over.

And I died inside.

Which, looking on the bright side, was half of a life-long task completed.

As I saw it, I had done everything right. I'd suffered and sinned, then taken it all and thrown it in into my art. I'd sacrificed. I'd gambled. I'd given it everything I had, most of what everyone else had, and a bunch of stuff I found in a skip.

I never played it safe. I never even played it wary.

And I wasn't some lazy fuck in a garret somewhere, painting nudes on the state's dime. I was a worker, a grafter, someone prepared to put their shoulder to the wheel. I didn't expect something for nothing. I expected everything, sure, but not for *nothing.*

Also, damn it all to Dante, I'd put in my ten thousand hours to become half-decent at what I did. Then surrounded myself, as you should, with other people who were much, much better than that.

And it didn't work.

Nobody gave a monkey's.

If I'd been well, or willing to listen to what almost everyone, up to and including strangers in the street, was telling me, this would have been a moment of clarity, a turning point. It should have been the final reel, when I discovered the true meaning of Christmas.

After all, I had survived trauma and madness and seven shades of stupidity to get here. I had children that I adored, people who loved me—and had been endlessly patient—and, be it ever so frustrating, a creative outlet, which is, let's face it, a luxury, not a right.

Okay, so it wasn't going to lead to fame and fortune. It was time to accept that. But, hey, since when had that been what it was all about?

But that was exactly the problem. It hadn't been about that. That kind of disappointment might have been navigable. I could have, in time, got over that. What it was actually about was something much darker.

I had to be *right*. I couldn't have gotten so much wrong, so often, and not be right. Not again.

If it all hadn't been part of some vast artistic odyssey, then I was just a very poorly boy who had put everyone through the ringer for a lark.

I wasn't ready to contemplate that.

So I didn't. I pretended none of it was happening and kept moving.

But not quickly.

Because that's what happens when your heart turns to ice. You end not with a bang, but a glacier.

I kept up appearances. I got through the days. I even tried, on occasion, to pull myself together, to give myself a stern talking to, to remind myself of everything I've written above and more.

The children became a dull, constant ache beneath my ribcage, a singular ventricle resisting the frost. I loved them and I knew that they needed me, but I was no longer sure what that meant. Or where to start. There was just enough gas left in the tank to manage a fair impression of a father, but neglect, in its devilish way, is in the details.

It was long past time to regroup. And I knew it.

So, I told myself it was a relief that I was taking a break from the merry-go-round I'd been on. I'd do something else; I'd do something new. I'd concentrate more on the kids. I'd be a better man.

But then one night, as I sat alone in the dark, tears mingling with Jim Beam and cheap diet cola, I looked up to see my shadow sitting opposite me. Which was odd, as we only had the one body between us.

He was smiling. He always bloody smiles. Personally, I think there's something wrong with his mouth.

"You look tired," he said, "How 'bout I drive for a while?"

***

In the midst of all of this, ordinary life rolled implacably on. It's a well-known fucker for it.

For the twins, this was not a period of any particular upheaval. No more so than for anyone reaching the grand old age of seven, anyway. If you told the story from their point-of-view, the nihilistic sea into which I was diving headlong wouldn't count for more than a couple of throwaway lines: "Dad's in a weird mood again. I wonder what's for dinner."

Some of that was because they had reached that point in their lives where not everything revolved around their parents. They wanted to be in control of their own destinies, provided, of course, that they could be underwritten.

"Going to the park" ceased to be a sufficiently exciting way of spending a Saturday—although it would come back around in a few chapters' time. They started to attend slumber parties and not call at three o'clock in the morning, begging to come home. They began to challenge—as they'd been encouraged to do—the beliefs with which they had been brought up.

That isn't the last you'll hear on that subject either.

Not that it was entirely a case of pulling away. In some areas, this new-found independence meant that they paid more attention to the adults in their lives. Because alongside a sudden and burning desire to participate in capitalism, their developing sense of the world brought with it a number of brutal truths.

People could be unhappy. People could get sick. People could, without warning, not be there anymore.

Both of them started offering "Don't die!" as their traditional farewell greeting. With Fathead, it was a plea, with Baldy, a command. They began to keep a suspicious and eagle-like eye on parents, grandparents, cousins, friends, pets—anything with a pulse that might, at any point, prove stupid enough to stop having one.

It was sweet and it was devastating. I can't bear a disappointed child—it knifes me in the kidneys and steals my grandfather's watch. To this day, I haven't told the girls about Santa. I *think* they've figured it out, but they are messenger murderers both and I don't need that on my slate.

So, it was particularly distressing to discover that the thing they wanted most from me was the one thing I couldn't give.

I was not even remotely okay.

The game, therefore, was to ensure that they remained as oblivious as possible. A forbidding task, but not an altogether uninvolving one.

Because while psychotic breaks are not as much fun as they sound—and they sound rubbish—they are, in hindsight, interesting. Like sharks. Or the Ebola virus.

For instance, I hope you never have a nervous breakdown, but if you do, I recommend attending a school assembly during it.

It's a hoot.

I should stress that, by this, I do not mean that you should actually hoot. You'll be trying to make a good impression and this is one of the many things at which the modern educational establishment is apt to look askance. In fact, if you want to continue to keep your imminent mental collapse on the down-low, I wouldn't recommend bird noises of any kind.

94

Besides, there's no need to try that hard. School events are triumphs of the bizarre under normal circumstances, let alone if you're unravelling like Theseus' sat nav.

For one thing, they have been patterned after a blueprint borrowed from the Catholic Church. They are always scheduled at the worst possible time and are designed to make you feel guilty if you don't attend, and unworthy if you do.

Fuck knows why anyone even thinks they're necessary. They're a disappointment to the kids, who are, briefly, excited about a respite from the classroom before, within seconds, leaving their boredom threshold in the rear-view mirror.

As for the adults, all I can say is that each and every one of us must have been extraordinarily cruel to some particularly adorable animals in a previous life.

The only reasonable conjecture, once you've discounted the idea of a dedicated purgatory for parents, is that assemblies are the educational equivalent of looking busy in front of the boss.

The chief message is this:

"Your children, as you can see, are in good hands. I mean, do you think that *bad* teachers could persuade a hundred and twenty children to sing a song about a happy cow, in more-or-less the same key? No, that's right. They couldn't. So, I think we can all agree that we've totally got this and there's absolutely no need to kick off at parents' evening this year. Mr Harrison has only just got back from rehab, and we don't want him falling off the wagon again."

But they can't come right out and say that, or Ofsted officials will appear from an unmarked van and take them to a hidden bunker where they teach nothing but beginner's violin.

So, instead, they trick you into going. Usually by giving your child an award. It doesn't matter what the award is for, it only matters that you would regret it for the rest of your life if you weren't there to watch them awkwardly snatch the certificate from the Headmistress' hand and run, mortified, back to their tittering friends.

One day, those memories will keep you warm.

That's not even a joke. They will, and the teachers know it. And that's how they will get you to sit through two hours of poetry recitation, fire drill reminders, event announcements, passive aggressive speeches by teachers whose classes are clearly falling behind—but for which they absolutely refuse to take the fall this time—and half-a-dozen flagrant blackmail attempts, designed to elicit free labour, cash money or baked goods that you will fully intend to make from scratch, but will, in fact, give the children money to pick up on the day.

Fathead and Baldy loved it when I came to an assembly. But not nearly as passionately, or as lastingly, as they held it against me when I did not. So, I did my best to show my face as often as possible.

But I couldn't tell them that, as much as my heart sang whenever they got up and recited the four words of French they could remember without laughing, or collected a genuinely pride-stirring award for citizenship or etiquette, the actual experience of attending, for a good portion of their school life, was literally torture.

This is going to sound petty. And heart-breaking.

Ten Canadian dollars to the first reader who gets that one.

Come on. Don't do me like that.

I know that every parent has their own cross to bear—which they likely stayed up all night making as part of their child's overdue Easter project—so I'm not pulling a "woe is me". But I don't think anyone realises how physically excruciating it can be when your mind is in the process of leaving the building. Once it's out on the open road, it's a different kind of pain. More nebulous. But as long as you're still making any attempt to hold on, the little things tear at your flesh like owls.

Don't let owls fool you, by the way. All that blinking and looking wise is a scam. They are bad-ass motherfuckers who will happily rip you a collection of new ones. But then, you can't trust any creature that can turn its head all the way around.

Your mother eats mice in hell, Karras!

They are not alligators, however, which is something.

Anyway, this is what a school assembly is like when you're losing the plot:

First of all, you have to get there, which is its own boutique brand of hell. Just the thought of it has been weighing on your mind since the badly mimeographed "save the date" went up on the refrigerator door. By the time the night before rolls around, it has amassed a level of anxiety that you might attach to impending brain surgery.

You sleep fitfully and fretfully. You have a nightmare that the Junior Netball team is trying to steal all of your canned goods. And you wake up the next morning with the same level of dread that you'd experience if you'd watched a haunted videotape the night before and then forgotten to switch off the television.

As you shower, for much longer than necessary, you try to convince yourself that it's not the event itself that's stressing you out, it's just the thought of all the people. Not that this is necessarily better, but it lends a little focus.

Crowds are not to your taste at the moment. In fact, they've temporarily overtaken arsenic and out-of-date milk in that department. In the presence of more than three people, you have begun to develop a series of arrhythmias that, under different circumstances, might net you the Grammy for Best Contemporary Jazz Album. You sweat and twitch like a police informant in an Italian restaurant.

Your desire to run away is so strong, Del Shannon would like to take you to dinner.

But you power through, somehow. You put on clothes, which you know from experience is preferred. You brush your hair and comb your teeth, then panic because you don't have time to correct the mistake.

You catch a bus—because you're Canadian and never got around to getting a driver's licence in your adopted country—and spend the entire journey worrying that this might be too personal an example for the tone to remain universal. You have an overwhelming feeling that you will one day explore your conflicted feelings about public transport in print but, for the moment, are both grateful that you don't have a pushchair and desperately sad that you no longer have need of one.

No matter how early you left the house or how short the distance to the school, you will be late. Everyone else will be prim, proper, seated and attentive and you're going to walk into the back of the room, looking like a scarecrow that invested overconfidently in a failing stock. You may as well just bang on the glass and steal the bride.

Necks, indeed, swivel on your arrival. The heady scent of smugness fills the air. Everybody else arrived yesterday, determined, whatever their other failings, not to be you.

Eventually, you spy the last remaining seat—conveniently located in the centre of a row of people with over-sized handbags at their feet—each containing a selection of their owner's favourite bricks.

You apologise as you brush your buttocks awkwardly against their chests—but you suspect you'd do that even under the most intimate of circumstances. To date, it has never come up.

Finally, you reach your tiny plastic chair, and collapse into it. There is a sound of protest from its paper-thin metal legs that feels like body-shaming.

You are damp with perspiration, shaking and already want to stand up, shout something vaguely political and bolt, screaming, from the building.

You need a cigarette.

You really need a cigarette.

97

Is there time for a cigarette?

There is not. The Headmistress is at the rostrum. She is eyeing the children with a mixture of trepidation and severity, as though they are a pack of circus lions that have been getting a bit frisky of late.

She bids you all welcome and thanks you for coming. She sounds, to your ears, like a supervillain, gloating while the Destructo-Ray finishes booting up.

You spot your children in amongst the mob, alternately waving at you and hiding their faces. You aren't entirely sure to which you are meant to respond. Had you not such a strong desire to throw up at the moment, you'd consider shouting, "Did you remember to put on clean pants?" just to see how they'd react.

It's time for a few important announcements. From what you can piece together later, a student has done a thing that has impressed those in charge of said thing, some sports have happened and the urinals in the upstairs boys' lavatories have become alarming in some ill-defined way. Also, there will be an assembly scheduled to discuss matters arising from this assembly at some point within the next few days.

You couldn't really hear any of it properly though, as you were distracted by the fact that you appear to have inadvertently clawed a hole in your own leg. You also have a disconcerting sense that you are starting to make people uncomfortable, and wonder if the keening in your head is starting to leak out. The mother next to you, in particular, plainly wants to hurl one of her precious bricks your way.

You need to get out of here. You can't breathe. And if you're going to not breathe anyway, you might as well be smoking.

Why are you not smoking?

Maybe you are smoking.

Maybe that's why everyone is looking at you.

Fuck's sake. There's a visibly nervous five-year-old up there spelling difficult words, albeit with a calculated lisp. Why are they looking at *you*?

The support act never gets any respect.

It's fine. It will be over soon. It has to be.

Awards next. Good. That's why you're here. If it gets too much, you can always slip out after this. Nip outside for some air. Lovely, nicotine-sodden air.

"First off," says the Headmistress, "We'd like to present the awards for attendance."

Jesus suffering fuck. Attendance? You look around the room. Unless you're much further gone than you think, the nine thousand children in this room are all, at least currently, in attendance.

Are they *all* going to get an award? What's the criteria here? How fierce is the competition? Do you have to show up on weekends or something?

Nope, it's going to be everyone but that one poor kid who had bronchitis for most of last April. And he's going to get a special certificate for Outstanding Resilience.

Then, on top of everything else, you realise that they're giving them out in alphabetical order. So, if there are, in your revised estimate, seventy-five thousand children here, and your two fall somewhere towards the end of the first third, then you can escape in about…

You're going to die here! You're actually going to die here! Archaeologists are going find a desiccated corpse slumped in a perfectly preserved, non-biodegradable chair and argue over what caused the deep scratch marks in its left femur.

Gently, you begin to rock back and forth and mutter invocations to random saints. In deference to your secular leanings, you eventually land on Etienne and Buffy Marie.

The first two million children collect their certificates at the speed of dirt. You keep expecting one of them—there's always one of them—to attempt an acceptance speech, which everyone else will think is eccentric and charming, but will make you reconsider your narrow-minded attitude to infanticide.

Then you hear the Headmistress call your daughters' names. Their real ones, not Fathead and Baldy. Apparently, despite that permission slip you both created and signed, they're not allowed to call them that.

There is a pause between their names, but it's obvious that everyone expects them to accept as a pair.

Which they do, shyly. But, at the same time, you notice a slight flush to their faces that suggests they aren't at all unhappy about it. They've been recognised for something—and they like it. Well, Fathead does. In a way that you find unnervingly familiar. Baldy's reaction is harder to read—but you'll later come to realise that though she hates the attention, she'd hate the feeling of being left out more. The look in her eyes is one of relief—she can now go back to not thinking about it at all.

And for a fleeting second, you are there with them—standing outside of your panic in a fragile little bubble of calm. Because a realisation has just smacked you in the face like a comedy frying pan—they aren't just your kids. They are people—with entire lives ahead of them. Ridiculous, complicated lives. And you are a large part of a small, dedicated team whose mission is to ensure that the balance of those lives is as weighted towards joy as is humanly possible.

So, you start to clap. Far too loudly, but fuck it. You love them so much and you've screwed up so much and even if they blush themselves unconscious, they are going to know that you're here, that you care and that you are proud.

You don't hoot though. That would be overkill.

It's a precious moment, but you know it won't last. In about five minutes, once they're safely returned to the bosom of their peers, you will flee, dizzy, nauseous and vibrating audibly, to the relative safety of the rest of the world.

And you will find your eyes are full of tears. Because it isn't right and it isn't fair that you'll never remember this properly. That you'll have to fill in the details with invention, and talk about yourself in the second person to take the sting out of it.

And because at this point, you don't know if it's ever going to get any better, or if this is the beginning of something worse to come.

Worst of all, because, for one shining moment, you saw what you've been missing.

And you don't know how to get it back.

For the first time in a long time, however, you will desperately want to believe.

Bi-furious

I've calmed down some now. As predicted, the little flurry of fresh bonkers melted before it settled and we can return to our regularly scheduled programme of contained outbursts and mild dyskinesia.

I'm sorry if I worried you.

But, as I am feeling more composed, it seems like as good a time as any to tackle a frequently noted symptom of bipolar disorder. One which, for me, has always nestled doggedly at the top of the list.

Anger.

You got a problem with that?

It won't shock you to learn that the principal research source for this book has been living through its contents in tedious real-time. Nonetheless, out of a desire to understand myself better, or at all, I have read a lot about bipolar disorder and I'm fascinated by the similarities and differences between myself and other sufferers. Especially when it comes to rage.

I know you can't tell from where you're sitting, but I've gone back and forth on the word "sufferers" for about an hour now. I nearly changed it. Isn't that odd? We have a disease and we suffer, but there's something about the word that makes us feel edgy. Like we're playing the victim.

It's an unfortunate thread that runs through the discourse about mental illness. In the attempt to empower people—a laudable goal—there is sometimes a tendency to downplay the fact that there's actually anything wrong.

Which is just denial with a fundraising ribbon pinned to its chest.

In any case, there's a chasm of difference between "you can still achieve your dreams" and "you're just like everybody else".

I'm not like everybody else.

I'm sure you're not either. You're one of only four people who bought this book, for starters. And I don't believe that I should get special dispensation—or even attention—for being bipolar, any more than you should for those jewellery boxes in the shape of film canisters you keep trying to flog online.

But the fact remains that my emotions and perceptions are adversely affected in a distinct and intemperate sub-set of ways. I would say it was outside the norm, but that's a can of nominative worms I have no desire to open.

Jesus. What's the least inflammatory way to put it?

How I experience life is to the extreme left of how the majority of people polled have reported experiencing it.

That seems vague enough to be acceptable.

The degree to which I get angry and the manner in which that manifests itself are excellent cases in point.

It's about the how, rather than the what. We all get irritated, and I'm sure, about many of the same things. When people waffle for pages and pages before they get to the point, for instance.

Injustice. Traffic. An absence of toilet paper at inopportune moments. Genocide. Bands who write songs about how hard it is to be rich. Prejudice. Right-wing politics. Left-wing politics. Chicken-wing shortages.

Cruelty. Stupidity. Greed.

These are all subjects bound to raise a hackle or two, or place your dander firmly in the upright position. And, often, quite rightly. There are things that shouldn't sit right, that should boil our blood.

Anger isn't necessarily wrong. It's simply volatile and needs handling with care. Or tongs.

I'm not claiming it as my sovereign province either. Even excess, or flat-out incomprehensible, anger is not uncommon. If you want corroboration, glance at any comments section on the Internet. Actually, don't. It's not much of an argument for anything other than a cull.

It definitely isn't just a bipolar thing. I know that much. There are scores of people with otherwise ordinary brains—this may include you—who find it an enormous challenge to process their rage or tame their temper.

One of them lives in my house.

No, the bipolar bit comes later. Bear with me. I promise it won't take you as long to get there as it did me.

I've been angry for as long as I can remember. Incandescently so. And, I'm informed, often unexpectedly. Which doesn't surprise me. My wrath is not equipped with an early warning system and its triggers are seldom predictable. By me or anyone else.

Therefore, I don't blame my loved ones for occasionally being caught off-guard. The all-time speed record, on my own personal mood shift scale, is post-coital to postal in three point five seconds.

Medication lessens the effects. It's one of the first things I noticed. Things just don't bother me as much as they used to. For the first time in my life, I find it possible to say, "Let's agree to disagree" without reaching for the first blunt instrument to hand.

But, once upon a time—or, more precisely, between my birth and eighteen months ago—I was a ticking time-bomb. And the constant ticking really got on my tits.

As a parent, this is the opposite of useful.

Fathead and Baldy have, once or twice, told me that I'm scary when I'm angry. I've never hit them or harmed them in any way and, frankly, they've never actually seen me at my worst, but even that statement is enough for me for to dedicate myself to controlling it. You shouldn't scare your children—it's so much more effective to be sneaky.

Although, to be fair, part of me suspects they overplay that hand. Once, I swear they slipped up and said, "You're scary when you don't give us money" instead, but they deny it and I'm honour-bound to give them the benefit of the doubt.

The odd fracas is unavoidable—children are anger factories. Nothing they do makes any sense to the adult mind, and they have literally zero concept of what the word "breakable" means or what anything costs.

But, for some reason known only to evolution, they are hard-wired to react ballistically on being told off.

So, basically, unless you are a complete brute, you will always come off worse when you get angry at children. No amount of fury that you can summon will ever match the amount of hurt they can cram into their weirdly large eyes.

On the rare occasion that I lose my rag with mine these days, it's over fairly quickly. Everyone stomps to their respective corners, swears creatively under their breath for a few minutes and then stomps back. Apologies are made on both sides—if occasionally grudgingly—and that's the end of it. If the argument is between me and Baldy, add an extra half hour of cooling down time, four ibuprofens and a stiff drink.

For me, I hasten to add, but I only give that a couple of years.

Even after these title bouts, it's not long before all returns to what passes for normal in our house. We're not grudge-holders.

Unless, of course, they're playing a long game.

What they don't see is that once we've had a nice, chilled evening to douse the memory of the firefight, I go to my bedroom and bawl like a mildly injured footballer. Pretty much every time. Being angry at them feels like swallowing acid. It's a bad idea, it doesn't taste nice and it burns.

I don't like being angry. I'm just good at it.

I am also aware—or have been made aware—that I have lost it over a bewildering assortment of topics over the years, with little difference in ferocity. A lyric I didn't rate could set me off, or it could be climate change denial. I once raged for about two hours, without a shred of irony, about how angry other people get.

But it's not so much that I get mad. That's a bog standard human problem and it can be addressed.

It's why I'm so relentlessly so that bothers me—and this is the bipolar element of the equation.

I get angry because I can't understand why you can't understand. In my head, everything is so crystal clear, so obvious, so perfectly logical, that, honestly, I have to believe that you are being deliberately obtuse. And why would you do that to me?

How can you deny what I *know* to be true?

Can't you appreciate how lonely that makes me feel?

It feels like gaslighting—albeit without any actual ill intent—and thus generates the same kind of wounded rage.

In order to cut that bullshit off at its source, I have had to learn that you can't see what I see. I've also had to accept that what I see isn't necessarily true—or, on the worst days, there.

Bipolar anger is that of a cornered animal. We don't hate you. You didn't do anything wrong. It isn't your fault.

We're as frightened of you as you are of us.

And that really pisses us off.

8: An Unexpected Inquisition

Is everybody okay?

I only ask because I'm not entirely sure what you expected from this story—join the club—and I'm concerned that some of the darker avenues down which we've motored may have taken the wind out of your sails little. Mixed metaphor fatigue may also be setting in.

I was recently in a bookshop—for the younger readers, that's a building you visit when you're out of Father's Day ideas—and I noticed that they'd erected a display containing their most popular releases on the subject of mental health. Always down for a bit of industrial espionage, I decided to check out the competition.

It was a bit of a blow, if I'm honest. After perusing a few volumes, I'm not entirely convinced I'm doing this right. At best, I have a radically different approach to the material.

They all have bright, clean covers proclaiming "You're Okay!" or "It's All Worth It!" or "£14.99 RRP £19.99!" in large, pleasant typefaces. There's a sort of scrubbed, antiseptic look about them—the kind of tomes you could take home to mother.

And, if the titles are anything to go by, they are exceptionally forthright about their objectives:

Ten Ways to Lift Depression—and Strengthen Those Inner Thighs

By the End of this Book, You Won't Notice Anymore—Conquering ODC

Men are from Mars and Karen is Self-Righteous—Surviving Marriage to a Self-Help Author

If any of the above are the kind of thing you were after, I'm terribly sorry. It was never my intention to entertain, enlighten or inform under false pretences.

Saying that, I think you'll find my style is less prosaic. Some authors barely use the word "fuck" at all, which suggests to me that their knowledge of mental illness is limited to the theoretical.

But I'm not trying to have a pop at writers who, I'm sure, are only trying to inject some positivity into the world. I have no reason to believe that they are driven by anything less than a Schweitzer-level reverence for life, especially considering the precarious state of the publishing industry.

Some of them even have letters after their names, which means they've either put in years of study—cause for respect—or have a terrible editor. I lean towards the latter, as it would best explain the number of fatuous platitudes that have crept into the text.

I'm kidding. Mostly. My low tolerance for the happy-clappy is my problem, not yours. Whatever gets you through the plight.

All I meant to say was that this is not one of those books. And there's nothing to suggest that I'd be capable of writing one, even if I'd a mind to. I don't have answers. I don't have professional training. I don't even have an author's photograph in which I show that many teeth.

What I don't want is for you to get the wrong idea. There is a special kind of disappointment that arises from expectation defied—and it can cut both ways.

Which is another thing you learn as a parent.

Segue!

***

By the time the girls were eight, I was not in a good place. I couldn't have pointed to it on a map, but I was pretty sure that any reputable guidebook would advise giving it a swerve. My head was full of cotton wool that had been soaked in lighter fluid and abandoned on a workbench next to an acetylene torch.

Unfortunately, having recently ceded control to the less diligent half of my personality, I wasn't able to express this. Every time I raised my hand to ask for help, he slapped it back down. He had his own plans, and he wasn't going to let my constant moaning undermine them.

He'd been around almost as long as I had, however, and knew that if he went too big, people around us would notice and start oiling the tranquiliser guns. In order to avoid this level of interference, he had learned to do an impression of me that I found a bit broad, but which did prove effective in small bursts.

It wasn't all fakery. He loved the same people that I did—he certainly loved the children. But he was a big picture guy. The minutiae were of no interest to him. He probably thought they were a dance troupe of some kind.

106

I hope it doesn't sound as if I'm making excuses for myself, because I'm not. I've just spent a long time isolating who I am from how I can be, and this is the simplest way I know to express the difference. It's not as though my preferred version of myself doesn't make mistakes. Or that my shadow doesn't, on occasion, accomplish things that I can't.

As it happens, I often envy him his clarity of thought and purpose. Since our working relationship was medically severed, I've missed it dearly. Everything is so much more complicated now; it's difficult to act decisively. That never used to be a problem. Decisive, I could do. Rational? Okay, not so much. But I never faltered, no matter how dumbass the move. Now, I'm overcome by this unfamiliar compulsion to think it all through first. At what feels like half-speed. It's a wonder anything gets done in this world, if everyone is putting in this level of consideration.

Oh, look! The newspaper has arrived.

Ah. I see.

Okay, so the knee-jerk reaction is not restricted to my tribe, but—outside of your more citrus-hued politicians—we still have a pretty good shot at the title. I know my own default setting has always been that of the exposed nerve. I see threats everywhere and, so, become perpetually guarded. And, as with most myopic concentrations on security, this is really only effective as a way of drawing fire.

When Fathead and Baldy were eight years old, they let loose the first of many volleys that, in my self-absorption, I did not see coming.

In the broadest sense, we're prepared for the fact that we will not always be thrilled with what our children bring home. We envision unsuitable romantic partners, stray animals, bad influences and disappointing report cards. We worry about underage alcohol or drugs. And we would take any of the above over lice.

Lice. Now that's a word that should have a trigger warning attached. Anyone who has ever wielded a nit-comb is having Nam-style flashbacks now.

"They're goddamn everywhere! Scramble! Scramble!"

The twins only topped the horror of those itch-making interlopers once— and only because they were playing to a very specific audience.

It was the kind of perfect day that almost always ends in murder. The sun was high, but the pollen low. The air was warm, but the breeze was pleasant. I was sober, but had been to the shop.

The girls, at their own request, had started to walk home from school with their friends, rather than their quasi-homosexual father. I retained responsibility for getting them there in the first place—I didn't yet trust them not to skip it altogether—but they assured me that they were big enough to handle their return.

Everything felt gruelling at the time, but the half-hour between the time they left school and arrived safely at their own front door, hangers-on in tow, was like removing fingernails with an anything. If they fell even five minutes behind schedule, I began to sweat from my eyebrows to my ankles. The worst thoughts imaginable shoved their way into my brain, like meth-heads crashing a bat mitzvah.

If anything happened to them, I genuinely didn't know what I would do. Or of what I would be capable. They'd only been around for a quarter of my life and, now, nothing before their birth felt like anything more than a ropey dress rehearsal. For someone with a splintered psyche, that level of connection was dread-inducing. The moment I realised how badly I needed something, it was usually taken away.

Of course, before I could even get to my master list of hospitals, police stations and travelling circuses,they'd roll up, laissez-faire and fancy-free, announce their imminent deaths from starvation, and cram the front room with schoolmates and din. Between breaths, I would slide from grateful mendicant to nervous wreck.

I was so desperately happy to see them that I immediately wanted to hide.

I'd typically duck into the kitchen, gather an unholy pick ''n' mix of unhealthy snacks and, using its delivery as a distraction, attempt to slip upstairs unnoticed.

As a rule, it worked impeccably. Provided they know where you are, children, in host-mode, are perfectly happy for that to be elsewhere.

This time, it was not to be.

There were five of them sprawled across the floor, reclining on cushions like Roman nobility. The twins, as the home team, formed the nucleus of the group. Orbiting them were a couple of the regulars and a nervous-looking newbie.

The television was airing one of a series of broadcasts in which pre-pubescent characters discovered they were not ordinary—despite facing a range of topical issues on a weekly basis. It was aspirational programming, if you aimed to be a member of an extra-terrestrial royal family who doubled as the bassist in a kick-ass band. Or a spy. Or a werewolf. Or both. Once, I think there was a story about a gang of apprentice welders with magic skates, but I couldn't swear to it. Between us, I never worked out whether it was a number of different shows, aired in rotation, or one with a fascinatingly broad remit.

All eyes were locked on the screen, hands moving robotically up and down between the bowl of treats I'd laid in front of them and their slack-jawed mouths.

I was three paces from the stairs when I heard Fathead's voice. Her head didn't move—but a piece of caramelised popcorn paused in mid-air.

"Dad?"

Frozen in mid-step, I cursed under my breath.

"Yes?"

There was a long pause and, out of morbid curiosity, I turned around. My gaze flicked to the TV, assuming one of the lycanthropic secret agents had done something cool or anti-authoritarian.

That wasn't it. Currently on-screen was a twelve-year-old actor discussing menstruation in heavily metaphorical terms, but nothing worthy of such a pregnant silence.

"I believe in God now," my eldest daughter said.

As the blood drained from my face, I turned to her sister. She threw me a challenging look, slightly undermined by the number of crisps attached to her face.

"Yeah. Me too. I want to go to church."

Two of their friends, the ones who kept toothbrushes in the upstairs bathroom, quickly excused themselves. They'd heard me on the subject once or twice and now had a burning desire to remember what their own houses looked like.

The new kid looked confused.

"Doesn't your Dad believe in God?" they stage-whispered to the twins.

Baldy stared me down, eyebrow hiked into a dare. She opened her mouth to speak, but was cut off.

"No, he doesn't," said Fathead, "His Mum and Dad weren't very nice to him, so he doesn't like Jesus anymore."

I made goldfish faces as I attempted to rally. My mouth was filling up with things that I knew I shouldn't say, like someone had turned on a garden hose and lost control of it.

"Yeah, he's an aphorist," added Baldy, a note of disappointment thickening her voice. She'd clearly been spoiling for more of a battle.

"Atheist," I corrected automatically.

Damn it.

"What's an atheist?" asked the girls' new friend, who I suddenly realised was the spitting image of Shirley Temple.

"Hey," I deflected, "Did you know that I'm half-gay?"

109

"Yes."

"Oh."

"My Mum says God looks after Grandma now."

Fuckity-fuck.

"Does she? She's probably right then."

"And my hamster."

"I'm sure they're both fine. Don't worry about it."

"Dad says we just go into the ground," chucked in Baldy, grenade-style, "And that's that." She dusted her hands togeher, to ehasise her point.

"The *ground*?! Why would they put my Grandma in the ground?"

"Well…"

"We put my hamster in the back garden, but Daddy said it was a tunnel to heaven."

I bet he did.

"Well, there you are. Your Grandma must have had her own tunnel."

"But she was scared of tunnels. We went to see this cave on holiday once, and she said, "Sod that" ' and had a cup of tea instead."

"Maybe God helped her not to be scared," offered Fathead helpfully.

Shirley T. smiled in relief.

"But Dad says there isn't a God," said Baldy, "So he couldn't have done. She was probably terrified."

Seriously?

"I don't think we have to be scared of anything once we're dead," I said evenly. "That's the good thing about it. No more fear. No more worries."

"Dad," said Baldy, "It's not good that her Grandma is dead."

"No, of course not."

"Or her hamster. It was very cute."

"I know. What I meant was…"

"That wasn't a very nice thing to say," added Fathead, with a pout.

"My Mummy cried for *ages*," Shirley informed us, "My Daddy had to take her to a special doctor, because she wasn't doing the dishes anymore."

The idea of a vengeful deity suddenly didn't seem so farfetched. And He apparently didn't fuck around when it came to unbelievers.

Would it, I wondered, be taking the piss to ask the ground to swallow me?

No one spoke for two moments too many, and I seriously considered just walking out of the door, catching the nearest coast-bound train and joining the crew of a merchant trawler. As you do.

But it seems that even heathens have patron saints, as, moments before I donned my sou'wester, I was saved by the bell. Or, more specifically, by

Debussy's *Clair de Lune,* arranged for soprano tannoy.

"Ice cream!" they all shouted and belted towards the door, all desire for theological debate forgotten.

I threw loose change at their backs and fled to my room. I sat on the bed, caught my breath, and shot an accusing look skyward.

"I thought I warned you," I said, "not to come round here anymore."

I neither waited for, nor expected a reply.

"I mean it," I continued, "You had your fun with me. But that's over now. Leave my kids the hell alone."

Someone laughed cheerlessly.

I hoped it was me.

∗∗∗

The girls did go to church, eventually, with some perfectly nice Christian friends from the end of their street. And, despite my misgivings, I didn't discourage them.

Not out loud, anyway.

Had I done so, I would have been no better than my parents. I'd always maintained that I would let them find their own way and support them to make their own decisions. God knows, I would adore them regardless. But this was the first real test of that philosophy and I very nearly failed it miserably.

My current operator was all for laying down the law, preferably via a histrionic speech about freedom. All in the children's best interests, of course. They were young and impressionable. They needed to be protected from that poisonous junk. It, emphatically, had nothing to do with revenge or retroactively palliating our own childhood ordeals.

Vengeance is mine, sayeth the asshat.

I'm not going to lie to you. Religion doesn't sit well with me. I think it detracts from the divinity of the human race and offers alibis to its devilry. Let us be good or bad on our own merits, rather than to please or defy our chosen holy pal. That's my motto. Despite the difficulty of fitting it on a t-shirt.

As it should, the true nature of the universe remains a mystery to me. But I have seen no compelling evidence for the existence of God, and much to suggest His or Her absence. Also, I'm pretty sure history is on my side.

Still, I've been cautioned, by some, to use the word "agnostic" rather than "atheist" because I acknowledge that I cannot know for sure. But I'm not a sceptic. I'm an infidel. I truly don't believe. Nor do I want to.

I am, however, no longer evangelical about it. It's very easy to be, especially when you were brought up with skills in that arena. But I've had too many frustrating conversations, ending in too many verbal conflagrations, not to have come to the conclusion that most people are going to believe what they want to believe, and live the lives they feel are best for them.

That probably shouldn't have taken as much working out.

When it came to the twins, however, I took their interest in religion—in the first instance—as a failure, on my part, to pass down my humanist values.

Much as my parents must have felt about their inability to turn me into a homophobic, patriarchal sermon machine.

I look back now and I realise that I'd actually succeeded beyond my wildest dreams. They were open-minded. They weren't irretrievably stuck in one way of thinking—especially not one that originated from without, rather than within. They didn't know how they felt about God—they'd heard good and bad things—so they trotted along to find out for themselves.

That was what I meant to teach them all along. And, by some fluke, they understood that better than I did.

Go team.

Yet, I worried, if it took, that we'd no longer have anything in common. That "Our Father" would appropriate the position of their father. That I would become an embarrassment to them or, worse, we'd lose the ability to respect one another.

Had I been in my right mind, I'd have seen it as a chance to be seized with both hands. There was nothing in this life or the putative next that could corrupt or diminish my devotion to my daughters. So, whatever path they took, my view of it would be coloured by trust in their choices and admiration of their constancy. I might even learn a thing or two.

As my right mind was on a gap year, I mainly felt wronged. Frightened. Violent. I wanted to scream. I wanted to bite. I wanted to scratch.

Bloody lice.

And it was then that the strangest thing happened.

I handled it correctly. Said all of the right things. Did all of the right things. The girls left our conversations on the subject with a sense of agency; they knew that they would be loved, no matter what.

And when, three weeks later, they declared church boring and went back to sleeping in on Sundays, I kept my joy in check and my celebrations restrained.

To this day, I have no idea how I managed it. We're not talking about keeping my temper, or being nice to their less appealing friends. Religion was the big one—it loomed large over the nurture portion of my defects. Compared to my hatred of everything doctrinal, Hell was a single, flickering candle.

So, if I *was* going to challenge my previous record for short-sightedness, this had all the hallmarks of an opportune time.

Yet, somehow, I kept my head and both the children's souls and my conscience escaped unscathed. Somehow, sanity prevailed.

It doesn't make a lick of sense and I doubt it ever will, but when I needed me the most, I showed up.

Frankly, it's a miracle.

Oh, hush. You saw that coming.

Gender Bi-as

I am the worst possible person to discuss the next topic, and, therefore, the only one who can.

Men.

Huh. Good god.

No. I'm not going there. I have come neither to bury nor to praise the gender into which I stumbled in my mother's womb. Either would be lazy and the former far too easy. And, if you've learned anything about me so far, it's that I habitually eschew the easy. I have never, for instance, been to New Orleans.

After all, those who identify as men—whether from birth or a later realisation—are legion, and available in most of the popular styles. Not to mention several that have fallen out of general favour, but still have their devotees. And, as is usual with selections from variety packs, not all will be to your taste. Some must, inevitably, be corn flakes.

And others will be rat poison, which is a hint that you should reorganise your cupboards.

It is fairly well-documented that men have caused a lot of trouble in the world. To pedant-proof this paragraph, yes, women have too. But, noticeably, on nothing like the same scale and with a more consistent level of repercussion.

The men have seen to that.

The next sentence that I type, therefore, might upset you at first, but only if you are the type of person who cannot understand how language works.

The problem is not men.

I ducked while typing that, which should reassure you that it is not something I say lightly. I am not an apologist.

Nor, and I want this bit on record, am I any kind of advocate for Men's Rights, as defined by the kind of people who believe political correctness is having a bad time of it and should seek professional help. As movements go, this ranks below bowel on the scale of things that should be allowed out in public.

Seriously, guys. Your inanity is showing.

Everything that is happening right now to address systemic abuses of power is both necessary and overdue. Misogyny remains rampant and if people choose not to believe this, it is because they are either benefiting from the effects of it in some way, or feel they are not benefiting sufficiently for it to be as big a deal as everyone is making out.

And while we're on the subject, defending yourself as the exception is a waste of everybody's time—time that would be better spent examining your behaviour and ensuring that it's true.

Because what I mean when I insist that the problem isn't men is that the ownership of male genitalia, or the inner knowledge that you should have born with same, does not, automatically, make you a bad person.

Being human does.

Stick with me on this.

We are selfish from birth. Not cruel, not malevolent, not instant assholes, just selfish. We couldn't be any other way. We're trapped in these flesh suits, watching the world through a singular set of whatever senses we've been granted and bound to a mysterious thing called consciousness that automatically places us at the centre of the narrative.

Instinctively, we have needs. Gradually, we develop wants. Pleasure and pain slip into the mix and sharpen both of these appetites. And through it all, we only ever see things *our* way.

Empathy, therefore, is a baffling concept and the only explanation for its existence is that, without it, the species wouldn't have survived its first argument about dinner plans.

The reason why it is men, rather than women, that have historically run roughshod over their fellow humans is not because of the aptly-named Y chromosome, but because, somewhere along the line, some idiot decided to tell them that they could.

The first man who heard the news had questions.

"Go through the first bit again."

"You are the superior sex."

"Right. Sounds good. Why?"

"Because you are a man."

"With you so far. What's a man?"

"You are."

"I'm Trevor."

"Yes. Trevor the man."

"Actually, it's Trevor Brannigan. Of the first-cave-on-the-right-after-the-thistle-patch Brannigans."

"Hmmm. Okay, let's try another tack. When you look down, what do you see between your legs?"

"Rex."

"I'm sorry. Hunting accident, was it?"

"Huh?"

"Sorry, I thought you meant... Never mind. Go on."

"When I look down, between my legs, I usually see my dog, Rex. He's always underfoot, the little scamp."

"Jesus."

"I told you, it's pronounced *Trevor*."

"That's not what I... Forget it. Won't make sense for a few million years. But think a little higher up, and attached to your body."

"Oh, the fleas? Yeah, they're a bit of a nightmare."

"Not the fleas. Part of *you*."

"Ah, I see. My wife-pleaser."

"Your what?"

"I call it that because my wife likes it when I..."

"She *likes* it?"

"Oh, yes."

"That doesn't seem right. No, we definitely need to crack down on that. You're supposed to like it, not her."

"Oh, I like it just fine."

"Good. Now we're getting somewhere. *Why* do you like it?"

"Because I enjoy that sound she makes when I..."

"Is there anyone else here I can talk to?"

"No, just me. It's my turn to have conversations with oddly-dressed strangers. We have a rota."

"Fuck's sake. No, no. Wait a minute. Yes. Who decides *when* you do that thing you like to do with your wife?"

"It's mutual. Sometimes she crawls under my bearskin, sometimes I crawl under hers. And if the other one says it's okay, then..."

"Wrong. You decide. You're the man. When you want something, you take it."

"Oh, I don't think she'd like that."

"Doesn't matter."

"Interesting. So that's being a man, is it? Having a wife-pleaser, but not necessarily pleasing your wife?"

"Stop going on about pleasing your wife. I'm starting to feel nauseous. Please *yourself*."

"Oh, I do that too. When's she off gathering berries or something."

"Saints preserve us."

"What's a saint?"

"If we're talking about patience, then I am. Look, is *any* of what I'm saying

116

getting through to you?"

"I can have whatever I want because bits of me dangle, except that one bit that sometimes doesn't?"

"Yes! Now you're getting it."

"And the ones who don't have anything dangling, they have to do what we say?"

"Yes."

"Because we're… *better*?"

"Yes. Stronger. More decisive. Smarter."

"Whoah, there. Smarter?"

"Absolutely."

"You obviously haven't met Jeremy. Fool brought a live mammoth back to the cave last month. Hadn't even bothered to check if he'd killed it. Strutted around like a big hero too, till it reared up and tried to take a chunk out of him. My wife had to chase it off with a stick."

"That's irrelevant. He was still right."

"He bloody wasn't. Rex nearly got trampled."

"What did the… uh… non-danglies say about it?"

"That they remembered him being dropped on his head as a baby and that probably explained it."

"And how many mammoths, live or otherwise, had they brought back that day?"

"Well, none."

"So what right did they have to make this…"

"…complete arse…"

"…fine *man*, Jeremy, feel worthless, when he had bravely wrestled this behemoth and brought it to heel?"

"He brought it to dinner. And not in the good way."

"Damn it, Trevor. Will you listen to what I'm telling you? Because you're a man, you can have everything you want. You'll always be right. If someone tells you that you're wrong or tries to make you do anything you don't want to do, you can hit them. Kill them, if you like that sort of thing. This world is yours."

"You're sure everyone is going to be okay with this? Because my wife gets a little shirty when I don't wash my beard."

"They won't have a choice."

"Hmmm. Well, I'll run it past the others, but I'm sure we're fine as we are."

Needless to say, the rest of the dangly half of the tribe—not all of whom were as placid as Trevor and some of whom had not yet found wives that wanted pleasing—found this an excellent proposition. And thus was born toxic masculinity. Whenever they identified something at which men seemed to excel, they'd chalk it up as one of the best things ever. Conversely, if a task came up with which they struggled, that became women's work and, logically, of lesser importance. And if, as often happened, a woman proved to be equal to or better than her male counterparts at anything from column A, they stuck their fingers in their ears and shouted, until she went away.

If the same offer had been made to women, I suspect they would have taken it too. Because individual humans can be awesome, but the human race is a dick. And dicks really aren't as great as everyone makes them out to be.

But that's not the way it played out, and this is where we find ourselves.

It is a tricky subject to tackle comically, as it has some desperately dark corners in which unspeakable things happen. It isn't just a case of "silly boys" who can't see how ridiculous their claims to supremacy appear. There's a lot of that, but it's not the bit that truly shames the species. Women are made to feel unsafe, daily, for the foulest possible reason.

They aren't safe.

But that is a subject for another time. Any attempt to unpick it here would be deceitfully slight. Also, as a man, I can have all the opinions about sexism that I like, but I'll never know how it feels to be on the receiving end of it. And, as I've cautioned with mental health, it would be a grave error to pretend that I could. Despite my protestations over the years, being a man is all I've ever known.

Not that I didn't resist the appellation. I've never had much of a desire to be masculine, in the traditional sense. I don't enjoy most of the clichés attached. I loathe the way other men behave. I like and respect women.

Yet, over the years, I've managed to make a lot of that behaviour work perfectly well in a nerdy, sensitive milieu. Because the world told me I could.

Nonetheless, when I was younger, I hated being a boy. The ability to urinate while standing was no trade-off for being disallowed tears, compassion or sensitivity. Or for being forced into a position of supposed dominance that you neither wanted, nor believed yourself to have merited.

Also, why do the guys that you hate seem to get all the girls?

It's a slippery slope.

In the 80s and 90s, when I was growing up, feminism had already made great strides when it came to gender equality—though there were, as there still are, many miles to left to travel. If nothing else, it had finally sunk in that it wasn't a conversation that was going away.

Unfortunately, those changes were anathema to the religion in which I was ensconced. I'd inherited a faith that set great store by a man being the head of his household and a woman knowing her place.

Oddly, none of the women with whom I grew up knew their place at all—as their ideal place was clearly a hundred miles in any direction from the fucknuts to whom they'd made themselves subservient.

My mother, for instance, has a genius level I.Q. and has done precisely nothing with it, because she submitted herself to her husband. Who did not. That part wasn't his fault, but he *was* to blame for buying into the idea that, due to an accident of genetics, he should, nonetheless, be the one in charge. As was she for going along with it.

I'm sure I was not the son for which either had hoped. I liked literature and music. Sci-fi and art. I despised sports and was bored by cars I didn't own. I was known to flounce on occasion. Even to sashay, if my blood was up. I couldn't have been less butch if I were Sundance.

Still, I was dazzled and entranced by women, and I wanted them to want me near them. Thus, part of me ached to find someone with more left-field tastes, another part of me ached to discover a less hockey-centric form of machismo, and one specific part of me just ached.

I received the usual mixed messages at home. My mother told me that women didn't want "girly" men—yet excoriated me when she discovered the softest of soft porn under my bed. My father once asked me if I was gay because he caught me crying over a girl. Okay, so he turned out to be twenty percent right, but it remains one of the most mystifying questions I've ever been asked.

Even without the additional line-blurring of bipolar disorder, my relationship with my own masculinity would undoubtedly have been strained.

Paradoxically, it was in regards to my illness that I became the most stereotypically male.

I can't speak with any real authority on what the world's twisted approached to manhood does to women, I just know it doesn't result in a surplus of puppies and chocolate. But I can tell you what it does to men.

It makes us dangerous. To ourselves and others.

As a man, you are told, by everyone, that your job is to be strong. You should be a rock—hard, unyielding and frequently found outdoors. Able to withstand any storm. Difficult to crack. Useful for building things. As character traits go, they don't sound too bad, until you factor in the impossibility of maintaining them over the course of a human life.

It can't be done, but we're told it must be done, so when we find ourselves wavering, or fraught, we lie. Or we conceal. We pretend everything is a-okay, then do our best to die early with our façade still in place.

If mental illness comes into play, this sense of failure is amplified a thousand percent. We fall back on silence as we frantically try to work it out, the way our father might have, or our grandfather. They dealt with worse than our puny little problems, we think—hell, they seem to have been at war half the bloody time—so surely we can cope. We can soldier on.

Soldiers are particularly good at dying early.

I believe in communication. I think that seeking help is one of the most courageous things you can do. Masculinity is, to me, in its current form, a relic of stupider times and needs to be jettisoned in favour of something that results in less young men, with endless potential and families that love them, making rash and final choices, because they don't see any other option.

And in spite of all that, Freud be damned, I do keep mum. I do pretend to be okay when I'm not. I yearn to prove that I can handle it. That I can be relied upon. That I can be a rock.

That I can be a man.

When I found out I was going to become a father, I hoped for girls. I imagined it would be a simpler task to teach girls to be strong than to teach boys it was acceptable to be vulnerable. Now that I have daughters, I most often wish I had the strength not to mask my fragility with so much bluster.

I have failed those that I have loved. I know I have. And while I also know—in my head—that this had nothing to do with the contents of my trousers, and everything to do with the individual wearing them, it's hard to shake the feeling that if I'd been like the other boys—the ones who don't break so easily—I'd be in a very different place.

But it's the actions that stemmed from those doubts that did the damage, not my limitations or my ailment. If I'd accepted what I couldn't do more readily, I could have done so much more. And if I'd asked for help more frequently, I would have been in a better state to offer support in return.

So, yeah. Who knows what drivel lurks in the hearts of men?

The shadow knows.

And so do I.

Intermission

We've reached the half-way point of our story now, so I thought it might be a good idea to pause for a moment and take stock.

Feel free to make a cup of tea, or a sandwich, or that phone call you keep putting off. I'm not going anywhere.

I might have a coffee myself.

Yes, very refreshing.

Now, it's worth knowing in advance that the landscape shifts considerably in the second half. The only way I can explain it, without pulling focus away from our primary subject matter, is to say that a lot happened. Some of it was wonderful, and some of it was terrible. And I handled both equally badly.

I can tell you that, as we resume our story, I have abandoned my life as a full-time musician and have become, instead, a full-time actor, writer and film-maker. This decision was taken, as with all of my unmedicated choices, under the misapprehension that it would make life easier.

It did not. Keep an eye out for a substantial reprise of something that happened in Part One.

Along the way, Fathead and Baldy will also gain a parent. This, I'm sure, would fill an entire second book with heart-warming and pithy observations, but it's not my story to tell.

The biggest difference is that, as the second half begins, the girls' childhoods are suddenly half-over, rather than just beginning.

For continuity's sake, however, I am still no closer to transitioning out of mine.

9: Future-Proofing

Thinking ahead was never my strong suit. Nor, indeed, my sturdy cardigan.

It's not that I didn't make plans for the future—I have dozens of notebooks, full of smudged, frenetic scrawl, that testify to my scheming—but they all, regrettably, relied heavily on the acquisition of magic beans.

Day-to-day, I favoured the reactive stance—what some would call "fire-fighting"—in which you leave everything to fate and deal with complications as they arise. It's not super efficient, but it does look cool, what with all the rushing about and the sexy uniforms.

I tried to add an element of control by setting the majority of fires myself, but all this accomplished was extending the list of things I was burning at both ends.

In a similar vein, for many years, I deliberately made no provision for my dotage. Why would I? I was chronically suicidal. I'd already lived far longer than I had expected, so accruing investments, savings, pensions or property felt pointless—a squandering of resources that could either be put to better use, or frittered with greater panache. Besides, I was due a windfall at any moment, so frugality could blow me.

Instead, I lived hand-to-mouth, an expression that derives from the frequency with which, on receiving bank statements, you cover your face in shock and alarm. I wasn't against money, per se, but I was adamant that any uptick in my financial position had to be the result of my work being recognised, and not the mind-numbing jobs I had been forced to take in the meantime.

To underscore how ingrained this attitude had become, I began to have a recurring nightmare about winning the Lottery.

Yes, you read that correctly.

I'd always been prone to bad dreams, on the rare occasions that my insomnia allowed sufficient sleep, but they usually alternated between one about a tea party—held by my mother and attended by every woman I'd ever dated—and an infinite series of heart-stompers in which the children faced peril. If I was feeling especially frazzled, either might feature alligators.

This new addition to the rotation was different. In it, I won a life-changing jackpot that would enable me to fulfil all of my ambitions and ensure the children wanted for nothing, but—the kind of "but" that tethers rappers to veracity—it would be at the expense of my credibility.

I usually woke up weeping, with a tooth or two mid-gnash.

According to my subconscious, apparently, having one's endeavours tainted by ease is one of the all-time Top Three undergarment-fouling experiences that existence has to offer.

I know, right?

At this point in our tale, though, I was, at last, starting to have my doubts. I was nearly twenty years into my working life and had nothing to show for it. And I'd worked hard too. I had not only busted my hump, I had knee-capped the rest of my camel. I had earned a reward.

But it had to be the right one. I still didn't hold with consolation prizes.

Or, it appeared, progress.

I was in my thirties now, with two children and a Sherpa-taunting mountain of responsibilities, but I still thought like the nineteen-year-old who had impulsively fled to this sceptred isle.

He had earned his tins of beans by busking in the town square. He had weathered the winter with his face pressed to the radiator, until a blister formed on the end of his nose. He had been content to spend his evenings in a nasty little bed-sit, listening as passing revellers pissed on his gate.

Because it was all temporary. Something would come along.

And he was right. Much did come along. A young woman came along, love came along, a marriage came along, a nervous breakdown came along, a divorce came along and tragedy came along. By the time he was twenty-three, he should have learned his lesson so thoroughly that he was awarded a professorship in it, with tenure.

Ten years later, he was me, and I was none the wiser.

Goo goo g'joob.

Luckily, one morning, I was informed by the radio that the *children* were our future. Which was a relief, as I was totally screwing the pooch. Armed with this new knowledge, I decided to cut my losses and concentrate on teaching them well and letting them lead the way.

Not that I could have stopped them.

One night, when Baldy was four years old, I found her, sitting on the edge of my bed, her elbows on her knees, staring at the small television that sat on

123

the bedside table. She was mesmerised. Whatever she was watching, it had grabbed her skittish attention, wrestled it to the ground and stood on its neck.

She was completely silent and unusually still. I rushed to her side to ensure she was still breathing.

Eventually, she registered my presence and looked up in annoyance.

"Shush," she said curtly and returned to her programme.

But it wasn't a movie to which she was riveted, or a show about teen witches, or even that advert for Jaffa Cakes she loved, where a family is menaced by a shark.

It was a medical documentary. Specifically, an incredibly detailed and blood-soaked one about gender reassignment procedures. A surgeon, elbows deep in gore, was cheerily explaining one such operation to camera, and Baldy was all but taking notes.

So it was not entirely unexpected when, approaching the end of her first decade, she announced her intention to become a doctor.

Often, when children make these kind of career declarations, it's a passing phase. By the time you've read all the literature, bought all the corresponding toys and started researching colleges, they've changed their minds and would now prefer to be an astronaut or someone who tests Wellington boots by jumping in and out of puddles.

Baldy stuck to her scalpels. Between then and now, the overall plan has mutated to include the adoption of five or more orphaned children and a possible side-line as a writer of Green Arrow fan fiction, but medicine continues to have her heart, the parts of which she will name at the drop of a hat.

I'm hoping she specialises in cardiology actually, because I'm going to be paying for it.

If you have enjoyed this book, please tell a friend.

Her dedication to her dreams, despite her knack for becoming distracted by passing dust particles, has always made me proud. Especially as, when she first started telling people, she walked face-first into the adult world's fascination with expectation management.

I'm all for being realistic—I'm not, but I'm working on it—but attempting to dissuade children from pursuing a career because it sounds "awfully hard" is tantamount to abuse. Yet, you can count the number of interested parties who lead with this on the fingers of a polydactyl convention.

Of course, Baldy is the type of child whose instinctive response to "You can't do that" is to do it twice. The second time for spite. It's a characteristic that is often a pain in the ass, but, in this instance, it manifested as fortitude.

And heaven help any less-than-woke relative who asked if she meant a nurse. Nursing is a noble profession in its own right, but the merest whiff of the suggestion being gender-motivated and you'd find yourself daubing antiseptic on a startled great-aunt and apologising insincerely.

The passage of time has done nothing to dilute the strength of her feelings on the subject. And don't even get her started on the words "actress" or "heroine".

In case this is an audiobook, or you're reading aloud, the latter has an "e" on the end of it. But please don't start her on heroin either.

Fathead has different ambitions. She wants me to worry myself to death. I discovered this, around the same time, when she rang me on the phone and informed me, solemnly, that we needed to talk.

I'd heard the phrase before. I may even have said it once or twice. In any case, it had never led anywhere enjoyable and hearing it from my daughter's mouth caused a distinct flutter of anxiety in my guts. Had she killed a man? Was she pregnant? Had she somehow got someone else pregnant? Jesus, what was the world coming to if a nine-year-old girl can get a dead man pregnant?

Nonetheless, I agreed to meet. The only other option—refusing to talk to her for the rest of her life—would not only be negligent but would also mean I'd never find out how all that mustard ended up in my sock drawer.

So, we arranged a time, after school, and headed to a nearby café. I ordered a very strong coffee, Fathead a hot chocolate topped with so much cream that it might have been a Prince remix. Beverages in hand, we headed to a quiet corner and sat opposite each other.

It was all very formal. She took a delicate sip of her drink and, so as to further unsettle me, wiped her face immediately afterwards. With a napkin. One of my knees began to jog nervously beneath the table.

Knocked-up corpse. It had to be.

Fathead interlaced her fingers, gathered her thoughts and exhaled heavily. Then she looked me straight in the eye.

"Father," she began.

"Nope," I said, leaving my chair.

"What do you mean, nope? I'm trying to tell you something."

"If it starts with Father, I don't want to know."

I'd learned the hard way that you should always pay close attention to how your children address you in conversation, especially in unusual circumstances. Some of the words may *seem* interchangeable, but don't be fooled. There are layers of subtext.

If they call you "Daddy", for instance, they are either under five, or want money. If they prefer "Papa", they are French, or have a concussion. And

125

"Progenitor" is a clear indication that you need to put a lock on the outside of their bedroom door.

"Dad" is usually okay. It depends on the length of the vowel.

But a full-strength "Father"? That's a six-letter word for ulcer. It's a rain of toads. A quartet of horsemen. A musical remake of *Citizen Kane*.

This applies regardless of additional parenting prefixes or gender identification. There is absolutely nothing that your child is going to say, following "father" or "mother", that isn't going to cause you some kind of distress.

And so it was in this case.

"Please sit down."

"Sit down, *who*?"

"Ugh. Why are you so *weird*?"

"Answer me, child."

"Dad. Okay? Please sit down, *Dad*."

"Right," I said, cautiously, "That's better."

I resumed my seat. Slowly. One eye on the exit and the other tracking Fathead, in case of sudden moves.

She was shaking her head in exasperation. Which was rich, I thought, considering she started it.

I picked up my coffee and tried to appear nonchalant.

"So," I said, "What did you want to talk about?"

"Well, I have some questions about what just happened, for starters."

"Another time. *Daughter*. What did you want to say before that?"

She fell silent again and I felt a twinge of guilt. This was obviously important to her.

"I hope you know that you can tell me anything," I added, softening my tone, "Anything at all."

(Why not try Tone-O-Soft? For *all* your potentially delicate conversational gambits!)

"Did you just do a fake commercial in your head?"

"No."

"*Dad*."

"Maybe."

"What is wrong with you?"

"I'll tell you when you're older."

The banter continued for another ten minutes or so, until it became apparent that not only was I the only one talking, but this had been the case for a while. The child was looking at me in a manner to which I had become accustomed. With diminishing patience.

I zipped it.

"Sorry."

"It's fine."

"No, I'm really sorry. You know how I get sometimes."

"You should really do something about that."

"In a few more chapters, I promise."

"You better. I can't imagine these conversations are going to get less complicated."

"Ain't that the truth."

"*Dad.*"

"What?"

"You went off on one again."

"I know. I'm trying to be funny."

"And how's that working out for you?"

"Wow."

"I'm sorry. It's just… Look, I wanted to tell you that I've decided what I want to be when I grow up."

I sat up straight in my chair. Not bad news, then, but big. That changed things. I pulled the emergency brake and ground myself, screeching, into a different gear.

Time for some full-service parenting.

"You have my undivided attention," I said, "Tell me all about it."

She hesitated.

"Well…"

"Don't be shy. Whatever it is, I will support you."

"Are you sure?"

"One hundred percent."

"And you won't try to talk me out of it?"

"Not as long as it's legal. And, depending on the sentencing restrictions, there may even be some wiggle room there."

"I don't think you'll be happy about it."

Even in my manic state, I sensed the enormity of the moment. This was prime fatherly advice territory. Anything I said now had a good chance of being repeated in my eulogy.

Thankfully, speeches are what Tiggers do best.

"My darling girl," I said, "First of all, I need you to know that I love you and your sister more than I will ever be able to express. For the last nine years, it has been my honour—my privilege—to watch you grow into young women that I am immensely proud to call my daughters. You have made my life better in countless ways. To be honest, you have made my life, period. And, every single day, I pray for an opportunity to return the favour. I know getting older is scary; I know there must be nights when you lie awake, wondering about the future and your place in it. Everyone does; it's a natural part of life. But here's the thing: You will never be alone. I will be there, every step of the way, cheering from the sidelines. I will, always, without fail, have your back. So, whatever you tell me now—whatever you want to do with your life—if it is something about which you feel passionate, that you will work at, that will make you *happy*, then we will figure out a way to make it happen. Together."

One of us definitely had tears in their eyes. I can't remember which.

Fathead nodded. She'd heard what she needed to hear. After one more deep breath for courage, she divested herself of her burden.

"I want to be a singer and an actor. Like you."

I drank the words in. Let them settle in my mind. Composed my response with care.

"Have you considered pole-dancing?"

"*Dad.*"

"Seriously. I hear it's very good exercise."

***

Like *me*. Jesus. Was she a masochist?

I know that a lot of parents dream of hearing those words. They'd enjoy nothing more than stencilling "& Child" on to the signage of their life's work. I suspect that's because they have been successful in their chosen field and they want their children to experience the same satisfaction. Or they've built a business—with their own two hands and the sweat of their brow—that they hope will be passed down from generation to generation.

This was not the situation in which I found myself.

Don't misunderstand me. I love what I do. I always will.

But it's entirely unrequited.

I've come to terms with that; I know that my need to continue, despite everything that's happened, is Stockholm-assisted, but I decided long ago that I'd see it through to the finish, come what may. I am who and what I am.

Trust me, I'm no happier about it than you are.

Still, how could I, in good conscience, recommend to my own flesh and blood the pursuit of a career that actively and frequently tries to kill you?

The life I chose—or which chose me—is so gruesomely unstable that even those who have reached the zenith of their professional lives spend the lion's share of their time battling imposter syndrome, dreading the inevitable moment when it all goes away, and they are back in the queue with the rest of us. It is frustrating. Anti-social. Soul-destroying. It messes with your conception of reality, of human connection and, most deleteriously, of self.

I'd rather she'd taken an interest in Russian roulette, though, basically, she had.

But I didn't want to be one of those parents you read about in biographies, the ones who, after years of warning their kids that they'd never make it in music, or acting, or dance or competitive ice sculpting, end up looking like complete assholes.

I *had* those parents. Admittedly, their primary concern was that I'd turn out gay and God would smite me, but they still did everything in their power to impede my progress in the Arts. If I have any residual yearning for splashier success, it revolves heavily around flipping them the bird. And while that can be handy in terms of maintaining motivation, it isn't the relationship I want with my children.

So, despite my initial chagrin, I pulled myself together and assured Fathead that she could count on my patronage.

✱✱✱

"I assure you that you can count on my patronage."

"I don't know what that means, but good," she said, "Because I need you to help me make my dreams come true."

Okay. No pressure then.

"I'll do my best," I said.

And I did.

Which was my first mistake.

Bi·ological Warfare

We've talked about the mind for long enough. It's time to turn our attention to the body.

Don't get overexcited, you filthy animals. It's my body we'll be discussing and, I can assure you, it's nothing to write home about. Not unless it's a letter that begins: "Dear Mum, I accidentally saw a Canadian man's body today and I don't think I want to live here anymore."

I *hate* my body.

I don't mean that I'm ambivalent towards it. It isn't that there are parts of it that I would tweak, given the chance. My judgement is unyielding and unequivocal: I loathe the fucker. From the tip of its most obstinate hair, to the gap between its oddly-shaped toes.

"The crazy doth protest too much," is what you're thinking now, I'm sure. But I promise you that I am neither fishing for compliments, nor exaggerating for comic effect. This is not, for once, an attempt to appear self-deprecating. If I could live as a brain in a jar, I would.

Of course, all things being equal, I'd also prefer a different brain. And an opaque jar.

I'm aware this isn't healthy. I know, rationally, that how I view myself is not how others see me. I've even met people with similar levels of self-disgust and wondered—as you might—why they can't accept that they look fine and that any belief to the contrary is just their brain warming up the branding irons.

So, yes, I know what's going on. I can see the moving parts, and where the grease should be applied. But, in my head, the gears still seize and the sparks still fly. I look into the funhouse mirror and see a photograph.

The word "dysmorphia" has been tossed around. Not by me, I should stress, although I suppose I wouldn't know.

The kerosene on this particular bushfire is that whenever I attempt to be proactive, in the cause of a more tolerable self-image, my primary disorder develops a case of the green-eyed monsters and demands to be involved.

Unfortunately, it has as skewed a view of its limitations as I have of myself. And, naturally, abhors the middle ground.

So, for weeks at a time, I will hit the gym every day, tottering atop a cresting wave of endorphins and shedding weight to the point that my friends start sending me leaflets for hospice care.

Following which, I will spend several months beneath a duvet, gnawing tearfully on a wheel of cheese.

I yo-yo, in other words. Though you should imagine the toy in question as being unspooled and retracted from the basket of an unweighted hot air balloon.

The thing is, I'm not entirely sure what I *would* like my body to be. I've no bodybuilding aspirations; I may not like my neck, but I'm glad it's there. Likewise, my testicles.

I just don't want to look like this. Or feel like this. Or be like this.

I suppose it's similar to money—the ideal amount to have is however much allows you to ignore it completely. That's what I'd really like—for my body never to cross my mind.

At the moment, it's never far from my thoughts.

Because it isn't just my weight, or the associated lumpiness. That's just the tip of the dressing-free iceberg. We must also consider the thickness of my ankles, and the slightness of my forearms, and how one of my eyelids is demonstrably puffier than the other.

Actual tears have been shed over how flaky my skin gets when I grow my beard in. The sun has risen and set as I've brooded about the shape of the back of my head. And I've a single rebellious eyebrow hair that has been known to spark off week-long benders.

Counterintuitively, the only parts of my body with which I am completely comfortable are the mismatched pair of scars on my wrists—one horizontal, one vertical. The former is a subtle reminder that one should always do their research before attempting a task, and both serve as a testament to how far I have come.

But the rest of it can get to fuck.

Speaking of which…

Sex.

What's that all about?

From the moment that my youthful hormones went into screaming overdrive, I have been utterly baffled by the erotic. I'm not against it—on the contrary, I consider myself a fan. But it doesn't make any sense. I've no idea why anyone would want to go to bed with me, and even less why anyone has.

I'm grateful, obviously—and I hope that has come across in my fumbling endeavours. But when I hear people kvetch about being desired for their body alone, I just nod and smile. Well, nod and shift my lips about; I'm not keen on my smile either.

Anyway, try as I might, it's not a problem I can fully wrap my head around. I can't remember a single occasion on which I have been treated like a piece of meat, or made to feel like a vibrator with shoes. And, let me assure you, it has not been for lack of trying. For some reason, I spent a large portion of my twenties *desperate* to be objectified. Which goes a long way to prove that, however feminine I consider myself, I have literally no idea what women go through.

Wouldn't it be nice, I thought, for someone to be overcome with lust, just from looking at you? Wouldn't that reassure you that you were physically acceptable?

As moronic as it sounds, I truly believed that anyone who was intimate with me because of *feelings* was doing it under duress.

It would take considerably more time than we have left—both in this book and as a species—to completely untangle everything that's wrong with that, but I think it's worth having a look at the abridged version.

To begin with, that's not how it works. Desire and arousal are predicated on, often quite literally, different strokes for different folks. A well-turned ankle can hoist your freak flag, as can a well-turned phrase. Yes, there are times in our lives when we succumb on purely physical grounds—when mutual, equally valid—but, in my experience, attraction to someone's entirety cranks the sexy up by several notches.

It's also one of a depressing number of instances in which we assume away the agency of others by putting thoughts into their minds and words into their mouths. You don't tell someone else *why* they have sex—that's creepy and weird. Even if you don't say it out loud. After all, you're as much a part of their story as they are of yours, and, most likely, an equally confounding and unwieldy one. In my case, probably more so.

Ultimately, with hindsight, I realise I had the whole thing back to front. Which, despite the context, is nowhere near as much fun as you're thinking.

Nor is it cause for your soft-hearted noises, as though I were a puppy who mistook a sprinkler for a biscuit. Insecurity is too readily weaponised. A nip and a tuck and it's jealousy. A twist and a turn and it's violence. Left unchecked for long enough, and it's downright predatory.

So while hating myself has consistently led to pain, it hasn't always been mine.

"Ooh, didn't Mummy love you enough?" is a taunt, for instance, that we love to employ. We aim it at the entitled and the passive aggressive, at brats of every stripe. It is an excellent—and effective—multi-purpose burn.

But how do you respond when the answer is an unambiguous "No, actually, she didn't"?

If you've ever loved someone broken, you know the answer. You try to pick up the pieces. Make up for the past. Fix it.

But the pieces are sharp and the past is far-flung. And some things just cannot be fixed.

It's not just a vicious circle, it's a psychopathic one. We'll run ourselves down. You'll try to rebuild us. We'll berate you for trying. You'll assure us we're wrong. And, little by little, with nothing but love on both sides, we'll both start to think less of the other.

It's the arena, for me, in which lions still lurk. With the aid of medication, I have greater clarity about my past. There are many mistakes I'll no longer repeat. My mood swings are manageable, my temper is sedated, my psyche is, at least, held together with sturdier twine. I am a better father and a more reliable man.

But I'm still not convinced that I'm worth all the effort. I don't feel attractive. I don't feel comfortable in my skin. The idea of performing—one of the great joys of my life—now makes me anxious, in a way it never used to, because I no longer want people to look at me. Every rejection, against which I once railed, now feels supremely reasonable.

I'm not without hope, though. I do *know* that I'm wrong. That's a big step forward. I have, finally, found comfort in remembering that I've been loved deeply by those I've loved madly. And I'm no longer tempted by my shadow's approach, which is to take the pauper he sees in the mirror and declare him king.

Something useful on the shop floor will do me fine.

I don't know if I can learn to love my body. For the moment, that still feels a leap too far. But, one day, I could well start to like myself. A little, at least.

If I behave.

∗∗∗

At the risk of being ritually murdered, I should probably tell you that wrestling with your own low self-esteem—whether focused on body or soul—is only the beginning. There is another, more crucial, task that tails it like a gumshoe.

You have to ensure that you don't pass it on.

That's not easy, especially if you have any kind of prolonged contact with other human beings. Or, if you have sensibly fled from society and taken to a cave, with particularly vulnerable bats.

Why?

Because we are not as isolated as we believe. For all that I've banged on about the intrinsic solitude of being alive, we cannot help but have an effect on others. There is always a reaction, whether big or small.

It's not always the one you'd expect though.

For example, we often tell children that a sunny disposition will, as a matter of course, inspire happiness in others.

This is nonsense, of course. I have often wanted to garrotte the cheerful with the nearest piece of piano wire. I'm sure you have too.

Okay, yes, sometimes a smile lights up a room. If it's the right teeth, in the right face, at least half-an-hour after I've had my coffee. But it doesn't happen nearly as often as legend purports, or we wouldn't be in the middle of an energy crisis.

The point is, thrill or throttle, mood has consequences.

Likewise, if self-loathing is released into a populated area, whether it's because you don't like the way you look, or how you speak, or how you think, it will have an impact. Or, rather, a series of wildly unpredictable, if uniformly distasteful, impacts.

Some will simply resent you for turning up and harshing their buzz. Others will tie themselves up in knots trying to identify what they did to cause you to feel this way. A few liberal-minded souls may even let *you* tie *them* up in knots, in the hopes that it will make you feel better. The combinations are endless, but no one's going home unbruised.

If you have children, the worst outcome is that they store it away with all the other hastily-assembled life templates you've provided.

I worry about damaging the girls' self-image in the same way I do about equipping them poorly for life—constantly and with a hyperawareness of my own inadequacies.

I am, after all, supremely underqualified for the vast majority of tasks I am called upon to perform, let alone encouraging self-respect. I am not a doctor, yet I have undertaken a score of emergency procedures. I am neither an exterminator nor a reaper, yet I've shepherded thousands of wasps and spiders to their final reward.

I am also not a chef, yet I repeatedly swear in my kitchen. But this is largely because they only like three foods, and still won't tell me which ones.

I do have skills. Even my shaky grasp of self allows for that. But, in terms of day-to-day life, they're pointlessly niche. English Literature getting you down? I'm your boy. Struggling to master the I–V–vi–IV chord progression? Whack your money on the barrelhead. Want to dissect the meaning of life and aren't yet old enough to inhale? Take a seat, child, and let your wise old Dad bore you to tears.

I'm an "ideas" guy. But, unfortunately, children cannot eat ideas. Though they will have a fair crack at crayons.

The upshot of all of the above is that I have to dabble in real life more frequently than my comfort zone appreciates. Which is fine—it's the price of doing business—but I know it will never be second nature.

On top of that, I've discovered, over the years, that their emotional requirements outstrip their physical ones by a factor of infinity to one. Which you'd think would be more in my wheelhouse, but I've never been much for maintaining the boat.

It's a shitty world out there at the best of times, let alone when you're still trying to figure out who you're supposed to be. Superficiality reigns supreme. There are pressures from every corner to act a certain way, look a certain way, think a certain way. For young women, this seems especially body-centric— with consistently wounding, and potentially tragic, results.

At the most basic level, of course, we're not dealing with anything we haven't before. The concept of "fitting in" is as old as childhood itself. But it's equally hard to deny that it's had some work done. Our now ubiquitous technological connection to one other, while not intrinsically to blame, does enable a level of propaganda bombardment that makes North Korea look like JD Salinger.

It is, therefore, up to me to provide the necessary guidance to ensure that they remain true to themselves, feel confident—but not arrogant—about their abilities and bodies, and develop rounded and balanced senses of self.

I mean, for fuck's sake. You may as well have employed the Pope to organise dress-down Friday.

So, how do I teach them to love themselves, when I can barely stand to be in same room as me? How do I help them to see their reflection and not a collection of faults?

Well, first, I contemplate the snaking queue of love-sick boys and girls outside my house. As none of them appear to have reached the level of maturity necessary to judge on personality, I can only conclude that, even discounting parental bias, the twins are aesthetically-pleasing.

And everyone says they look just like me.

Reverse-engineering takes care of the rest.

Then—and it gets a little corny now—I think about the fact that I love them so much that there are times when I think my heart might actually burst. (Baldy says it's because of all the salt in my diet, but she has no room to talk. I've seen her treat chips like Lot's wife.)

The big finish is reminding myself, for the millionth time, that, for whatever reason, they love me back. They want me around. They need me. I am *fundamental* to them.

So, I can't be all *that* bad, can I?

The answer you're looking for is "No", but I would also have accepted "You mean well".

From that point onwards, it's about paying it forward. You blow gently on those tiny sparks of confidence, till you've all felt the heat on your face.

It's not a perfect plan and it doesn't always work. And even when it does, it's far from permanent. You almost always end up where you started, and must face the whole process again.

But, where it counts, it takes the edge off, just enough, to prevent the children from having to use it themselves.

I only wish I'd thought of it sooner.

10: National Expression

I spent most of 2012 in the back of a coach.

No, you're absolutely right. Of course I didn't. That would be insane.

It just *felt* that way.

Which, for those of you keeping score, is also a lie.

Sort of.

At this point, feel free to slap me. Just avoid the face; I've got kids to feed.

Prevarication aside, I did spend a perverse amount of time, for professional reasons, in the back of a coach that year. The days were long, the nights were errant and the rejection flowed like wine. Which also flowed like wine. I was suffering from exhaustion, mania, anxiety, depression and, for a couple of really rough months, sciatica.

Yet, it was also a year that contained some of my happiest ever moments. The kind about which songs are and, indeed, were composed.

To paraphrase Charlie D, it was the best of times, it was the most thoroughly fucked of times.

Still, I can assure you that when I dream of those days, as I often do, it is not of the lonely stretches I spent on the road, folded like a deck chair, watching in horror as each of my electronic devices died, one after the other, leaving me with nothing to occupy the hours but my splintered thoughts, a feeble overhead light and the ominous dry heaves of the drunken gentleman to my immediate left.

My reveries, instead, feature wondrous things. Beautiful seconds that seemed to last for years. Words that seared themselves on every chamber of my heart. Impressions on my skin that will never fade.

None of which, I'm sorry to report, will be detailed here. As lyrical as I could wax, and as hard as I could make you cry, I shall continue to guard them jealously.

It's the right decision, but it does raise a question that's concerned me from the moment I started writing this story.

How honest am I really being, when I'm leaving so much out?

I guess you'll just have to trust that I've haven't cut anything that would distort what I'm trying to say. There are no suspicious mounds of freshly-dug earth in my garden. I don't wear socks with sandals.

It isn't the whole truth, but it remains nothing but.

Less gallingly for me, but possibly more so for you, I will also be skipping over the handful of celebrity encounters that occurred during the course of plying my trade. I know it's probably not a smart commercial decision, but they don't feel organic to the piece, which is wanker for "Do I *look* like a gossip columnist?"

I understand this may come as a disappointment. With all the heavy emotional material through which you've had to trudge, it must seem churlish to deny you a palate cleanser of Hollywood intrigue.

"Bring on the dancing bears!" you scream, with near sexual intensity. "Show us the fancy folk and tell us of their ways!"

Hey, it's not as if I'm not torn. An author wants to please his readers, even if their attitude sucks. And there are some very funny stories to be had, featuring a litany of exceptionally famous people. If I cared to, I could drop names like a DJ dropping the bass.

Then again, I have enough trouble staying on topic without additional tangents to navigate, especially ones that are better-looking and more successful than me.

It's a conundrum and no mistake.

Still, I suppose I can afford to throw you a bone. Especially as, otherwise, I'm going to have to answer some tough questions about why I have all these bones lying around.

So, by way of a compromise, here are all of my celebrity workplace encounters, condensed into one easy-to-carry anecdote.

"Hello, famous person. I hope you are well and enjoying this unseasonably clement weather. It certainly is pleasant to be working alongside you on this film/television programme/oddly low-rent advertisement. I have long been an admirer of your work."

"Why, thank ou, woing stiff. Please tell me your name, so that I can repeat it back to you and prove that I am just an ordinary person, who knows the names of underlings and absolutely does not have a pet squid called Balthazar."

"That is very kind of you. And please do not feel bad that I have informed you of my name several times, and you have consistently repeated it back to me as "'Bubba" ' despite it containing none of those letters."

"You are gracious to say so, although, most likely, I am already in the process of forgetting this ever happened."

"I completely understand."

And scene.

Everybody happy now? Itch sufficiently scratched?

Good.

Because our ride is leaving in a minute, and I don't want to wind up next to the toilets again.

***

Outside of the coaches and the redacted glories either side of them, there is one day of that year that would, in any civilised society, go on to live in infamy. Or, at least, on the outskirts, where the rent is cheaper.

As you can imagine, I've crossed many lines in my life. I admit it freely. I've scuffed others out and redrawn them to suit. Once, I even maintained with such fervour that lines were, in fact, round things with spots on, that the person on the other side got confused and went home.

But what I did on this particular day was so beyond any conceivable boundary that I've never been able to completely forgive myself for it.

I missed the twins' tenth birthday.

For a job.

It wasn't even an exceptionally lucrative one, really, but that's not the point. Nor am I pointing fingers at anyone else who, in the cause of earning their scratch, has made difficult choices. There are endless instances of loving, devoted parents doing what they have to do, even as their hearts break.

But I, of all people, should have known better. This shit was important to me. It was personal. I grew up without birthdays, for Christ's sake.

That's not just a prepositional outburst, by the way. One of the many charming quirks of my parents' faith was its full-scale boycott of any holiday that might be considered in any way "fun" or "nice". Birthdays came in for a particular kicking, as they were not only pagan in origin but self-centred in application.

Consider the story of John the Baptist, they'd say, by way of backing up their claims.

To which I now reply, "Why not?"

***

The Bible, though hot on begatting, actually mentions very few birthdays, another point that is considered a mark against the practice. But it does take

139

pains to record the shindig of a certain Herod Antipas, Tetrarch of Galilee and Perea and, to be fair, I'm not surprised. Being royal, it was a lavish affair and, as the setting for a moral lesson, bacchanalian. Like a hog roast in a strip club, but posh.

At the time, you'd have thought King H would have had his fill of elaborate events. He had, after all, recently married his brother's wife—the way people do in Biblical stories or Arkansas.

It's worth mentioning that his brother's name was also Herod and, even more oddly, their joint wife was called Herodias. This should tell you all you need to know about the kind of people with whom we're dealing.

For further colour, the two Herods' father—Herod, natch—had achieved fame of his own, 30 years previously, when he had ordered a bunch of babies to be murdered, in an attempt to wipe out a single Messiah-y one.

If the family existed today, they would absolutely have their own show.

The spouse-nabbing had largely been shrugged off by the general populace, who had better things to do with their time, like ploughing stuff or dying young. There may have been a "Tch, what are they like?" or two at the dinner table, but they mostly left them to it.

The newlyweds, however, had not accounted for the ire of the world's worst swimming instructor.

Because, unfortunately for the Herods, the Baptist was a traditionalist, and, as such, had taken a dim view of the union. And like most religious extremists, he didn't hold with quiet disapproval or living and letting live, and instead took to denouncing the couple publicly at every opportunity.

"Come on!" he would shout, in the town square, "His brother's wife! How messed up is that?"

I'm assured it sounds better in the original Aramaic.

At first, Herod—thinking John a holy man and knowing that fucking with them never plays well in the provinces—was content to turn a blind eye. But Herodias became increasingly pissed, both at the insult and her new man's seeming lack of spine. She began to dream, nightly, of revenge. And of, one day, meeting a man called Geoff or Barry.

And then, thanks to the laws of narrative momentum, her husband's birthday party provided her with a perfect opportunity to settle the score.

For, somewhere between the streamers and the endless pairs of tube socks, Herod—rather than just downing a bottle of tequila and murdering *Paradise by the Dashboard Light* like a normal person—called upon his new wife's daughter—and, let us not forget, his niece—to dance all sexy-like for the assembled company.

We've all done it.

Her name was Salome, and being an accommodating sort, she duly busted a veil-wafting move and earned herself a standing O. Her step-daddy-uncle, in return, offered her anything she desired as a reward.

Torn between a new pair of shoes and money for college, she consulted with Mummy.

After which, she asked for John's head on a plate.

I'd like to point out at this stage that I am not making any of this up. Nor will I spoil the ending, in case you suffer a bout of insomnia in the near future and want to read it for yourself.

Suffice it to say, the *only* possible conclusion to draw from any of this, if you are either a cult member or enjoy hitting yourself repeatedly in the temple with a claw hammer, is that if you celebrate your birthday, there is a greater than average chance that you will end up with someone's cranial fluid leaking on to your good china.

For my parents and their ilk, it was the Judean version of *Reefer Madness*. Birthdays. The gateway holiday.

Not that it stopped there. Christmas, Easter, Halloween, Canada Day—they had similarly flimsy excuses for banning all of them. Wedding anniversaries were the only exception, as this was the one occasion on which *they* received presents.

Of course, as a child, the worst part was the endless questions you had to field from your peers.

"What do you mean, you don't have Christmas?"

"I'm not sure how else to say it. We don't have Christmas. Nous ne fêtons pas Noël."

"I don't understand. Doesn't Santa bring you any presents?"

We'd been relentlessly prepped for that one. If anyone needled us about not receiving birthday or Christmas presents, we were supposed to reply, "It's okay. We get presents at other times."

I was excited by that for a while, until I eventually realised that "at other times" was a largely hypothetical construct.

The point is, when I finally got out of the asylum, I made a solemn vow that I would celebrate all holidays within an inch of their lives, stopping just short of prophet-based buffets. And Fathead and Baldy definitely weren't going to know what hit them when festivities rolled around.

So, why, on the day of their transition into double digits, was I not at their side, as they mainlined sugar and shredded wrapping paper with eager fingers? Why was I, instead, somewhere in a frozen corner of Wales, covered in fake blood and pretending to be murdered?

Have a guess.

Yep, got it in one. Despite having been gifted an unmerited number of fresh starts, I was still struggling with the concept of balance. I'd transferred all of my obsession with making it as a musician into making it as an actor, which is like escaping a shark attack by head-butting a tiger.

The greatest hazard, however, was my desperation. I wanted so badly to be a provider, to stand on my own two feet and lessen my reliance on those who propped me up at every turn—gladly, but with swiftly hardening feelings. At the same time, fear of failure, of proving to be ordinary, kept me from exploring any of the sensible options for achieving that. I continued to insist that the dam was going to break any second; I just had to keep going.

I was not correct. Instead, it wouldn't be long before Shergar's corpse and I required a safe word.

Further driving spikes into my heart was how well the twins seemed to be taking my regular absences. They barely batted an eye, accepting it as just the way things were. This was both a relief and a kick in the balls. I obviously didn't want to them to suffer, but I didn't want to be extraneous either. I think I was hoping for them to adopt a stiff upper lip approach, for which I would later reward them.

Like a good little truant, I rang them on the day and tried to keep the guilt out of my voice. Baldy answered.

"What?"

This is still how she answers the phone.

"Hey, kiddo."

"Oh, hi, Dad."

"You okay?"

"Uh-huh."

"Happy birthday."

"Thank you."

"Are you having a good day?"

"I guess so. We had to go to school."

"I know."

"Even though it was our birthday. Molly never has to go to school on her birthday."

"Well, that's up to Molly's parents."

She growled and I changed the subject.

"I'm really sorry I'm not there. But we'll do something at the weekend when I get home. I promise."

"That's okay. I know you have to work."

"Thank you for understanding. How's your sister?"

Rookie mistake.

"She's an idiot."

"Don't say that."

"YES, YOU ARE!"

Sigh.

"Right. What's happening?"

"She took my trainers and now she won't give them back. YES, YOU DID! NO, YOU CAN'T TALK TO HIM! I'M TALKING TO HIM!"

This was followed by a series of noises that, if recorded, would make for a serviceable set of World War I sound effects, before the phone grudgingly changed hands.

"The *reason* I took her trainers, is because she put mine somewhere and now I can't find them, and what was I supposed to do? Get glass in my feet and catch a disease and *die*?"

"Happy birthday."

"Thank you."

"Do you think you and your sister could try to make up? For me?"

"I'll make up with her when she stops being a little bitch."

"Hey. Come on. There's no need for that."

"I'm only telling the truth, like you taught me. She *is* a little bitch. YOU ARE SO! NO, YOU SHUT UP! Dad, *tell* her."

Children take a hypocritical approach to the level of authority that you hold over them. If they don't want to do something, you are a tyrant who, come the revolution, had best watch their back. If they don't want their sibling to do something, or want them to stop doing something, then you become the arbiter of all, upon whose mercy they will happily throw themselves.

"Come on, girls. It's your birthday. You should be nice to each another."

"But she's so *annoying*. YES, YOU ARE!"

"I'm sure you annoy her too."

"I doubt it. I'm lovely. YES, I AM!"

"Where's your mother, by the way?"

"I think she's hiding."

"Fair enough. When she comes out, tell her I'm sorry."

"What for?"

"Dealer's choice. Look, I've got to go back to set now. Are you sure you're going to be okay?"

"Yes."

"You'll be good? And not kill each other?"

"We'll try."

"All I can ask. I love you both. I hope you've had the best birthday. And I really wish I was there."

"We wish you were here too."

And there it was. The dagger in the parental chest. The wish you can't fulfil. There are many of those, in the course of raising a child, but when it's something as basic as your presence, you feel like the worst Dad ever.

Because you don't miss children the way you miss adults. If you're away from a lover, you count the days until you are reunited. If you are away from your child, you count the days that are lost to you forever.

You just don't always count them straight away.

Children, in turn, miss you like oxygen. They don't acknowledge it or appreciate it, but remove it from the room and they soon notice. The only difference, in this case, is that, if deprived long enough, they will learn to breathe something else.

I'd love to be able to tell you that I completely understand why I made the decision to take that job. Some of my past choices make a twisted kind of sense when gazed upon with a sound mind. You can point to a moment when the disease took hold of a perfectly sensible idea and spun it off in the wrong direction.

This wasn't like that. I knew it was a bad idea and I did it anyway. I knew that I would regret it, yet convinced myself it was a price that needed paying. I hated every second and, somehow, that reassured me that I was doing the right thing.

Even my shadow was tapping me on the shoulder and asking if I was okay.

The fact was that a more profound set of dysfunctions had come into play, and a more integral deficiency.

I still had no idea who I was.

***

Identity is a peculiar beast. I don't know to what degree other people wrestle with it, but, for me, it was always a grudge match.

To, very nearly, the death.

And yet, for all that, I did have a broad concept of myself, a picture in my head to which I aspired. I wanted to be funny, literate and clever. They had always been the qualities I treasured in others, and, with my tastes and my ostensible skills, I thought I might, with a prevailing wind, be able to pull them off.

144

Sure, I'd have loved to have been sexy, it might have been fun to be popular, and I wouldn't have turned down successful, provided the fine print was in order, but those were fantasies, rather than goals.

Lamentably, you can't just go around telling people that you are funny, literate and clever without looking a prat. Or being wrong. Adjectives must be bestowed upon you by others; you can't commandeer them. Besides, they are of little use in isolation; they must be both elicited and housed.

I hoped to achieve mine through writing. From the time I was five years old, that's what I told people I was. Well, that and a Time Lord. Songs, films, long-winded treatises on mental illness—it didn't much matter to me in which medium I ended up toiling, provided I got to muck about with words.

There's a disconnect, however, between saying you're a writer and people believing it. If they haven't heard of you, or you can't point to a piece of work that can be exchanged for cash, they are only two breaths away from tossing out the word "hobby" and abruptly stripping you of the single layer of self you've so far identified. I don't think plumbers have this problem. Provided they have regular contact with pipes and wrenches, folk are willing to take them at their word. But writers are considered to be kidding themselves, until external agents declare otherwise.

The same misgivings haunt us, of course, which is why we are always trying to read things at you. We pursue reassurance as though it were an escaped arsonist in a heavily-forested area.

My personal solution was to gradually add hyphenates to my job description, on the baseless grounds that, if I played the averages, one of them was bound to take off.

Actor. Writer. Musician. Director. Have you ever heard of a less suitable collection of roles for someone with low self-esteem and a stress management system based largely on nicotine and scotch?

Yet, I have defined myself, internally and externally, as each of those things in turn. And not a one is who I am. Not even when they're going well. They are a result of who I am, a by-product.

This has taken most of my life to figure out and I'm not sure it would ever have clicked into place if it hadn't been for the children. Over the course of their lives, I've seen them ask questions, make mistakes, experience doubts, all the while trying on various metaphorical—and actual—hats and gradually edging towards a foundation on which to build.

Their putative careers are separate. What their various parental figures want for them is separate. Everything other than whatever is going on in their mad little heads is separate.

By way of proof, I offer into evidence the following interview, conducted shortly after the murders.

Sorry. Got distracted for a moment there. Obviously, what I meant to say was "in preparation for this chapter".

Officer.

"Please state your name for the record."

"What record?"

"Just go with me on this."

"Ugh. Fine. Do I really have to say Fathead?"

"Yes."

"Can't I just say my real name and you can write it as Fathead?"

"How would anyone know?"

"I'd know."

"Fine. Please state your name."

"Fathead."

"Better?"

"Not really."

"There's no pleasing some people. Speaking of which, where's your sister?"

"The next chapter?"

"Smart arse."

"Genetics. Can we hurry this up? I've got places to be."

"Okay. So, in this bit, you're ten years old. I just want to know what you remember about that time."

"You better not be saying anything embarrassing about me."

"I'm not. I promise."

"Because I know where you sleep."

"Look down a few paragraphs. It's all nice stuff."

"Don't be weird. Anyway, what do you mean, what I remember? I was ten. We went to school, we did stuff, we had our friends round. It wasn't complicated."

"But who *were* ou?"

"Am I allowed to sw in this book?"

"No."

"Then I cannot answer that."

"What I mean is, when you thought about yourself, what kind of stuff did you think?"

"I wish I had boobs?"

"No, about who you were. As a person."

"I don't know. I hoped that people would see that I was nice and they'd like me. That sort of thing."

"You also wanted to be an actor. And a singer. Did you think "'I'm Fathead—the actor?" ?' or anything like that?"

"You're really stuck on this Fathead thing, aren't you?"

"It's a device. Answer the question."

"No, I didn't. That would have been stupid."

"Why?"

"Because I'm not a thing, I'm a person. Why, do *you* think you're… what's your name in this, anyway?"

"I don't have one. I'm more of a subjective narrator."

"And you're absolutely sure your medication is working properly?"

"Yes."

"Just checking. In the book, do we still call you Dad?"

"Obviously."

"But that's not your name."

"No, because I'm not just a Dad, I'm…"

"Hah!"

"Alright, very clever…"

"Did I win?"

"It wasn't a competition."

"I know, but did I win?"

"You only made the point I was trying to get to anyway."

"By winning."

"Interview terminated at…"

"Spoilsport. Oh, by the way, can I have some money?"

This is yet another example of how they are naturally smarter than me, although if you ask me in their presence, I shall deny having said any such thing.

Kids pick up a lot from us—good and bad—which can make us both proud and peaky in equal measure. I think we forget, however, that this can sometimes form a useful trail of breadcrumbs back to our better selves. Whatever pieces of us they carry, they do so without the additional weight of our disappointments or missteps. If you want to know who you *could* be, watch your children.

Personally, I'd quite like to be mine when I grow up. They are flawed and fabulous, like all the best people. They are talented, bright, inquisitive, spirited and caring.

And quite extraordinarily lazy.

Loathe as I am to admit it, that one's totally on me. Sure, I've done a bunch of stuff, but that doesn't mean I was ever happy about it. In fact, I have long held and twice defended the title of laziest workaholic in the world. Sans interference, I would do nothing. I would sit on my couch, consuming art and macaroni and consider it a full and fulfilling life. In fact, I often think my compulsion to create is my body's way of preventing me from slipping into Howard Hughes-style hermitry.

And, God, do I ever resent doing anything I don't want to do. I'm sure that's not individual to me, but I think I take it to an unnatural extreme. To say I perform tasks outside of that narrow definition grudgingly is like saying that Christian fundamentalists protest abortion clinics in a bit of a huff.

Unfortunately, Fathead and Baldy have inherited this, to the degree that asking them to perform chores consistently runs the risk of sparking a riot.

It's not a fatal flaw, of course, nor has it remained unchallenged. The point is that seeing it from the outside has been enlightening. For one thing, I've learned exactly how fucking maddening it is, and added it to the list of areas in which I need to improve as much as they do.

Once again, however, my faults and bad habits are not who I am. As theirs are not who they are. As yours are not who you are. And so on.

So, if I am not my passions, my legacy or my blemishes, who am I?

My nationality, perhaps?

I certainly wouldn't be the first person to fall back on geography in the midst of an existential crisis. And, let's admit it, I do come from a pretty sweet place. Chill and production values—what more do you really want from a country? Also, I can't say that being a Canadian abroad does not have its advantages, especially as we currently seem less intent on dragging the world into hell by its genitals than some nations.

But as a demarcation of identity, it doesn't ring true. It doesn't feel sufficient for something as complex as a person.

In fact, at the risk of infuriating the flag-fond, I find the whole concept of patriotism bizarre and a little distasteful. How can you define yourself by something as arbitrary as where you were born? How can you be proud of something over which you've had no influence? And why is everyone so intent on insisting that their homeland is the best country that ever countried? What's wrong with just being a nice place to live?

Answers on a postcard, from wherever you find yourself.

Which is not to say that where you grew up has no bearing on the discussion. It may not be who you are, but it does influence it.

For instance, I apologise constantly and I love maple syrup. I have an inferiority complex and a predilection for quilted jackets. I cherish politeness and I am fantastically strange when I think nobody is looking.

Perhaps none of the above would be the case had I not been Canadian, if I'd slithered out of my mother in Reykjavik, rather than Saskatchewan. But I'd still be me. I'd still have bipolar disorder, I'd still find the world and other people perplexing and, I suspect, fight a daily battle to survive even remotely intact. I'd just do it nearer to geysers.

Weirdly enough, when I was little, I wanted nothing more than to be British, like my parents. So much so, that, when I was six and we made one of our infrequent trips to the UK, I came back proudly demanding "To-MAH-toes" in place of "To-MAY-toes"—a bold move for a child who was already bullied.

Of course, since moving to England, I have clung to my Canadian identity like a limpet with abandonment issues. I bleed beer and back bacon, I'll throw folk a grudging "aboot" when they need cheering up, and, despite my allergy to jingoism, I do pull myself up to my full lack of height whenever I see the old red, white, no blue.

Basically, I think I just want to be different. Or, even more likely, because I *am* different and have little choice in the matter, I lean into it.

With Fathead and Baldy, this process has been reversed. They refer to themselves as half-Canadian, their Canadian cousins have been elevated, in their minds, to mythic status and you could embroider the word "Canada" on to a dead cat and they'd wear it proudly round the town.

But the only thing it really changes about them, by comparison to their contemporaries, is that they've had a tree described to them accurately.

To me, hand on heart, it makes no difference. The people in my life simply are, they don't have component parts. They aren't Canadian or British, they aren't writers or musicians, film-makers or educators, artists or audiences. Love welds all the fragments together, leaving the whole not only greater, but in lieu.

So, why do I feel so distraught when I can't say "I am a such-and-such" with confidence? Fuck, why would I even *want* to be a such-and-such? The hours are a bear and the pay is terrible.

And, moreover, what the hell would be wrong with just hoping that people saw I was nice and wanted to be my friend? Despite that sounding far creepier when a grown man says it.

My other working theory, of course, is that no one knows who they are, but we all think everyone else does, and that's what fucks us up.

That one feels closest to the truth, actually. Because even when we do experience a fleeting sensation of self, it always seems to dance through our fingers like a bar of soap, just out of the reach of our words.

Perhaps we are reliant, for good or ill, on those who look at what we are and think it's pretty darned swell. And on the person they make us want to be.

And, maybe, it *is* a matter of national pride after all. Only we are the nation and our success is dependent on our immigration policy.

We are who we love. I've both heard and proffered worse notions. I'll allow for exceptions, such as if you've fallen for a serial killer or someone who chews with their mouth open, but in the broadest sense, I'm standing by it. Choosing to love is a decision made in extremis, always, and that, as we all know, is where your true self winters.

This means, however, that if we plump for safety over risk, if we—blatant political metaphor alert—decide instead to build a wall, then we will never become everything we could be.

Or know any Mexicans.

Bi One, Get One Free

At this juncture, I'd like you to join me for another flying visit to the present day.

I'll try not to lose your luggage this time.

You will discover momentarily that this is an entirely appropriate joke, if undoubtedly a Dad one. I also believe that you will swiftly forgive me the latter.

And this is why:

A few days ago, my daughters—whom I love more than anything else on Earth and have sworn, violently, to protect—boarded an airplane and headed off to meet, for the very first time, my family.

Having read this far and, therefore, knowing what you know, I'd like to imagine that your expression is now one of shock and dismay. With maybe a hint of indigestion.

Indeed, when the idea was first floated, I was horrified—if moved by the lengths to which they were willing to go to provide me with fresh material.

It was almost as if they'd read my notes.

If I made notes, of course, rather than just typing and screaming.

Eventually, however, it dawned on me that this was not, in fact, an act of self-sacrifice on their parts. They were excited about it. Frantically so. In fact, I don't think I've ever seen them in such a comprehensive state of bliss and I once fell over an ottoman in the middle of telling them off. Baldy smiled for five whole consecutive minutes and fifteen further non-consecutive ones, even though I had forgotten to buy her a new phone charger. Fathead wept openly and thanked the Academy.

In the end, it was hard not to get swept up in it, despite my complicated feelings on the subject. I do like it when they're happy. I get shouted at less and, sometimes, if I've had anything to do with the source of their joy, I even get a cup of coffee out of it.

When they get home, I'm owed a vow of silence and a cappuccino maker.

I do think the element of surprise might have had something to do with it. They'd been begging to visit Canada since they could speak, and I'd been trying to get my head round the idea for even longer. But I don't imagine they believed for a moment that it would ever happen. And neither did I.

It had, at least consciously, been a matter of expense. My homeland is far away and scenic, so the airlines can pretty much charge what they like— up to and including firstborns, which would have negated the point of the exercise. And with no pressing desire on my part to return, it never managed to clamber very far up the list of justifiable debt.

Deep down, however, I knew that the question would, one day, have to be revisited. The girls were getting older, and like it or not, my history was their history, and they would eventually want to investigate their roots.

And when that moment came, I instructed myself, I was not to stand in their way. I haven't been home for twenty years, for reasons detailed everywhere in this volume, but if the twins wanted a relationship with my parents or my siblings, so be it.

Besides, my brother and sisters haven't done anything wrong; I just don't know them. The oldest was seventeen when I left and the youngest, four. Our paths diverged in a wood and, as it worked out, I never found my way back. After all, there are a significant number of wooded areas in my country and this was before satellite navigation.

But now they all have children of their own, including a raft of adorable-looking babies, and the girls' grief over not being able to fuss and cuddle them was en route to achieving sentience.

So, when it came to light that my erstwhile tribe had put the money together to bring them over for a few weeks of the summer, there was little for me to do but watch as they packed every item of clothing that they'd stolen from my dresser and set off on their grand Canuck adventure.

And then teeter precariously on the precipice of spoiling it for them.

Because once it was actually happening, once my vague sense of dread had been transformed into tickets and suitcases and passports and timetables, all of my good intentions and zen musings were forcibly defenestrated. And it wasn't because I didn't understand why it mattered to them or because I really believed that any harm would come to them.

It was shittier than that. It was punitive.

They, my brain was screaming at me, didn't *deserve* to know them. I assumed "they" were my parents, although you can never be sure with that asshole. It was definitely either them or the piss artists who write fragrance commercials, and, to the best of my knowledge, the children have never expressed an interest in calling the latter "Grandma".

Not that it mattered. For once, my brain and I were of one mind. So to speak. After everything my mother and father had done, why should they be granted access to my children, whose lives had already been adversely affected by the aftermath of their mistakes, time and time again?

I became aware of a cold fury rising inside of me, though, for their sake, I did my level best to damp it down. I made conciliatory noises, smiled anaemically and, under my breath, muttered my go-to mantra:

"This isn't about you, dumbass."

Unfortunately, Fathead and Baldy are not stupid, and I have been honest, if not explicit, about the fact that my childhood was unhappy. Not to poison them against my Mom and Dad, but to allow them the opportunity to know and understand me better. And, yes, occasionally, as part of a lecture about how they should be thankful for the three much nicer parents they'd ended up with.

The result was that, try as I might to reassure them, I could sense they felt guilty for wanting to go, in case it hurt me, and that, in turn, made me feel terrible. I wasn't the least bit angry about their desire to meet the other side of their family—that was the most natural thing in the world and I wanted it for them. In fact, I hated that my past might be robbing them of something they needed to feel complete. It was bad enough that it had done it to me and everyone else who had ever loved me.

What I *was* angry about was my family's presumption that I would be fine with it. Although, as time passed, this was steadily replaced by a nagging worry as to why.

See, after my parents split, a big deal in their community, most of my siblings ceased to have much to do with our father. It's one of the few things we have in common. But, unlike me, they've never seemed to have a problem with our mother. I often see pictures of them, posted online, all gathered together, playing happy families, and my first thought is never "I wish I was there" but always "What the fuck is wrong with you people?"

Why don't they feel the way I do? Why do they stay? Why are they *smiling*?

But having bellied up to the fact that my memories and my emotions can, at times, be suspect, I found myself overtaken by the sudden, nauseating fear that maybe the problem was *me*.

Had I remembered it wrong? Had I cut myself off from everything I knew, run halfway around the world and rechristened myself as an only child because of something my addled brain *made up*?

After two decades of self-inflicted isolation, I'm not sure what I would have done with that information.

Thankfully, if that's the right word, it turned out to be bollocks.

If any of the others had great childhoods, then yay. Misery is not as fond of company as we are led to believe; it prefers a quiet night in. All I'd like to know is how, why, and were opiates involved?

Because mine, to put it bluntly, was a shit-show. A perfect storm of madness, within and without.

Which rather neatly brings me to the subject of this portion of our communion:

Nature versus nurture.

It's something I've spent a lot of time pondering, as I did get rather passionately screwed on both fronts and it is a brick wall into which I have repeatedly run, coyote-style.

First things first, though. Does anyone else find it suspicious how similar those two words are? Nature? Nurture? Awfully convenient, if you ask me. As if decades of contrast and comparison had somehow been planned in advance. In fact, were I prone to over-thinking things—which, of course, I am not—I might be tempted to investigate who in the psychiatric community stood to benefit most, and which linguists had recently bought second homes.

On the other hand, if it is simply a coincidence, I have to assume that whoever first joined up the dots celebrated with a bout of furious masturbation. I know I would have. And then taken a victory lap of the room.

Because it's worth commemorating. The aesthetics of word choice have had a greater influence on the development of our culture than we'd like to admit. Even the most fascinating of subjects doesn't successfully trickle down to the masses without a catchy title. If this chapter were about "Environment versus Cultivation" you'd currently be fighting dual urges—to sew patches on to the elbows of your jacket and to nap.

Nonetheless, the concept itself captivates me. If I'd had the same childhood, but no mental health issues, what would I be like? Would I have been a better man? A more consistent one?

Or if I'd still been ill, but had been loved without qualification and supported without rancour, would I have healed less erratically? If I hadn't had to contend with the demands of the divine, would my path have been strewn with fewer thunderbolts?

These questions plague me on a daily basis.

But would they, if things had been different?

It's enough of a rabbit hole that you will occasionally find an obese bear wedged into it. And I've been told by half a dozen people with degrees—mostly in psychiatry, but at least one in film theory—that the pursuit of circular arguments is something I should avoid. Still, when that weight starts to press down on my chest, it's hard to keep perilous thoughts at bay.

Thoughts such as: "It didn't have to be like this."

That's a dangerous line of enquiry for a lot of reasons, not least of which

154

is the fact that it probably did. Unpick a single thread, and the person who wishes their past revised begins to unravel entirely.

Also, however much you try to keep an open mind, if you take that road, it always circles back to blame. And blame has no upside. It's sugar water in a diabetic's thermos.

Not that it doesn't taste sweet. When you have been abused—and again, look away if this hits too close to home—you carry a burden that is as hefty as it is unjust: other people's sins. Your firQAst impulse is always going to be to shift that load elsewhere, preferably back from whence it came.

As you might imagine, this seldom works. It's like working out a restaurant bill. The person who had starters and a second glass of wine is always the fiercest proponent of splitting it equally.

The hard truth is, at this stage of my life, it may not matter anymore. There are barely enough hours in the day to audit my actions, let alone take inventory of their origins.

That said, no amount of chemical intervention can mend a broken heart and the off-kilter thump of mine still vibrates the floorboards, all the more audible for the quietening of my thoughts. It might not hurt to whack the ceiling with a broomstick a bit.

So, having given it some thought, this is how I reckon it breaks down:

Nature made me crazy. Nurture—or the lack thereof—made me infuriating. And both have evinced an industrial-strength hard-on for dissipating my potential.

Trouble is, when in full flower, each obscures the other. This makes it difficult for anyone in my orbit to feel much sympathy for either, and impossible for me to understand why they're crying.

I am not, for instance, farcically desperate for validation because I have bipolar disorder. Nor is mental illness the reason why I have passively allowed people who've loved me to become subsumed by my needs, at the expense of their own. That's textbook battered child behaviour.

What bipolar brings to the party, alongside its own acid-tabbed carnival sideshow, is the inability to process the effect you are having on other people. Or, at least, to process it accurately.

"Do you know what?" you might think to yourself. "I need to address some of these issues. After all, I care about the life I've built for myself and I truly love the people in it. It won't be easy, but I'm not that frightened little boy anymore. I'm a grown man and I can do better."

And having thought that, you might even make attempts to put it into action. You might co-opt professional help to work through how your past has affected you, and what you might do to effect change. You may choose to share your thinking with your loved ones, make sincere apologies and ask for support.

The bipolar part of your brain, alas, translates this as: "I am the worst person who has ever lived. I'm going to drink some vodka out of this shoe and then hitchhike to Serbia."

It's only since I've been back on medication that I've had any real understanding of how I've made other people feel. In the past, I'd catch a glimpse of it out of the corner of my eye, and immediately run screaming in the opposite direction. I couldn't contemplate the hurt I was causing, because I literally had no idea how to stop, and that might mean that I was not broken, but simply bad.

Which is what I'd been told I was, all those years ago, over and over again.

Somewhere, a therapist I've never met is cursing a lost fortune.

When I put it all down on paper, it seems so obvious. Clichéd, even. If you wrote me into a novel, you'd get the manuscript back, red pen flooding the margins.

Thankfully, neither nature nor nurture get the final word on any of this. This does:

I have never fallen in love because I was broken. I have never been proud of my children because I was hurt. I have never been loved because I was crazy. And my children have never needed me because I needed them to.

So fuck nature and fuck nurture. They're just window blinds. Sometimes pretty and tasteful, sometimes vile and beige.

It's what lies beyond that matters. Do you look out on a meadow or a trash fire?

In a few weeks, when Fathead and Baldy come home, they will have seen where I come from. It will have become a part of them, in an utterly different way to how it did for me. They may have questions. They will absolutely have laundry.

But they still won't really give a shit where I came from. They'll want to know where I'm going.

And if I'll pick up doughnuts while I'm there.

I can live with that.

11: These Things Will Not Bite You…

Once upon a time, a Princess met a Prince.

The Princess, it's worth noting, was no entitled royal; she had ambitions and talent and even a proper job at which she worked incredibly hard. Actually, perhaps you should consider "Princess" as more of an honorary title, used here to conjure a sense of grace and tap into your childhood memories of admittedly reductive fairy tales.

We're talking about a multi-dimensional protagonist whose entire existence does not revolve around her romantic life, is what I'm trying to say.

Glad we cleared that up.

That being said, she did, on occasion, make decisions in accordance with the demands of her heart, rather than those of her health or sanity.

I hear it's all the rage.

It was following one such incident that she, much to her own surprise, had found herself hand-in-hand and nose-slightly-to-the-side-of-nose with the youngish and erratic Prince, despite every ounce of common sense that she had eagerly squirrelled away over the years suggesting that hitting herself repeatedly in the face with a pan might be a safer long term bet.

Prince Alarming, for his part, had his own concerns about the wisdom of her choice, but he certainly wasn't going to complain. As Princes went, he had remained more amphibian than most and had, therefore, long relied on the blindness of strangers. Moreover, though he didn't know much, he knew that his often fickle fortunes had taken an unexpected turn for the better.

To be perfectly honest, he had inadvertently set fire to his last couple of castles, and by rights, should have been sleeping in a ditch, so it was all an unexpected bonus.

Besides, he truly loved the Princess, even if he didn't always know how to express it without the need for regular apologies.

It was a rare and beautiful thing. I'm not even joking.

So, if you are expecting a poison apple or childhood curse to rear their ugly heads at this point, then congratulations. Your gift voucher is in the post.

Because the difference between fairy tales and real-life love stories is that the complications don't evaporate after the first kiss.

They multiply.

In this case, by a factor of two.

Because Prince Alarming did not come alone.

***

Obviously, keeping in mind the rules I put in place from the outset, the above story should not be taken as anything more than a decorative flourish, an amuse-bouche to get the chapter started with a bang.

It is also the most accurate thing I've written so far.

Saying that, I would hate for it to be misunderstood. I can see that on first reading, it might appear that I am suggesting that the already complex business of relationships is made even more taxing by the presence of children.

Well, shows what you know.

In fact, I've half a mind to cancel that gift voucher. You can buy your own bloody face cream.

Oh, I'm sure there's a gut-busting chapter to be written about the many ways in which parenting undermines our shallowest romantic notions—the sort of piece that could be handily excerpted in your chosen Sunday periodical and chuckled at on tube or toilet.

If you expect me to write it, however, then I'm not convinced that you've been paying attention. I still maintain that having kids is the best thing I've ever done and that my personal life would be more of a shambles without my children, not less.

Fuck knows what that would entail, but I can only assume I'd be serving time for mail fraud or playing in a covers band.

The other reason why I am grateful, despite the hole in my heart, for some of the ways in which things turned out is that for all I lost, I also gained a couple of things I didn't realise I needed.

Tell us more, I hear you say.

Well, since you asked nicely.

You may recall that I spoke early on about what constitutes my version of single parenting, and what that means to me. But while there's no denying that it's a handy shorthand, the more I think about it, the more uncomfortable I am with the label.

Sure, I lie awake at night, staring at the ceiling through watery eyes.

wondering how I'm ever going to manage. Yes, my day-to-day life involves picking far too many bras off the floor that I had no part in placing there. There are, indeed, times when I feel utterly isolated and weighted down with responsibilities.

It would be a lot, even without my collection of cerebral idiosyncrasies.

But the fact remains that I parent single, not solo. There's a massive difference between the two.

While we're on the subject, anyone who actually does it completely on their own deserves a medal. I'm serious. Give them free money and regular massages. Name holidays and airports and streets in their honour.

Because I have my own crosses, but I don't have to make any excuses for anyone, or bite my tongue when anyone's name comes up. I don't have to compensate for anyone's shortcomings other than my own.

And, most importantly, there are two numbers in my phone to which I can send messages that read "I'm selling the children" and receive the reply, "What have they done this time?" rather than a knock on the door from the local constabulary.

Because the two people I know best and trust most are those who love Fathead and Baldy as much as I do.

How could that not be the case?

Even the knowledge that both of these people are, without a shadow of a doubt, primarily grateful for my presence in their life because the children were part of the package, doesn't bother me.

There's no argument to be had. It is the best thing I gave either of them. And I would be nothing without what I received in return.

Therefore, while I have repeatedly committed sins of omission and remission, and, as a result, there are now specific absences in my life that form the foundation of my unhappiness, I know it could have been so much worse.

And they say I don't do pep talks.

***

What constitutes a family?

No, really. I'm asking. Because, for me, the word carries more baggage than a steroid-jacked camel. And, though it might seem obvious to you, it's taken me years to fully grasp why.

It isn't what you might think. I know we've established that my initial experience of the phenomenon was problematic. On those grounds alone, mixed feelings are to be expected.

But it's more complicated than that.

I'm not against family. I have dreamed of having one of my own since before I can remember, and pursued it for as long as I've had opportunity. Yet, when confronted by those ties that bind, I've always ended up in knots.

And like so many things that have flummoxed me or at which I've proved not to be a natural, like sport or relaxation or life, I eventually convinced myself that I never liked them much in the first place.

When other people tell me, for example, that they are spending their weekends or holidays with their extended family, condolences bubble into my throat like acid reflux. I can't think of anything worse.

I'm exaggerating, of course. I can think of four things worse, but three of them involve colonoscopies.

Besides, recently, I've come to realise that I've been lying through my face.

I would adore being part of a large family. I'd like to have a clan. I'd like to be surrounded by fat babies and daft puppies and sanctimonious cats. If the budget stretched to it, I'd also enjoy a teapot-sized pig.

Bring hither, say I, the picket fence and the mailbox with a flag on its side.

But the definition of family, to me, is not only people that love you, but people that understand you.

And those have always been thin on the ground.

In the first instance, with my parents, it was a case of genuine bafflement on their part. I was so different, so eccentric, so angry at everything they considered normal, that they threw their hands up.

Sometimes, they also threw their hands directly at me, but we're not dwelling on that for the moment.

Still, if there is one emotion that I have experienced more often than any other, and I have a few repeat customers, it is loneliness. Not necessarily the loneliness of being alone in a room—I'm quite good at occupying myself, though I do eventually go a bit peculiar—but the loneliness of feeling as though you were designed for some other world than this.

With its tendency to over-personalise your perspective, bipolar disorder amplifies that sensation. But I don't think it's entirely to blame. There is a wire loose, somewhere in my soul, a disconnect that I have never entirely been able to bridge.

Even with the twins, it's a struggle. I go to great lengths to try and understand them, so they won't feel that crushing sense of singularity. But it doesn't always, through no fault of theirs, feel reciprocal.

I'm still on my own.

Eventually, though, that becomes a self-fulfilling prophecy. It's true that many people since have tried and failed to understand me. And, at times, I've relished being an enigma wrapped in a mystery, wrapped in a patchwork quilt.

But others have made it within striking distance and, instead of dropping to my knees and offering tearful thanks, I have become immediately spooked.

That isn't to say that I don't have people in my life, or that they are less devoted to me than I am to them. I have wonderful friends and two glorious children. I'm even loved, albeit from a safe distance.

For the twins, happily, this is not something they appear to have inherited. They *get* family. They always have. And theirs is a broad church. Blood relatives, self-adopted siblings, neighbours, ex-babysitters, friends—they all come under the protection of that dual-headed *soror familia*.

When they were eleven, because, yes, I am still telling this chronologically, this open door policy was put to its first real test.

***

Co-parenting is stupidly hard. Step-parenting is stupidly hard. I know I'm breaking my self-imposed rules here, but I wanted to acknowledge both. Also, *self*-imposed rules, so hah.

If you have a baby with someone, it's considered a natural extension of the relationship you've had up until that point, whether that has followed the traditional path of falling in love or careened from the road after a meeting of minds and tequila. You may conceive that child, you may adopt them, there may be a surrogate involved. If you step on board on the parenting train from the initial point of departure, it's a very different experience from joining further down the line.

Because even though it bears little resemblance to most people's reality, we still hold in our heads this image of the perfect little nuclear set-up: Mum, Dad, kids. So when life has its wicked way with you and that picture shifts or expands, it can be unnerving for everyone concerned.

The hardest part, in my experience, is not the potential for jealousy or territorial disputes. It's not even the massive step-parenting fuck-you that the Brothers Grimm and their colleagues lent to the language.

It's that the late arrival didn't get them as babies, when they are vulnerable and at the mercy of adults. They got them as children, when the reverse is true. Some Cat-in-the-Hat-looking motherfucker charmed their way into their house, cracked open a box, and these feral little creatures bounced out and into their lives, without any of the build-up or bonding they had been brought up to expect.

161

While across the aisle, the original parent with whom they share an approximate role is thinking, "Fucking great. Someone is feeding them who hasn't spent the last ten years trying to get them to clean their room. There's no way they're not going to prefer that."

And if anyone involved in this purely hypothetical triangle, square or, in extreme circumstances, pentangle is, say, differently mentalled, then all bets are off.

However, if you get lucky with the people involved, and I did, everyone puts the children first, loves them madly regardless of the method of acquisition, and the best is made of a weird situation.

The only remaining concern is how the Things themselves are going to react.

Well, in this case, despite the misleading end-of-section crescendo above, the new status quo didn't actually rattle Fathead and Baldy much. As far as they were concerned, the more people they had looking after them and occasionally showing up with gifts the better. And, as they saw it, if I had someone looking after me, it was seventy-three percent less likely that I'd suffer an injury that would inconvenience them or their dinner. There were about four seconds during which Baldy pondered whether she'd be breaking faith with her mother by accepting someone else into her life, but once reassured on that front, she did what felt natural, which was to work out how to get biscuits.

As for me and my slowly collapsing psyche—well, we were fine with the surface details. This wasn't a situation where anyone was at anyone else's throat. Nobody hated anybody. Within the finite barriers of human weakness, it was all very amicable and supportive.

But while I didn't have any issues with the set-up, the execution was seriously throwing me off my stride.

Because I was suddenly forced to see my own parenting through two very different perspectives, at a time in my life where, unbeknownst even to me, I was coming apart at the seams.

In hindsight, it was the best thing that ever happened to me. At the time, however, I felt besieged. I was dimly aware that I wasn't at the top of my game, but remained pathologically incapable of admitting it or asking for help.

So, when their mother would call and want to talk about Baldy's temper, or Fathead's stubbornness, I heard "they're just like you and I'm paying the price for it".

When their stepmother queried whether it was really super-awesome that Baldy ate peas with her hands, I heard "you're fucking this up".

Neither of these women were saying any such things. Both were simply asking for help and prioritising the children's best interests, which is pretty much verbatim what I'll request of them in my will, as soon as I have something more substantial to bequeath than a wall full of *Doctor Who* novels and some pre-loved guitars.

Today, I couldn't be more appreciative of the fact that they understood that the one thing I truly cared about more than anything else was being a good father, and were willing to put themselves in the crossfire to ensure that I achieved that.

At the time, I was defensive and combative.

I've always been slow.

The twins themselves, at eleven, were also in flux, which was admittedly chipping away at my resilience. They weren't teenagers yet, but they'd already begun the process of testing their adult limits, challenging the world—as now represented by the three people who wanted them to eat healthily, do well at school, and stop calling each other "bitch-face"—at every opportunity.

Baldy was still a temperamental beast, short-fused and gimlet-eyed. And Fathead, after a lifetime of playing sugar to her sister's spice, was experimenting with a few tantrums of her own, largely directed at her mother, to whom she was as similar as Baldy was to me.

None of it was out of the ordinary. They weren't knocking over convenience stores, or shooting up behind the bike sheds. They were just a handful.

In fact, for the most part, they were lovely and, very often, stone-cold hilarious. Their unfiltered worldview was a joy to listen to, and I'd record more of it here if it didn't reveal that my approach to confronting profanity at the time was, arguably, too lax.

The elephant in the room was not their growing pains. It was me. I had overworked my self into a corner. I had out-sized ambitions and nada dinero. And I'd somehow convinced myself—again—that, having made big life changes, I was finally sauntering down the road to recovery, despite the roughly-hewn blocks of good intentions clearly visible beneath my feet.

Something had to be done.

And, oh, did I do something.

***

If things had gone differently, this chapter might have been the one you skip to in a celebrity biography, having grown bored of overly detailed descriptions of the streets in which they once kicked footballs or got felt up.

Because we're rapidly racing towards the moment when I will have a bright idea that will change the course of the rest of my life.

As I intimated in the prologue, I have no desire to retread that ground. But it is a part of my life, and there is no better nexus point between my experiences with bipolar disorder and my life with my daughters.

If only there were a way to tell you what you needed to know, without going into all of the gory details.

***

One morning, some years later, Prince Alarming woke with a start.

"I've got it!" he said, sitting bolt upright and smacking the eiderdown with the palm of his hand, "I know how to save the kingdom!"

"Shush now," said the Princess, eyes still closed, but patting his arm sleepily, "It was just a bad dream. Go back to sleep."

"No, I mean it. This is going to change everything! I can't believe I never thought of it before."

There was something in the tone of his voice that snapped the Princess' eyes open.

She too sat up.

"Sorry, what?"

"You know how we were talking yesterday about how the coffers always seem to be empty…"

"Well, I remember saying that you probably shouldn't have spent so much on that war with the neighbouring village."

"…and that you've had to take up blacksmithery on the side just to pay the privy cleaner."

"It's not a privy. It's a moat. The fact that you can't tell the difference is why I had to get a cleaner."

"What?"

"Never mind. What's your big idea?"

"I am going to write an epic poem."

"Right."

"I know what you're going to say. It will be difficult."

"That's not *exactly* what I was going to say…"

"Anyway, I haven't told you the best part. Not only am I going to write an epic poem, but I shall then entice the finest mummers in the land to perform it. I reckon twelve should be sufficient."

"Dear Gods."

"What was that?"

"Oh, nothing. Bit of a scratchy throat. Spot of plague, I shouldn't wonder."

164

"Hmmm. If I didn't know better, I'd say you weren't particularly excited by my idea."

"Trust me, I am full of emotion right now."

"Good, good. Well, I'm sure you have a lot of questions."

"That I do."

"Fire away, my love."

"This epic poem…"

"Yes?"

"What's it about?"

"The princesses. Their lives and times."

"I see."

"Well, they say such charming and good-humoured things. I'm sure the entire kingdom would pay good coin to hear them set in verse."

The Princess sighed. Heavily.

"Yeah, we'll put a pin in that one for a moment. I want to hear more about these mummers you mentioned. They'll be doing you a favour, will they?"

"Oh, no. I shall require the very best, and, in turn, they shall require coin of the realm."

"Didn't we just agree that the realm is not exactly coin-adjacent at the moment?"

Prince Alarming looked suddenly crest-fallen.

"Fuck's sake," thought the Princess, lifting it off him, "I told him it was too heavy to hang over the bed. Besides, just look at the thing. A beaver and a moose on a helm of wheat? Ridiculous." She quickly checked for signs of concussion, then dusted him down and took his hands in hers.

"Hey. Don't look like that. You know that I think you are a wonderful poet. Any troupe of mummers would be lucky to have your epic in their repertoire. And you're right, the princesses would make an excellent subject. It's just… Remember that time you went out to draw some water from the well, and came back all singed because you'd wandered off the trail and ended up fighting a dragon?"

"I won, didn't I?"

"I know. But your eyebrows took ages to grow back."

"It was a look."

"It was also an iguana. There are no such things as dragons."

The Prince grew serious.

"I just think… I could do this. I could finally make something of myself."

"You're a *Prince*."

"No, I'm not. This is a thinly veiled allusion to real life, that I'm using to avoid having to talk more directly about a sensitive subject."

"I'm aware of that. I didn't get to be a Princess *and* a renowned metal worker by being just a pretty face. But you're a Prince to me. And to them."

An impatient voice sounded from beyond the bedroom door.

"Hey!"

The Prince and Princess both looked up.

"Umm, yes?" they said in unison.

The voice continued.

"Are we getting a walk-on part in this bit or what? Cause we've had some ideas about our costumes."

The Prince and Princess exchanged a glance.

"Don't look at me," said the Princess, "It's your psychological deflection."

"I don't think so, honey," said the Prince finally, "We're getting towards the end of the chapter."

"Ah, goddamn it."

"Language!" said the Princess.

"Dad's writing it!"

"Even so."

"*Fine.* We're going to watch… Hey, where's the TV?"

"Not invented yet."

"This is bullshit."

"Hey!"

"Sorry."

The couple sat in silence until the sounds of muttering and stomping feet disappeared into the bowels of the castle.

Finally, the Prince spoke.

"I think I need to do this."

The Princess looked at him, sadly.

"I know. And I'll help in any way I can. I just worry about you. And about the girls."

"I promise. I can handle this."

"I'll hold you to that."

"I know."

And so the Prince set to work on his *magnum opus*. Night after night, he burned candles to the wick, pausing only to raid the larder and, occasionally, howl at the moon.

He did not, however, do it alone. The Princess, despite her misgivings, was as good as her word. She gave fully of her time and talents, while simultaneously running the kingdom, fulfilling a rather large order for broadswords that had come in and trying to build a relationship with the two Princesses for whom she would already take an arrow to the chest.

And they all lived... more or less.

***

Can we talk about something else now?

Bi-focal

The word "obsession" is an interesting one.

Well, interesting to me, which is why I have spent the better part of a day, when I really should have been writing, researching its origins. All for the sake of what I envisage to be half a page of text.

I am aware of the irony.

However, in fear of this entire section turning into one long etymological digression, I'll keep my report brief.

Because there really is a first time for everything.

The root of obsession, obsess, is, unsurprisingly, derived from the Latin. Most things are. According to the last set of blood tests I had done, both of my knees, my left nostril and the belt I was wearing that day are Latin in origin.

In this case, it is the word *obsessus,* which, for all the alliteration fans out there, is the perfect passive participle of *obsideō*, meaning to sit opposite to, or to besiege. In late Middle English, round about the 1500s, the connotation twisted slightly to describe the experience of being tormented from without by an evil spirit. Obsession is, after all, a close relation of possession; it's just more stalker than squatter.

According to all the sources I consulted, this is considered to be different from our modern understanding of the word—the sense of being preoccupied by something or someone, to the exclusion of all else.

I'd argue that the meaning hasn't changed a jot. Besieged is a word I use a lot when talking about my illness—as recently as the last chapter, in fact— and if my shadow isn't an evil spirit sitting opposite to me, then I don't know what is. When my obsessions are at their most potent, it does feel as though I have been surrounded. Off in the distance, I can hear the unmistakeable sound of a trebuchet being lumbered into position.

Still, some of my enthusiasms are harmless enough, in isolation. I go full dork for fictional universes, for instance. The more intensive the world-building, the better. I like continuity and detail and I'll happily while away the hours studying the political histories of made-up countries. Not only do they usually make more sense than their real world equivalents, but, fan fiction notwithstanding, there's half a chance that they represent the definitive versions.

Along similar lines, I am a completist, which is basically just an organised hoarder. It's one of the many reasons why there are more books in my house than in some decently stocked public libraries. I'll stumble on an author, or a series, and I have to collect the set. And then file the lot in alphabetical order.

It has crossed my mind—in both senses—that I've unconsciously taken the same approach to mental illnesses.

Under other circumstances, such as being rich, these traits would be designated quirks or eccentricities. Some might even find them endearing. Others, of course, would be vexed to distraction. All according to taste.

The issue is that when I feel I have to do something, I do not mean "I quite fancy the idea and may give it the old college try" as you might. I mean I *have* to, or I will be in large amounts of psychic pain.

It's been that way since I was very small. For starters, I've always had a collection—a relief valve for stress or confusion or rage. The comic strip adventures of an overfed cat. Books about earnest, talented young sleuths with a passion for law and order and a propensity for casual racism.

An entire village of Smurfs that my father smashed up because he thought they might be possessed by the Devil.

Okay, I'm starting to see it now. My stories really do go sideways a *lot*.

Collecting might seem like perfectly ordinary childhood behaviour, but I assure you: not the way I did it. When I became fixated on something new—and, even medicated, I retain a weakness on this front—everything unconnected to it might as well have taken the year off.

The same was true of projects. I had my first nervous breakdown when I was twelve, when I wrote and performed in a satirical play about the pursuit of riches over wisdom, which was subsequently entered into a regional competition and knocked out in the semi-final.

I also spent three months attempting to prove that you could defuse nuclear weapons with magnets. I do not recall what the point of that was, but I know I lost sleep over it.

When the fever is upon me, I cannot be stopped. I am incapable of thinking outside the box in which I am currently rummaging.

Unfortunately, once it reaches that point, it isn't even fun anymore. It's the second hit of heroin, rather than the first. The tension builds until it feels as though my bones are going to burst through my skin. I need a fix.

Just to take the edge off. Just to get me through.

Come on, mate, I *need* it.

All in all, I'm not a half-measures sort of guy. Even this book started out as a note to the children to pick up some milk. I just got carried away.

It has its benefits, from time to time. Thanks to medication and, you know, life, I seldom have sufficient time or energy for the creative work that brings me real fulfilment. Often, I barely have enough to manage the stuff that pisses me off. Which is everything else.

However, once I have decided to do something, I do it. Professional pride and old school bloody-mindedness play their parts, but bubbling underneath it all is the knowledge that if I do not complete the task, it will hurt.

Take writing, for example. It is often said to consist of ten percent inspiration and ninety percent perspiration. Whereas, for me, it's only about four percent inspiration, with the remaining ninety-six split equally between seething hatred and abject terror.

And yet I'm still typing.

I'm sure you won't be surprised to learn, given the context, that another synonym for obsession is mania. You'll have heard it used, pinned to the end of Beatle and Dalek—indeed following the name of anything or anyone sufficiently zeitgeist-fellating to have been clasped roughly to the public's bosom. It's been diluted by overuse, and now seems to indicate a sort of extreme fondness, but you only have to look at footage of monochrome teenagers going critical over the Fab Four to get a more accurate sense of why it was originally chosen as a suffix.

Those screams, that palpable sexual insanity, that's the pitch at which mania resonates. Even if, from the street, it looks like a party, inside the house, someone's poisoned the punch.

So, while I can tell myself—tell you—that I have an obsessive personality, it doesn't even begin to do it justice. Obsession isn't about collecting books, or organising spice racks by grain size or even looking very seriously at trains. Those are minor, incidental offshoots. Like the headache you might get if you were stabbed.

Obsession is agonising. For everyone concerned. You're in a dark, hot room, screaming and banging on a soundproof door, while in the hall beyond, your neglected loved ones are convinced that you're in there having a whale of time, with something you clearly prefer to them.

I have been tortured—inquisition-style—by ideas, by delusions, by regrets and by fears. I have sat up for days at a time, sending out emails to promote a project, convinced beyond all doubt that if I didn't, the world might end.

I've cried every night for a month because I believed that something was going to happen for which I had no evidence whatsoever.

170

I have undertaken extraordinary feats of physical and emotional endurance, receiving applause for their lunatic bravado, when, in fact, I was terrified that if I didn't finish what I started, I might die.

Even the scars on my wrists happened, not in moments of sadness or despair, but in the grip of an obsession—a conviction I had developed that if I switched off the world, my world, it would reboot and I would return to my life without pain and with all troubling elements of the past rewritten.

As I had once believed in God and his vengeance, I believed in this. It played on my mind every second of every day. I didn't wonder if it might happen. It wasn't a theory. It was the truth.

I just had to push through. I just had to put in the work.

Psychosis. That's the big, scary word that doctors and bad screenwriters use. But I've always referred to it as "looping".

It's one of the hardest symptoms to control, because its roots cannot be dug out completely. Everyday stresses, ordinary worries, actual problems—they can all set off a loop. Some small fragment of some stray thought burrows under your skin, settles into the warmth and the black, and grows.

I'll assume you've heard the phrase "blowing things out of proportion". Well, looping is a little like that, only you forget how to spell proportion and, in any case, believe it to be a type of fish.

It is the most painful thing I have ever experienced. And I have lost toenails, in public, on more than one occasion.

Actually, I take that back. Experiencing it is the second most painful thing, just ahead of every instance in which something has hit my testicles without permission.

Number one, with a bullet, is the pain that occurs once you've taken the blinders off.

Because do you know what you're not allowed to possess unchallenged when you are known to be obsessive?

Devotion.

There are times when I find myself wanting to punch a wall with the frustration of it. I have been so wrapped up with meaningless pursuits in the past, that when I want to be committed to something real, when someone deserves me to be willing to do *anything* for them, I have lost the right to say so and be believed.

I've been willing to do so much for so little, it is no longer a trustworthy measure of worth.

How could they ever feel settled in their minds that they were not something else onto which I'd locked, that my exertions on their behalf, or

171

my protestations of love, were not my shadow monologue-ing?

It's particularly galling because I know it's not true. And the reason I can say this with certainty, is because I also know exactly what's changed:

I've stopped thinking about myself.

I don't mean that to sound as though I've become some kind of altruistic zen master. Trust me, I'm still the same idiot I've always been.

Neither have I conquered obsession completely. I doubt I ever will. The inconsequential still calls to me like a siren. I still need my little hits, just to keep the demons at bay. But I have found myself doing the right thing more and more often, doing things for the people I love for no other reason than the—arguably still a little selfish—fact that I like doing so. But not for reward and not for fear of ill consequences if I don't.

And not because I *have* to.

It's gutting to contemplate what I lost along the way. But it's also hard to describe how liberating it is to find myself capable of loving without asking anything in return. I have needed so much, for so long. I have *demanded* so much, intentionally or not.

But now, by letting go, I appear to have finally got a grip.

It's possible that you've worked out why we're talking about this now. Even if I've been a bit stingy with the details, it can't have escaped your notice that, back in the primary timeline, if I've done my job properly, there has been a growing sense of foreboding.

I wish I could tell you that you were wrong.

But then, if this story were about a man who did all the right things and, as a result, got everything he wanted, there wouldn't be much scope for drama. And even less for comedy.

I can reassure you though that this is not a tragedy. Something beautiful will rise from the ashes.

At least, I hope so. We do have a few chapters to go, so I could still be hit by a truck.

If that does happen and this book ends abruptly, I apologise.

My mind was probably on something else.

12: Reel to Real

Look, let's get it out in the open. We are entirely at cross-purposes, as audience and author, when it comes to this chapter. If it were up to me, we'd skip it entirely. If it were up to you, this page would have a free sachet of microwave popcorn stapled to it.

Not that I can't see it from your point-of-view. I made a feature film. That's quite an exciting thing to have done. More than that, it starred the actual Fathead and Baldy, to whose alter egos you may well have become attached over the course of the last sixty thousand words or so.

Furthermore, and don't pretend you hadn't noticed, I've made several provocative insinuations about the movie being at least partly responsible for the shit that's about to go down in the final act. If I were you, I'd want details and lots of them.

Of course, part of you may even suspect that I've been deliberately building up to this, and my reticence to tackle the subject is a pose, or, worse, some sort of humblebrag.

I guess you'll just have to wait and see.

From my perspective, I'm fighting a battle on multiple fronts. I've spent this entire book attempting to be frank and transparent about my experiences. Not because I think that mine is necessarily a universal story, or even know for certain that it'll be helpful to anyone—I am no longer that arrogant—but because I've learned that not talking about mental illness ends up with people getting hurt.

And that not talking about parenting leads to waking up naked in a yurt with a lay preacher and a donkey.

But I haven't the distance from what's coming up that I have from other parts of my life, and, yes, it is more difficult to write about. I'm a little worried that I won't know where the jokes go.

Besides, this isn't the story of a filmmaker, or a musician, or an actor, it's the story of a guy with a fucked-up brain and a couple of reliably zany but,

173

nonetheless, vulnerable kids. I don't want to talk about what I did, in what passed for my career. I'm more interested in who I was, in what passed for my existence.

I have a confession to make, however. When we started this journey together, to my everlasting shame, I lied to you. Only the once, but it was a doozy.

Making the film didn't break me at all.

I did.

And, what's more, I'd been working assiduously towards it for years. I'd ignored every warning sign that I might be getting ill again and turned a deaf ear, a blind eye and a slightly dodgy back to anyone who tried to bring that to my attention.

By the time I decided to pitch myself headlong into yet another all-or-nothing situation, despite everything I'd learned and suffered in the past, it was already too late. If my line of work had been landscape gardening or intimate waxing, it wouldn't have played out any differently.

Or to put it more poetically, the movie was not the noose, but the tree.

The truly stupid thing—so stupid that it could run for public office and win—is that I probably wouldn't have got my relationship with my daughters back on track if I hadn't done it. That's not the same thing as saying I *couldn't* have, but in the state I was in at the time, I really don't think I'd have managed it.

Because, for all that I was in no fit state to do so, I looked at them down a lens.

And they looked back.

***

INT. LIVING ROOM—EVENING

A pair of identical twelve-year-old girls, FATHEAD and BALDY, are sitting on a sofa in a sparsely decorated room. The space is clearly tidy, yet somehow still feels as though a horse has been recently shooed from it. Movie posters and bookshelves line every wall, the latter full to bursting.

Each girl holds a mug of tea, which, every few moments, casually sloshes its contents on to the front of a once white school shirt. This does not seem to faze them.

Largely because their attention is fixed entirely on someone off-camera, whom they address with a mixture of pity and concern.

174

BALDY
I'm warning you. Don't do it.

FATHEAD
You're better than this. Think of the children.

BALDY
(to Fathead, whispering)
But we're the children.

FATHEAD
Exactly.

SUBJECTIVE NARRATOR (O.S.)
I don't know what either of you are talking about.

BALDY
Yes, you do. A scripted section? Really?

SUBJECTIVE NARRATOR (O.S.)
(slightly embarrassed)
Oh, that. Well, we were talking about the film and, I just thought, maybe it would be appropriate and, hopefully, funny if…

FATHEAD
Bit on the nose, don't you think?

SUBJECTIVE NARRATOR (O.S.)
I know, I know. But you don't understand what it's like. If I don't do it, some idiot is going to write a review complaining that I missed an obvious trick, further illustrating my lack of commitment to the form. Or something.

BALDY
Jesus. Who talks like that?

SUBJECTIVE NARRATOR (O.S.)
Critics.

FATHEAD
Then is it really a good idea to make fun of them?

SUBJECTIVE NARRATOR (O.S.)

Probably not. Although, one of my primary themes is self-destructive behaviour, so...

FATHEAD

Any chance I could not grow up? Cause it sounds awful.

SUBJECTIVE NARRATOR (O.S.)

Fine by me.

BALDY

Anyway, what's all this about you having a problem with the film? We had a great time.

FATHEAD

Yeah. I mean, I told you I wanted to be an actress and you gave me my own movie to star in.

BALDY

Our own movie, thank you. And don't say "actress". We're "actors".

FATHEAD

Why are so you so hung up about the word "actress"?

BALDY

I don't want to be considered different, just because I'm a woman.

FATHEAD

Trust me, that's not why you're considered different.

BALDY

Rude.

FATHEAD

Man, I forgot how much fun it was to be twelve.

BALDY

Yeah, well, maybe you won't make thirteen this time round.

176

SUBJECTIVE NARRATOR (O.S.)
Guys, please. Focus.

He breaks off, puzzled.

SUBJECTIVE NARRATOR (O.S.)
Why does that feel so familiar?

FATHEAD
(quickly interrupting)
What I was trying to say is, that was some pretty cool Dadding.

BALDY
Yeah. Molly's Dad won't even take her ice skating.

SUBJECTIVE NARRATOR (O.S.)
But I was so tired. So stressed all the time. And I put you both under a lot of pressure. I shouldn't have done that.

FATHEAD
You are such a dope sometimes. Dad, I learned so much. It was an experience that no one else could have given us and one that I will never forget.

BALDY
Besides, we got to come to work with you every day.

SUBJECTIVE NARRATOR (O.S.)
(unconvinced)
You hated going to work.

BALDY
Well, it was bloody early.

SUBJECTIVE NARRATOR (O.S.)
So, you both enjoyed it? Really? It didn't, like, screw you up or anything?

FATHEAD
Of course we did. And no, it didn't. We saw you doing
what you love, we got to meet some brilliant people. We
got to be in a film, for God's sake.

BALDY
And the sandwiches were amazing.

FATHEAD
It kind of makes us sad that you didn't have a good time
though.

SUBJECTIVE NARRATOR (O.S.)
I'm sorry.

FATHEAD sighs.

FATHEAD
So Canadian. You don't have anything to be sorry about.
We just don't get it.

BALDY
Yeah, if it made you so unhappy, then why did you do it
at all?

The SUBJECTIVE NARRATOR pauses somewhat melodramatically, as
if to give the audience the impression that he is wrestling
with his thoughts. Or possibly a bear. It's difficult to tell.

Finally, he speaks.

SUBJECTIVE NARRATOR (O.S.)
You know how, in a couple of years, I'm going to have
to start taking medication again?

BALDY
So that you don't murder us all in our beds, yes.

SUBJECTIVE NARRATOR (O.S.)
I've asked you to stop saying that.

BALDY
Not yet, you haven't!

SUBJECTIVE NARRATOR (O.S.)
Touché. Well, anyway, it turns out that I wasn't quite
as well as I thought at the time and the film sort of…

FATHEAD
Took over everything?

BALDY
Became the only thing you thought about?

FATHEAD
Came up in casual conversation more often than if you'd
attended a really expensive school of some kind?

BALDY
Put further distance between you and the real world and,
in turn, your adult relationships?

SUBJECTIVE NARRATOR (O.S.)
Umm. Yeah.

BALDY
Oh, we knew that. We were twelve, not idiots.

FATHEAD
Well, I wasn't.

BALDY
Shut up.

SUBJECTIVE NARRATOR (O.S.)
And none of that bothered you?

FATHEAD
We were making a movie with our Dad. We were happy.

There is an uncomfortably long pause. And the sound of sniffling.

BALDY turns to her sister and rolls her eyes.

179

BALDY
Oh, God. He's crying again.

FATHEAD shakes her head and reluctantly stands.

FATHEAD
I'll get the macaroni. You put on the whale song CD.

***

Every story is *Rashomon*. Except *Rashomon,* obviously, which is clearly an allegory for the development of the Faroese fishing industry following the end of the Danish Royal Trade Monopoly.

Kurosawa was a complex artist. And much misunderstood.

And perspective is everything.

Do you ever wonder why we concern ourselves to such an unnatural degree with what other people think of us? Why we torture ourselves with something over which we have so little control?

We think they know something we don't.

Relationships are difficult for the same reason. Imagine two people are in a room. It doesn't matter what they're doing, whether it's knitting or making love. It's seldom both, unless they've really run out of ideas. The point is this: same place, same time, same confusing use of the word "purling" and, yet, two utterly different experiences.

The sequence of events, no doubt, could be boiled down to its essentials. He made a scarf. She felt a crushing sense of disappointment. Et cetera.

But their respective concepts of what *happened*? Totally different story. Or, more correctly, stories.

We live in a world where the existence of "truth" is continually up for debate. At the time of writing, in any case. If you're reading this in the future and a consensus has finally been reached, then I am both glad you finally got your shit together and have a list of graves I'd like to you to dance upon on my behalf.

Now, some of what gets said, even by the slimiest commentators, is technically correct. Objective truth is very difficult to quantify.

Facts, however, are still facts.

Trying to get the two to marry up in any meaningful way requires a shotgun and a father with a regressive view of parental authority.

But what does any of this have to do with me, my daughters or the events of 2014, which I have been told, in no uncertain terms, to stop calling the "incident"?

Well, thanks to bipolar disorder, my life is *Rashomon* as a one-man show.

Barring the odd episode of true psychosis, I share approximately the same reality as everyone else. My interpretation of it, however, even when I'm fairly level, has been called into question on a sufficient number of occasions to make me gun-shy.

And so I exist in two parallel but distinct realms. What I remember and what I've been told. Emotionally, my instinct is to react to the former. Intellectually, I've come to rely on the latter. And the two are constantly at each other's throats.

It requires, as it would, an extraordinary amount of trust on my part to accept the contradiction of events to which my brain is testifying with its hand on a Bible.

As a result, I am suspicious of most people. Partly because of the number of them that have attempted to take advantage of my uncertainty for their own ends. Which makes them sound rather more like supervillains than I intended. Mostly, it's just been humans doing their thing.

Even those who have earned my faith aren't infallible. If my mind goes to a dark place, it's always possible, considering the nature of the universe, that I'm right on the money and all my illness is doing is preventing me from denying it.

When it comes to the year in question, and those that followed, I have a very particular take:

Shit done got fucked up, and it was primarily my fault.

And by mine, I mean his.

Because while I remember everything I said, I did and I thought, I do not remember what happened.

We all make boneheaded decisions. I have an extensive list of my own that has sod all to do with my mental health.

But, as I've said, there are also periods in my life where not only do my decisions not make rational sense, they are entirely contrary to my values, my beliefs and my heart.

When you can't trust yourself, your life is constantly in freefall. Plus, you're forever having to change your banking password. All in all, it's hard not to become disenchanted with the whole business of living.

That, in a nutshell, is why I hold on to the concept of my shadow. I need someone to siphon off blame, when the guilt becomes too much. I'm still not sure if that's healthy or not. I know I need to forgive myself for those mistakes I made when I wasn't in control. But I have no desire to cement in the minds of others the idea that I am undependable. Nor to make excuses.

My solution is to study the children. Them, I trust them implicitly and not simply out of love. Their needs are my central concern, so even if they chose to be pricks and play me, it wouldn't matter. As long as I'm the father they need, I feel as though I'm on solid ground. Their view of me is the one to which I default, and the one upon which I base any adjustments to be made.

I'm aware, of course, that part of being that father is also distinguishing between what they need and what they simply want, so I do have to remain autonomous to a degree. Still, the confidence I draw, from theirs in me, can't be overstated.

The year I made the film, I began to lose track of myself in ways I thought were long behind me. I don't think I was consciously aware of it—that's kind of how it works—but some part of me must have clocked it and switched on the emergency systems. Otherwise, how, even as I was sliding back towards madness, did I manage not only to protect the twins, but to leave them with positive memories? How else did I foster the renewed closeness that I was soon going to need desperately?

I would change everything about that year, except for that. I wasn't to know it at the time, convinced as I was that I was embarking on a grand adventure that would finally set everything right, but I was laying the groundwork for an enormous loss, one from which I would struggle to recover.

But that's only one version of the story.

The other is that, somehow, I turned a dozen failures into a single success. The one that mattered most.

Both of these tales co-exist in my head, their characters equally compelling and their plots worthy of sequels.

One, I watch in the dead of night, when I feel the need to set tears free. The other when I need to be reminded why all of this is worth it, and why I am still here.

And I always watch both until the end of the credits.

Who knows? There may be one more scene.

Bi-partisan

We've covered religion a lot, and sex enough to bother the religious people, so, for the sake of the hat trick, we should probably have a look at politics.

There's no point in groaning. I can't hear you. And, frankly, I wouldn't pay you much mind if I could. I have a limited amount of patience for those whose reaction to politics is to cover their eyes and pretend it can't see them.

It's an understandable position, considering how overwhelmingly fucked everything is, but, in my opinion, it is demonstrably unsustainable. The political sphere keeps turning, regardless of whether or not you choose to engage with it.

Look at it this way. If you lived in a jungle full of lions—underfed ones, who, incidentally, lost their mothers to hunters on their birthdays—and insisted that because lions were preoccupied with slashing throats and consuming entrails, you preferred to pretend that they didn't exist, most people would accept that you needed specialist educational support of some kind.

Such as being shown a lion.

Yet, more and more, because the lion's share—ah, shut up—of politicians is comprised, particularly in the top tier, of morally dubious and shifty motherfuckers, the first instinct of many is to retreat into a fantasy world where politics is something that happens to other people.

Clearly this is not the case. Ask anyone.

They said what?

The bastards.

My own history with politics is convoluted, which brings the running total of problematic relationships in my life to forty-six. And a half. (Mint chocolate, in case you were wondering.)

I grew up in a neutral household. Our allegiance was to the fascist wonderland that was God's Kingdom, and it had been made abundantly clear that treason would be dealt with harshly. We were to obey laws and "render Caesar's things unto Caesar", but we were not to participate.

This was an easy out, and prevented you from thinking too deeply about world issues, which was obviously the point. You were encouraged to keep a tally of everything wrong in society, for decrying purposes, but activism was restricted to pointing and shouting "Hah!"

The word on the street was that God was on His way to sort it out and humans would soon feel foolish for imagining they could do the job in His stead. Also, there would be smiting.

Yet, even after ucked off the rest of my upbringing, I remained Switzerlandesque. Even with my newly secular perspective, I had no desire to ally myself with those on either side of the aisle, steeped as they were in agendas and Machiavellian schemes.

But I wasn't waiting for a deity to turn up and clean house anymore.

I intended to do it.

Through the medium of art.

My early political views, therefore, owed as much to *Bill and & Ted's Excellent Adventure* as anything else. And they were bipolar-fed. My inner conviction that I had been born and torn for a purpose made details irrelevant. I was playing my part just by doing what I had been planning on doing anyway.

Obviously, once I had achieved my inevitable position atop the food chain, *then* I could start to feed the hungry and house the homeless and wreak vengeance on my enemies. Perhaps on the weekends, as a change of pace.

Thankfully, my thinking gradually evolved. And in the usual way: I came into contact with other, more nuanced minds and I listened to a bunch of Bob Dylan records. I still maintained that I had a destiny, but I was willing to entertain the possibility that, in the meantime, it might be worth tackling what was going on in the here and now.

To this too, I took a traditional approach. Give me an issue of the day and, by God, I could shout at it. Often to musical accompaniment.

And now?

Let's do the math.

I am an atheist and former cult member who believes in equality and individuality. I am drawn to and protective of the LGBTQI+ community on an eighty percent ally, twenty percent curious basis, think a woman's body is her own business, that human rights trump—don't worry, I see it—any national advantage and that a subscription to the vast majority of -isms is indicative of a lack of higher brain function. I believe that an enlightened society has a responsibility to protect its most vulnerable members, and even though there are those who may take advantage of that, it is to both our individual and collective benefits that we err on the side of mercy, rather than cynicism.

I also enjoy folk music.

So, obviously, I am a dyed-in-the-wool conservative. Or would be if I hadn't shot all the sheep.

But seriously, comrades.

If you hadn't worked it out already, I veer to the left. So hard to the left that I'm up on the curb kerb and heading for your neighbour's fence. I am the face Rush Limbaugh sees before he wakes up screaming.

However—he says, preparing to alienate a healthy proportion of his target demographic—I do not believe that everyone who swerves right is evil. It's tempting, especially when many of their representatives and a vocal portion of their membership do such apparently callous things. But, for starters, they're hardly alone in that and, besides, the supposed basis of left-wing philosophies is concern for all people, regardless of status.

This, by its very nature, has to include assholes, however you happen to define them.

I'm not saying that you shouldn't call things or people out, just that we've reached a point at which both sides are more concerned with dragging each other down than actually articulating a position. The sad truth is, many of them would despise the change they support, as what they really enjoy is the screaming.

When invective has supplanted reason, both sides are traitors to their causes.

Here's where we most often go wrong, in my opinion:

We consider our own value systems to be self-evident, and those of others to be a malicious repudiation thereof. Whereas, they're thinking the same thing.

Now, it is my belief that if you lead with kindness—not nearly as simplistic or woolly a concept as it seems —you can't go far wrong. Personally, I struggle to understand how you could argue with that.

Yet, the fact remains that many do. Often quite forcefully. And, yes, it is as confounding to me as it is frustrating. Nonetheless, as appealing as the idea may be, it seems statistically unlikely that they are all, in fact, Satan.

The lack of dress sense alone ought to be a clue.

We've talked at length about the selfishness of the human race, and it's this, as with so many squiffy things in life, that is actually the root cause of political divides. We protect our interests. Unilaterally.

Now, it may be that you consider your interests to be less insular than most. You may see yourself as one of the good guys. But, here's the kicker: the moment at which you take satisfaction in that? In fighting the good fight? Boom, you guessed it. Selfish. You may talk about leaving a better world for our children and grandchildren—but you really mean *your* children and grandchildren, or any other descendant member of your inner circle. You may say you want a kinder, gentler society, but what you mean is that the one we have currently makes you feel bad.

There is nothing wrong with any of that. Entirely pure motivations are incredibly difficult to comeby, and, overall,positive actions beat murky feelings. In fact, I think most people fall into this category: generally well-disposed towards others, but never at the expense of their own.

I would murder every single one of you, quite brutally, if it kept my children from harm. That's evolution, not politics.

Still, it cannot be denied—well, it can, but it'd be hard to keep a straight face—that there are those,— left and right, —whose motivations are unkind, unfeeling, unpleasant and dark. Driven by anger, jealousy and hatred.

But the most common cause of awfulness? That would be fear. Like all animals, we strike out most often when we are hungry and when we are afraid. And if we're afraid *of* being hungry, then hoo doggie.

Sometimes, those fears are well-founded—nature's form of self-defence. Others are irrational and need addressing before they have disastrous consequences.

Those are called phobias. And they are not evils, they are disorders.

There is, for example, a marked difference between someone who has not yet been motivated to challenge their racist beliefs or feelings and someone who has no inclination to do so. One may simply be afraid, while the other is patently hateful. The actions they take, as a result, may be equally despicable, but one person clearly has a better chance of redemption than the other. Not a guarantee of it—they might just as easily slide from stupidity to spite—but a shot, at least.

So, if we're so progressive and humane on the left, why do we spend so little time delineating the two? Is it that much easier to say that once someone has an unworthy thought they are immediately and forever *non grata*?

We hate people on the right because we are afraid of them. Their attitudes—as we understand them—are so cold, so backwards, so antithetical to our own that we are terrified about what they're going to do next. In our heads, it becomes the worst thing we can imagine.

They are going to eat a baby, while wearing a giraffe-skin suit.

Equally, they hate us because we seem to have so little regard for their safety, for their way of life, for their traditions. Things that bring as much comfort to them as they do discomfort to us. And are much higher up on their list of priorities. They see us as unrealistic and therefore unpredictable.

We're going to adopt a baby and name it Giraffe.

And so an impasse is reached.

I do need to hop off the fence though. Conservatism, neo or otherwise, is not a philosophy I can get behind. It makes assumptions about what people shouldn't be. (Just as liberalism has begun to make assumptions about what people *should* be.) Its priorities are not my priorities.

In my bowels, I feel it. I will never be that.

But I don't believe for a second that everyone who considers themselves a conservative holds those views for unworthy reasons.

I used to. Oh my God, I used to. I had a recurring nightmare in my twenties, in which I woke up naked next to a Tory amour, and had to either castrate myself or forfeit my honour. I mean, obviously, I just made do without the honour. But I missed it.

But every so often, someone on the other side, by dint of being a human being, says something that is sensible and wise and heartfelt. I think it speaks to my growth as a person that I can acknowledge that without bleeding from the eyes.

I would like to think that even if our respective views were less diametrically opposed, I would find it too extreme a compromise to ally myself with the worst offenders. If I were fiscally conservative, for instance, I don't think it would justify belonging to a group who, while sharing my monetary outlook, also wanted to scoff infants or flay those majestic runway models of the savanna.

You could, however, say the same thing about the left. I often do. The buzzwords, the name-calling, the personal attacks in lieu of debate, the assumption of guilt based on ever-changing vocabularies. It's fucking nonsense, and undercuts everything we should be trying to accomplish. Often, the only thing they are truly liberal with is the truth.

It's just that their stated intentions and mine dovetail, more so than with the other lot. I have no illusions about how infrequently they—or I—live up to them.

These are my politics:

I think if you don't understand something, you should, at least, make an attempt to rectify that before offering an opinion. And if you put in that effort, and it still doesn't make sense to you? Well, who fucking cares? Who made you the Great Understander, anyway? I think if you are not immediately affected by an issue, you should shut your pie-hole and listen to those who are.

I think we have a responsibility to the human race as a whole, and not to any arbitrarily-decided subset thereof.

I believe I can fly. I believe I can touch the sky.

I believe that if our society requires a government to function, as appears to be the case, then that body should work to the benefit of the greatest number of people, not merely those who have been deemed worthy by the current set of bozos in charge.

I don't think power corrupts, as much as it enables. We're all a little corrupt, and we all have things we'd do if we thought we could get away with it.

I would go pants-less in a bank.

Governments should, at all times, be accountable to the people. But I also think the people need to remember that it's not always about them individually.

I'll take a permissive society over a proscriptive one, any day. Neither is perfect, but I'd rather rein myself in than fight my way out.

The world is full of so much pain and misery, wrought by its own inhabitants upon each other, that anger is inevitable.

Cruelty, however, is a choice.

That's what left means to me. Maybe for you, some version of the same thoughts has tugged you to the right. I don't know. We've never met. Unless that was you in the garden last night, in which case, you owe me a lawn chair.

There hasn't been a party assembled that manages to keep all of those plates in the air. There couldn't be. Political parties have people in them. People are ridiculous. Contrary. Hypocritical. Wonderful, tragic and inane. Their attendance precludes perfection.

Consider how our political awakenings often begin: with a single issue. Something that speaks to us on a personal level. And we step up, because it feels like the right thing to do. Then we step up some more, because the notion of influence is intoxicating. Very often, this happens when we're young, a period of time when the fire always smoulders, and thus takes little stoking.

Naturally, we ally ourselves with those who appear like-minded; we seek out safety in numbers. We feed on the power of our army and dream of the victories it will accrue.

Then, one day, our siblings-in-arms decide to run some other disputes up the flagpole for consideration—issues about which we hadn't previously given a toss, but which seem to similarly exercise their spleens.

And, before we know it, we find ourselves adding a verse to the battle hymn. For the sake of team morale. Then another. And another.

In for a penny, in for a pounding.

That's party politics. Buy one, get dumb free. Nobody believes exactly the same thing, it's logistically impossible. Religion. Politics. Relationships. We gather together for warmth and convince ourselves it's for similarity.

188

The twins are sixteen now, several years into their political development, and it has been both inspirational and soul-crushing to watch. Inspirational in that they think for themselves and their first thoughts are often for others. And soul-crushing because of what we've given them to work with.

We become immune over time, even the most socially conscious of us, to how deeply fucking horrible much of what happens on this planet actually is, but children are only just finding this out. Their bullshit detectors aren't caked in detritus just yet.

One Saturday afternoon, when the girls were about seven or eight, we went into a bookshop to kill some time before their bedtime and my bottle.

Our browsing methods were very different. I would wander from shelf to shelf, idling wondering how many hardbacks I could fit under my coat, if I weren't so intent on setting a good example. Whereas they viewed most places as outsized pinball machines. The bell above the door would chime, and they'd launch into the building, pinging off of walls and into each other, all the while screeching at the top of their lungs.

If you haven't heard it before, or have blocked out the memories, this is a sound unique to children let loose in an adult environment. Just pain-like enough to make other shoppers stare accusingly at the weary parent, yet sufficiently joyous to keep said parent from running away when they're not looking.

Anyway, the girls had finished their first thirty laps of the store, when they took a breather and happened to glance at one of the actual books.

On the cover was a tall, distinguished African American man, who I knew to be the recently elected President of the United States, but imagined Fathead and Baldy wouldn't have known from Adam, other than that he was fully dressed.

"Obama!" shouted Fathead.

"Brick Obama!" replied Baldy.

They were both clearly in favour of the gentleman and celebrated his leadership by shrieking half an octave higher than previously and running around in ever decreasing circles until they bumped heads and fell over.

That was a gut reaction. They liked Obama. He looked nice to them. Hardly a detailed political analysis, but illustrative of how children see the world.

Eight years later, they saw his Orangeness for the first time, and their reaction was very different.

"Who's that, Dad?"

"Donald Trump."

"Well, he's an arsehole."

The reality, obviously, is far more complex and there are seldom clear-cut heroes and villains. Except Trump, who is an asshole. But the reason why young people have historically provided the bulk of our firebrands is because they still expect things to be right. Which is exhausting to watch, so we tell them they're wrong until they start to believe us.

There has to be a middle ground, where we expect good to prevail, accept that it won't always, and resist becoming overly despondent.

A boy can dream.

I've tried to support my two as they've sighed their way to a better understanding of how the world is run, off-setting every new "What? *Really*?" with a "Yes, but also there is beauty."

At the same time, I want them to stand up and fight for what they believe in. When Baldy discovered there was a tampon tax, she went full Jane Fonda. There were speeches and petitions. And an award-winning film about a dance marathon. Probably. Likewise, Fathead only has to hear of animal cruelty and a red rage descends. They are articulate, passionate and caring women. And not shy about speaking out.

And I'm the jerk who has to manage their expectations. So far, I think I've done it without dampening their spirits and, on a good day, while reviving my own. Besides, my real job is to, over time, teach them to marshal their anger and focus it, and not dissipate it through mud-slinging.

No one tells you about that in parenting school. Because it doesn't exist. Though I have written to my MP about it.

What all of this has to do with our story should be obvious. I mean, it isn't. But if I'd written it properly, it would have been.

Like many people with a particular set of symptoms, I used to be pretty good at spotting them in others. I could spot mania from the glint in someone's eye. I could sense depression like a drop in air pressure.

But when I watch the news now, it's like sensory overload. Everyone on every channel appears to be bipolar, and they are totally not taking their medication. The inflated senses of self, the capacity to talk with complete confidence and zero accuracy, the heightened, frantic tones followed by Cassandra-baiting prophecies—that's the shit for which I get hardcore professional help.

Is there such a thing as psychological appropriation? Because the politicians, the journalists, the pundits—all of the fuckers, whatever their leanings—are lifting my act and blowing the punchlines.

My children and my friends' children (and probably some other children—I lost count after about seventeen) are having their impressions of the world moulded by people who are pretending to be mentally ill for kicks.

190

And it's spreading. Social media is like the inside of my head on a bad day. Full of sound and fury and signifying fuck all. We are normalising distortion and calling it democratisation.

However, as with any mental illness, what we need now is not judgement, but treatment. And the realisation that it is not the symptoms that destroy, but their impact. The first sign of true recovery, after all, is the capacity to see more than a single step down the line, the reclamation of our sense of consequences.

Our world would be infinitely better off if everyone who espoused a philosophy or political opinion was immediately shown the entire chain of events—good and bad—that would occur if it were seriously taken up. If you could see every ripple in the pond, you'd think more carefully about where to chuck your stone.

If we were very lucky, perhaps that might *actually* change hearts and minds.

Though, at this point, I'd be content with shock and awe.

13: Teenage Mutant Ninja Hurdles

Great. Another chapter I don't want to write. Honestly, this is getting silly now.

In this instance, it's not because I know what's coming. I've been awake for about twenty-four hours, so much of it we'll be discovering together.

It's more that we're speeding straight into cliché central, with the brakes off and a blindfold on. Smoking with one hand and texting with the other.

Teenagers, eh? Whaddya gonna do?

Maybe I'm overly concerned with originality, but I don't want to trot out the hoary old trope about the sweet kid who suddenly turns into a Neanderthal the moment they enter their teens.

Also, strictly speaking, that isn't what happened with Fathead and Baldy. They decided to keep me on my toes by becoming each other, like some sort of weird *Parent Trap/Freaky Friday* crossover.

Fucking Disney Channel has a lot to answer for.

Actually, while we're on the subject, the entire media could do with a bit of a slap. Ever since James Dean first flicked up the collar of his jacket, parents have been conditioned—by films, by television, by comedians and commentators—to fear the inevitable transformation of their children into egomaniacal monsters, monosyllabic hormone junkies whose only goals in life are to cause worry and erode patience.

They're not wrong, per se, but the build-up doesn't help. We expect conflict and, *quelle surprise*, conflict is exactly we get.

The girls and I had joked about it, frequently, over the preceding years.

"Hah hah," I would laugh, casually, "I bet you two will be terrors when you become teenagers."

And they'd just look at me and smile, like possessed dolls, until my hair began to sweat.

I'm not sure what I was specifically worried about. It's not as though moodiness and contrariness hadn't featured in our lives together. If the archetype had any merit, Baldy had been a teenager since she was three months old.

As had I.

But it has to be said, there was something unsettlingly new in the air.

My mental state didn't help. My anxiety was through the roof—and afraid of heights—and I'd recently pulled into an enchanting little side street of my condition known as rapid cycling. Instead of days or weeks of mania, followed by the equivalent period of depression, my mood could shift from one pole to the other and back again within hours. Sometimes, it even got confused and attempted to be in both places at once.

Not that I was doing much to combat it. Thanks to the workload I'd taken on, I hadn't slept properly for about eighteen months. I hadn't been taking care of myself and I hadn't been taking care of the person who was trying desperately to take care of me in my stead.

It was disorientating to the point that I'd given up trying and was now simply riding the wave. Which was exactly as good an idea as it sounds.

This was only compounded by the fear that Baldy might, against all odds, discover hitherto unexplored levels of irascibility and the concern that, with Fathead joining her on the dark side, I'd be facing it without an ally.

The gunpowder trail led straight to the barrel and the cowboy was holding a match.

And do you want to know what I would have said to you if you'd asked me how I was?

Well, first off, "Who wants to know?" But once the pleasantries were out of the way, I'd have gifted you this gem:

"I'm fine. Just tired."

To this day, if I repeat that combination of words to anyone close to me, they immediately arrange an intervention. If necessary, at gunpoint.

Because I was not in any way fine, and there was no "just" about my tiredness.

Not that I was quite ready to throw in the towel. In a desperate effort to counteract how scattershot I felt on the inside—and control one of the few aspects of my life I, erroneously, believed I still could—I'd started to tighten the reins at home.

I'd never wanted to be a stern father—I'd seen how that played out—and any rules I'd laid down in the past had tended to run along the lines of, 'Could you please not throw things at Daddy when he's hungover?' But now, I realised that, for better or worse, the girls were changing. They had different needs, faced new challenges and dangers. They were, whether I liked it or not, headed for the starting line of their adult lives, and all that entailed.

193

If they were to going to navigate their futures successfully, I would have to provide structure and, dare I say it, discipline, a word I had previously only associated with hurriedly deleted internet histories.

By realise, I must stress, I mean that it had been pointed out to me by smarter people and I had grudgingly taken it on board.

This was, of course, another instance in which having clever children complicated proceedings.

"Dad?" said Fathead, one afternoon. She was leaning insouciantly against a picnic table, a glass of cola in one hand and her recently acquired and much-loved phone in the other, looking somehow both thirteen and forty. Her tone was serious, but calm.

"Yes?" I replied eventually, having failed to come up with anything better.

"Can I ask you a question?"

"Apparently so."

I couldn't see beneath the dark lenses she was, obviously, sporting, but I know she rolled her eyes.

"Of course you can," I course-corrected, tensing from the rectum upwards.

She pulled her sunglasses down her nose, and looked at me, over the top of them. I blame American television.

"Are you trying to make up for something?"

Suddenly, I was the killer in her bad cop drama. How did she know? I'd been so careful.

"What do you mean?"

"Well, we've been talking…"

"You and your sister?"

"Yes."

"Do you mean arguing?"

"No."

This *was* serious.

"Right. Go on then."

"… and it seems to us as though you've been extra strict about stuff lately, and we wondered if it was because you thought you hadn't been around as much the last few years."

Honestly, how do you reply to that?

Sorry, what I meant to say was:

How do you reply to that? Honestly.

"Probably," I said, after a moment. Bipolar disorder has its occasional advantages, one of which is random acts of transparency.

Plus, she totally wasn't expecting it, and the element of surprise can be very useful when dealing with teenagers. Their default setting is the assumption that they know exactly what adults think about every subject, and how they will react. Whereas, I seldom know what I think about any subject and never know how I'm going to react. This is usually a pain, but for once it was pulling its weight.

It's good for the soul to have one's expectations confounded sometimes. All the time is a bit much, admittedly, but you work with what you've got.

"Oh, right," said Fathead, suddenly on the back foot. The sunglasses came off altogether, and she was suddenly a child again, a trick she and her sister would pull off repeatedly over the next few years. Teenagers, especially the rookies, are like those rudimentary holograms you used to get at the bottom of cereal packets, the picture dependent on the angle at which you held it.

From one viewpoint, they seemed so appallingly grown-up. From another, still so tiny and vulnerable. Just like their father, if you discounted the grown-up part.

My heart swelled and broke as the image twisted in the sun.

Baldy bobbed up from beneath the table, where she had been chasing an errant crisp.

"You think we're growing up too fast," she offered, daring me to say yes.

"Yes," I said.

I was half-aware that I was straying into dangerous territory, but I was too tired to care.

"Do you?" I added, lobbing the ball back into their court, despite my distinct unease at employing a sports metaphor.

They both looked at me with steel in their gazes. Steel and cotton candy, in fact, which is properly unsettling.

I braced myself for a fight. I was on the cusp of a manic episode and, therefore, all in on this one. I couldn't tell if this was going to be a glorious victory or a devastating failure, but I was beyond retreat.

And, then, for whatever reason, and in the blink of one of my bloodshot eyes, everyone's guard fell down.

"I don't know," said Baldy.

"Maybe," said Fathead.

"Why?"

"I don't know," said Fathead.

"Maybe," said Baldy, who, having dropped another crisp, had lost track of the conversation.

"Why do *you* think we are?" asked her sister.

I felt abruptly feverish. My brain was racing with all the things I desperately wanted to say:

"Because I haven't got it anywhere close to right yet. Because I haven't done half of what I set out to do and what kind of example is that? Because you're going to leave me, and go out into the same world that has beaten me down and I don't have any idea if I've prepared you for it or not. Because I look at you standing there and I realise how much time has passed and how badly I've spent it. Because I don't know what you think of me. Because I have a terrible feeling that I'm about to lose everything else that I care about, and you will be all I have left. Because very soon I will have to let you go and I'm not ready for that."

I didn't say any of that out loud. Unfortunately, I did say it in my head, which took a while.

"Dad?" asked Baldy, eventually, "Are you okay?"

"I'm fine," I said, "Just tired."

***

The reality of life with teenage daughters is not half as bad as people make out. It's not even as bad as I make out.

It is upsetting, though, especially if you overthink it. And adults have a terrible habit of transforming their natural sadness into frustration at its cause. And bipolar adults can turn frustration into crusades.

I was galloping towards the Holy Land at a thundering pace. To escape the war at home.

Just when I would have gladly clung to them, all of my constants had been turned on their heads. In particular, Baldy, after years of raging and snapping, had suddenly softened and Fathead, having spent the same years largely pliant and affable, had done the reverse.

The latter and I had always been different to one another and, as such, had got along famously. But, if the media had taught her anything, it was that fame and rebellion went hand in hand. Overnight, she began to reject anything I told her and balk at every—admittedly overdue—attempt to exert my authority.

I found myself uttering phrases I'd so far managed to avoid. Like, "Because I said so" and "Because I am the parent" and "Who pays for everything around here?" and, my personal favourite, "You'll understand when you're older."

She didn't know that I was falling apart. She didn't know that I sought peace and quiet—through shouting—because I couldn't quiet the voices in my head. She just knew that she needed to work out who she was, and that it

196

felt equally good to push back and, disconcertingly, to regret having pushed back so hard. It made her feel alive.

And that frightened the life out of me.

Baldy, on the other hand, had stepped down her campaign of terror by three or twelve notches. We'd discovered common ground in, amongst other things, our obsession with the minutiae of fantasy and science fiction and our shared bewilderment at ordinary people and the ease with which they appeared to sail through the world.

But she was pulling closer to me—something of which I had dreamed since the day she was born—at a time when I was pulling away from everything and everyone.

I would sit and listen to her for hours, because I knew she deserved it, with every nerve jangling and screaming. It was agonising to sit still and every more painful to realise that if my head hadn't had all those acid-drenched nails being hammered into it, I would have been in heaven.

All the while, my other little girl, the one who had once curled into my arms, and rubbed her snot-encrusted face against my cheek with genuine adoration, was now raving in the next room because I opposed her plan to pierce something or lacquer something else.

And I was raving back. Because I was furious. Livid that all of this important stuff—good and bad—was being torn into confetti and tossed into the wind by the chemicals in my brain. Outraged by the brutal flashbacks to my own teenage years and their God-mandated self-loathing. Indignant at my continued and increasingly delusional conviction that everyone just needed to hold on a few more months, just chill the fuck out for a second, and watch, amazed, as my grand plan paid off.

It would all get better. So fucking soon. Why couldn't everyone just put all this life stuff on pause until I could dot all my i's and row all my ducks?

I had never been so scared. I had never felt so incompetent.

Because I had never been a teenager. Sure, I'd had the years and I'd had the hormones, but I'd skipped calamitously over the experience. No poorly concealed hangovers, no golden-hued abandon, no wide-eyed and ham-fisted amorous escapades.

My overwhelming memory of adolescence was finding myself, only a few years older than the girls were then, in a hospital bed, having the painkillers and muscle relaxants and—don't even ask—crème de menthe leached from my body by an IV stand at my elbow. There were still tar stains on my crumpled paper gown.

I remember crying and shaking and staring incredulously as the social worker in the chair next to me idly wondered aloud if perhaps the religion in which I'd been raised bore some responsibility for my despair. Had I, for instance, considered not being in it?

So, what the fuck did I know about turning teenagers into functioning adults? I'd never managed it before, and there was only one of me.

More or less.

I know all of the above feels disconnected—not to mention the opposite of the hilarious teenage antics you might have imagined to have been forthcoming.

Well, good. I've finally managed to get something down exactly as it happened.

Until this moment, I don't think I've ever truly admitted how bad things were. Ordinarily, I tell the same stories that all parents tell. Albeit with more flamboyant gestures and the requisite soupçon of showbiz élan.

Oh my godGod, they were *so* moody. They hid in their room. They played their loud music. They were off with their friends doing God knows what, while I sat at home and worried myself sick.

But I'm grasping at a universal experience, because I feel that I must be owed *one*. And why not that one? The one with which I could tease them, and through which I might claim retroactive apologies when, one day, their own kids get snide.

My gratitude, however, remains bolted to those around me at the time. The ones who took up the slack, and ensured that when I returned from my most recent sojourn to the underworld, I did so to women who had come through that crucible of growing up, that hideous, confusing time that, let's try to remember, is much, much harder on the person experiencing it than the baffled adults around them, not only intact but thriving.

Oh, I could tell you tales of the many ways in which they mystified me. Of the daily struggle to support them through an experience I had never really had. Of the funny things they said—which I know you're probably gagging for right now—and the bonkers things they did.

Those stories exist, but, in a way, I feel like I experienced them secondhand. I'm just glad we all got through it.

Sixteen, on the other hand, I've been entirely present for. And that's been an absolute nonsense.

So, as you might want to tell any teenagers in your own life, don't lose hope.

It'll get funny again soon.

Bi the Light of the Silvery Moon

I am writing this in an airport.

Though it would please me even more than it would you, this is not because I am headed anywhere exciting. My ship has not come in between chapters.

If it had, what would I be doing in an airport? I'd be on my ship. Think it through.

No, what I'm doing is sitting in the weakest link of a popular chain of coffee shops, staring groggily at the International Arrivals gate of a busy and deeply unpleasant terminal in the south of England.

Why, you may ask, am I doing this? Is it, you may add, *sotto voce*, a cry for help?

Well, yes and no. In fact, I am waiting for Fathead and Baldy to return home from their Canadian excursion. But that doesn't mean I haven't found a way to bizarre it up.

You see, they won't get back for another eight hours or so and I've already been here for four. Thanks to the unique way in which I am funded, I have had to forego the luxury of a hotel room and pull an old-fashioned all-nighter, the kind that once made up half of my working week.

Thus, I have, at this point, been awake for about thirty hours, six of which were spent on yet another coach. Again, something I could have done, in the past, with my eyes not even remotely closed. But here in my dotage, things are beginning to get weird.

I have mistaken fourteen people for Englebert Humperdinck so far.

Fifteen.

Anyway, if you were wondering why the last chapter was a bit all over the place, there's half your answer.

Sorry about that, by the way. I was trying to make better use of my time than simply humming "Release Me" under my breath at strangers.

Sixteen. Actually, that one could easily have been him, if it hadn't been a baby.

Or possibly a dog.

It was in a harness, so one or the other.

Did you know that Englebert Humperdinck's real name is Arnold George Dorsey?

That fact just floated up from my once pristine and now waterlogged filing system, for reasons best known to itself.

When I was younger, I had an eidetic memory and a mind like the proverbial steel trap. Or, at least, *a* proverbial steel trap. I never examined its provenance. Either way, everything I read—every book, every magazine, every newspaper, every bilingual cereal box and can of condensed soup—lodged verbatim and, I thought, permanently into my mind palace.

These days, tourists swarm through in groups, whistling at the ruins.

I used to joke that bipolar disorder had Swiss-cheesed my brain, but only because I wanted to be Scott Bakula. By my twenties, I knew I was no longer as sharp as I had been at eighteen, but I tried not to think about it too deeply. By my thirties, any increase in jaw slackness was easy to lay at alcohol's door. Everything after that, age.

But it turns out that my jest was more accurate than I'd intended it to be. I know, because I looked it up. My illness *has* been repeatedly punching my cognitive function in the junk, from the day it moved in. Apparently, it's a whole thing.

My head, therefore, is still full of stuff, but my access to it is intermittent. I'm just glad I didn't know what was happening at the time, especially during the years when the bulk of my identity was tied up in being a clever little shit. Or maybe I did know and I've just forgotten.

How did we get on to this?

Seventeen.

In many ways, I am just relieved to be here. The girls have been gone for nearly a month, and I've been rattling around the house like a ghost. It's been ludicrously quiet, bar the clanking chains, and I've hated every second. Well, other than the occasional ones in which I've been able to play video games in my pants and watch stand-up specials without high-pitched complaint. At other times, in an effort to fill the void, I've whinged piteously at myself to put something else on and, if possible, make dinner. But it hasn't been the same.

Meanwhile, they've been with my mother, so I'm now struggling to shake the image of them bursting through the gates in front of me with beatific smiles on their beautiful mugs and Bibles tucked under their arms.

It's not likely, I know. They'd never make it through a book with so many boring bits. Like pages.

But the thought is terrifying.

Damn, my brain is all over the place tonight.

When you are diagnosed with bipolar disorder, in addition to the bags of medication and the yearly visit to a psychiatrist who has no idea who you are, you are often given a long speech about self-care and its importance to your recovery and maintenance. Self-care, it turns out, is very different to self-love, although I've also found that useful.

A balanced diet, regular exercise and plenty of sleep can do much, you're told, to lessen the severity of symptoms and allow your medication to do its work.

The first two, if I'm paying attention, I can just about handle, although not terribly consistently. As we've discussed, my body and I are not on cordial terms. From time to time, I'll let it go for a run, in exchange for a dime bag of endorphins and a two percent reduction in sexual insecurity. In return, it lets me read all the books I like, provided I remember to put on my glasses. It's an uneasy détente, but we just about get away with it.

Sleep is a different matter. Our loathing is mutual. We just hook up from time to time, when we both need to get something out of our systems.

You know what it's like.

There are multiple reasons for this. Firstly, I've never been good at it and we've discussed how I feel about that. Secondly, I am prone to nightmares, which, considering what my daytime life has often been like, seems unfair.

Finally, I like what happens when I don't sleep. I shouldn't, but I do.

I spend most of my life digging in my heels, trying to keep my shadow from running towards whatever edge he has his eye on—every muscle straining, every vein popping. It's draining.

But I still crave the fall. Which is glorious. You're flying. You're free. And best of all, you can let go. Relax and surrender to the inevitable. It's a relief.

Because I have vowed never to deliberately pursue that feeling again, and have asked others to go for the knees if it looks like I'm taking a run-up, I secretly relish times like these, when it has been forced upon me by circumstance. Like an addict on post-surgery painkillers.

So, yeah, it's been a long time, but here he comes. Feeling frisky and ready to play. I can hear him whooping and whispering inside me, playing my vocal chords like a washboard bass.

Don't worry. It's a contained environment, so he can't do much damage. I've deliberately left my passport at home and I don't have enough cash on me for him to buy into any illegal poker tournaments.

We're just going to sit here and watch the world through his eyes for a while. Play cards. Perhaps indulge in the kind of uncomfortable catch-up favoured by ex-lovers and heads of state.

What could possibly go wrong?

Eighteen.

***

He arrives, as he always does, without fanfare. As if he's been there the whole time.

Which he has.

"Hey," I say, as nonchalantly as I can manage.

"Hey yourself."

I tip half of my coffee into an abandoned paper cup and slide it to one side, both to show willing and to cover the extremely awkward pause.

He sips. Savours. Smacks his lips grotesquely.

I try not to grimace.

"How have you been?" I say, finally.

He cough-laughs.

"You know exactly how I've been, man. Let's not start by bullshitting one another. Not after all we've been through."

I nod. Take a sip myself.

"I'm sorry, you know."

"No, you're not."

"No, I'm not. Had to do it. Had no choice."

"Well, two out of three ain't bad, I suppose."

I swivel to face him. Which must look pretty odd from the outside.

"What do you mean?"

He sighs.

"You haven't changed then. Why do you have to make everything so complicated?"

"I'm not trying to. Honestly."

"The sad thing is, I believe you. Look, cock. I get why you did it. But don't pretend you didn't have a choice."

"Are you doing an accent, or are you just calling me a cock?"

"If the penis fits…"

"Jesus Christ! What is your problem?"

I smack the counter in frustration, inadvertently startling a sleeping businessman to my right. His head jerks back with a snort and he mumbles a few important-sounding numbers before realising what's happened. I look away but not before he shoots me a look that says he'd invite me outside if his legs were currently working.

"Sorry," I mutter.

"Fucking hippy," he slurs, before resuming a wildly erotic dream about unlimited expense accounts.

"Ooh, I like him."

"You would."

"Wake him up again. Maybe we can get a fight going."

"We're not starting a fight."

"Steal his watch, then."

"No."

"Drink his coffee."

"For God's sake, why?"

"Because it will make me laugh. You used to like it when I laughed."

"*You* used to like it when you laughed. I used to get a migraine."

"Potato."

He fixes me with a stare and a rictus grin and slowly and deliberately pours the rest of his cappuccino on to the floor. I try to poker face and fail.

He steps aside nimbly as I jump from my stool with a handful of napkins and start cleaning up his mess. Again.

"I don't know what you want from me," I say, half to myself. Well, all to myself. But you know what I mean. "You're here. Isn't that enough?"

"You know it isn't. I've been trapped down there for what, two years? Because *you* wussed out and drank the Kool-Aid. You think a few hours compassionate leave is going to make up for that? Spent, may I add, in a fucking airport?"

I lower my voice to a hiss.

"You know what you did. You *know*. I gave you every chance and you blew it."

There is a brief Mexican stand-off. Then a slightly longer Japanese stand-off. And finally, a stationary queue comprised of half-a-dozen bemused looking Norwegians.

It's a busy flight path.

Suddenly, the tension breaks and he laughs. It sounds like a steam train running over a platypus.

"That was a ridiculous joke."

I can't help but snicker back. He's infectious. Well, genetic, but near enough.

"I know, right?"

"And the platypus simile. Fuck me. What did that even mean?"

"I have no idea."

We lose it a little, cackling till tears run down our face. The businessman gets up slowly and edges to the other side of the café.

Thankfully, there's a chair free next to Englebert Humperdinck.

"I was worried you didn't have it in you anymore," he says, wiping my eyes, "Without me, I mean. I don't know whether to be relieved or hurt."

"You never did."

"Ouch. Good one."

"Thank you."

He takes a steadying breath and goes to straighten our clothes, before remembering that never accomplishes anything.

"Let's take a walk."

***

We sit atop the terminal, gazing down on strips of light and taxi-ing planes.

At least, that's how he sees it and, for the moment, I see no reason to take that away from him. This may be his last meal. Let him have the steak.

We drain the last of our coffee. The wind whips at our hair, somehow managing to make it slightly tidier.

"How are the girls?" he asks.

I hesitate. He clocks it.

"Come on, you know I love them as much as you do."

There's a note of genuine grief in his voice.

"I know."

It's his turn to pause.

"I wouldn't have hurt them, you know. I couldn't have."

I shake my head.

"You don't know that. I didn't know that. And that's why you had to go."

"Hah."

"What?"

"I said, hah."

"I heard you say hah. Why did you say hah?"

"You didn't get rid of me for them. You got rid of me for…"

"Shut up."

"It's true."

"I said, shut *up*."

"Wow. You're cranky when you're sane."

I rub my eyes, the weariness setting back in.

"Can we not fight? Just this once? Can we not just sit here together and, I don't know, look at the planes? Imagine all the places we always wanted to visit? All the incredible things we were going to do and see? Come on, make it all real for me, one last time. Play to your goddamn strengths."

"You really didn't know me at all, did you?"

"What?"

"Okay. I might not get the chance to say this again, so listen up, sweetie.

204

I get that you're pissed at me. That last time, I went a bit overboard. And I'm sorry about that. But let's not forget it was you who handed me the keys."

"I know."

"The Rolls, as it were, was always going to end up in the pool."

"I suppose so."

"At least we agree on something."

"What's your point?"

"My point is that you blame me—and, I suppose, with good reason—for all of the things that you've lost. But did you ever stop to think that you wouldn't have had any of those things in the first place without me?"

"What?"

"Do you remember what we were like as a kid? Timid? Afraid? Awkward? All godbothering and brown-nosing?"

"Yes, of course I do."

"Then I woke up."

"I remember."

"And suddenly, we felt like we could do anything. We could change the world. We could talk to the girl. We could play the guitar. We could be movie stars."

"Appalling scansion."

"Fuck you. I'm out of practice."

"Look, if this is going somewhere, then move it along."

"What I'm saying is, do you think you would have stood on those stages or in front of those cameras without me? Would you have scratched and bitten and clawed your way out of the hole you were born into, without me? Would you have found the courage to be someone's Dad, after all you've been through, without me? Would you have leant forward that night and kissed her? Without *me*?"

The words snap out into the crisp, dawn air like a challenge. Like a glove across the face.

I take a breath and let it out, watching it drift visibly from my lips against the cold.

"I guess we'll never know."

"That's all I'm saying."

"But do you know what?"

"What?"

"I never had the chance to find out, asshole. And I'll never forgive you for that. Because you weren't my mojo; you weren't my groove. You were a disease. You didn't just lift me up, you also repeatedly dropped me from a great height. On to big fucking spiky rocks. You weren't just the highs, you know."

He pouts.

"Alright, fine. It was only a theory."

But I'm nowhere near finished.

"You told me lie after lie and made me repeat them. You convinced me I was bulletproof and fireproof. Then, when I was burning and bleeding, you laughed at what a twat I'd been for listening to you in the first place. You were a shitty friend."

"I never said we were friends."

This stops me short.

"No, I guess you didn't. That one's on me."

We sit in wounded silence for what feels like hours. The sun moves wonkily up the sky like a timelapse shot by Dali.

And then, suddenly, it's morning. He rises, stretches and scratches his belly.

"We had some fun though, didn't we?"

"We did."

"If you ever fancy doing it again…"

"I won't."

"Your call. I'm not going anywhere."

"That I do know."

He looks at his watch. Which surprises me, as we don't wear one.

"Almost time. I guess I should be on my way."

He steps towards the edge, glances over it with his usual degree of fascination, then starts to fade, slowly, like a low budget special effect. But as he does, I catch an expression on his face. And curse under my breath.

"Hold on," I say, against my better judgement.

***

We're standing together at the gate, when the girls walk through. They're wheeling enormous suitcases and are festooned from head to toe in maple leaves and other Canadian paraphernalia. They look like a walking tourist board.

He catches his breath.

"Oh my God," he says, "I've missed them so much."

"I know."

"I've always meant to ask. Do they know about me?"

"A little. They know you were around."

206

"Do they hate me?"

"No, they don't hate you. I mean, not as much as I do, anyway."

He nods. Smiles in a way I don't think he ever has before.

On purpose.

"I loved being their Dad, you know. Even when it didn't seem like it."

"You still are their Dad. Let's face it, you always will be. But you have to admit it. You can't do what I can do. Or try to do, at least."

He looks over at he girls, who are now smiling, waving anrying to work out how much money I have on me by the way my jacket is hanging.

"You're right. I can't. Why is that, do you think?"

"Because right now, when you look at them, you can't bear it. I can see it on your face. It's too much. It's killing you. You love them *so* much that your first thought is that they'd be better off without you. And your second thought. And your third. The fourth is, "'I wonder if a drink will make it easier?" ?' And the less said about the fifth, the better."

"And you?"

"I love them so much that I'm prepared to overlook their poor choice in fathers."

"Hah."

"Yep."

He bites his bottom lip, his eyes never leaving the twins.

"It's better this way, isn't it?"

"For them? Yes. I think so."

Then a single tear runs down his face. Multiple times.

"Thank you," he says.

And, just like that, he's gone. Wherever it is he goes when I'm in charge.

Like an idiot, I already miss him.

Fathead and Baldy are now at my side. They seem older somehow. Probably because time has passed.

"Who was that, Dad?"

I give a little whoop, a last sacrifice to sate the departed, then grab them both, pull them in close and hold on tight. After a moment, they struggle free, deeply concerned about the state of their hair.

"That, my loves," I announce, as they rifle my pockets affectionately, "was Arnold Dorsey."

14: Fifty Ways to Lose Your Marbles

So, yeah. A bad thing happened.

It doesn't matter what; it doesn't matter how. All you need to know is that, shortly after, the levee finally broke.

Or maybe I was just dazed and confused. I don't really care to remember.

Ah, fuck. You're not going to let this go, are you?

Fine. If you must have specifics, then I'll put it this way: my second worst fear, and thus the worst fear I allow myself to consciously acknowledge, came shatteringly to pass, and, in the following months, I lost my mind.

Not, it's very important to note, because of the bad thing. That just broke my heart.

This is yet another phrase that we have imbued with commonality, as though it were one experience rather than a billion. Broken hearts are like broken records—they move through the same revolutions, but always to a different snatch of tune. Which is why books on the subject make better paperweights than medicine. And why this isn't going to be one of them.

Short version: I lost someone. Or maybe they lost me. I'm pretty sure it's the former, but I hate to make assumptions. Just because I know where I am, doesn't mean they do.

And, again, that is not what tore my mind from its moorings.

It just so happened that the nature of the blow meant that I was left alone for a sufficient period of time, worn down by years of denial and mental self-harm, to make the decision I'd spent my life trying to avoid.

I gave up.

There was, of course, an element of camels and spinal distress. I was angry at the world and angry at myself, and devastated in an utterly natural way.

But I was also unmedicated, frightened and tired of fighting. And keeping a rather important fact to myself.

I had started, over the previous few months, to see and hear things that were not there. Shadows. Whispers. Ghosts. Or, as a doctor might have put it, if I hadn't been industriously avoiding them, I was suffering from visual and auditory hallucinations.

I hadn't told anyone this, because that's how mental illness gets you. It makes connections on your behalf—lines up dominoes over months, even years, and then, with a smirk on its face, flicks the first.

This is how it all went down.

After the film had proved to be a longer and more expensive struggle than my mania had assured me, I began to sink into a depression. In the midst of my depression, I began to suffer paranoia about what my loved ones thought of me. I was a failure. A bad provider. (That masculinity bullshit doesn't wash out easily.) A terrible father. An awful partner.

A bad person.

Crazy.

No one thought these things but me. Don't get me wrong, nothing about any relationship is simple and I am by no means low maintenance. But the wholesale demolition of my character was in my head, not my world.

I just couldn't tell the difference anymore.

Off the back of that paranoia, I began to make the kind of grand gestures I'd always made, just facing in a different direction. This, I mistook for change. Took a dead-end job, to prove I was responsible. Moved somewhere that made everyone uneasy, to demonstrate I could live within my means. Made all the right noises and all the wrong calls.

I tossed off odd decisions, in sequence and at speed, and grew resentful that no one was throwing me a parade. Why didn't anyone appreciate my sacrifices?

Oh, right. I forgot. They thought I was a bad, crazy person. But that was okay. The setbacks were only sweeteners for when it all came good and they realised how badly they'd underestimated me.

Still, there was no way, in the midst of all of that, that I was going stand up and announce that I was now also seeing and hearing things. Because I knew what that meant. What it led to. It had happened before, when my disorder was still shiny and new. No one in their right minds was going to stick around for that car crash. And that, I would be unable to bear.

So, I went into lockdown. Redoubled my efforts. Avoided the subject whenever I could and when I couldn't quite fake it, maintained it would pass. Fine. Just tired.

In fact, I was only surviving because the people I assumed thought so little of me were propping me up. And so discreetly were they doing so, for the sake of my pride, that I believed I was doing it myself.

But no one was looking after them. No one was thinking about their feelings, or doubts, or responsibilities, or battles. And no one was throwing them a parade, when they were the one making the actual sacrifice.

Of themselves.

I thought I was parenting, because the children still loved me. And they thought I was too, because I still loved them. And we were all still afloat because I had a desperate Cyrano speaking softly in my ear.

I didn't talk back to the voices. Not even the one that was real.

The bad thing was bound to happen. If I'd been looking at it from the outside, feeling the way I did about everyone concerned, I'd have wanted it to happen.

But when it did, I found myself with one less thing to fight for. And one thing less to fight for, was all I that needed.

To let go.

If I'd had any hope that mania would swoop in and rescue me from the immediate pain, it was swiftly quashed.

Instead, the floodgates opened. Fifteen years' worth of pent-up sorrow, rage, confusion and fear tore into my bloodstream like a speedball.

I cried and cried. And screamed and screamed.

I kept the latter from the girls, and considered it a victory. When they caught sight of the former, I told them half-truths and dressed them as candour. I was sad, I said. Very sad. But that was normal. And they were not to worry. I would get through this.

I think they believed me, which is a sick testament to my dramatic training. I had no such belief.

I went to work. I fed the kids. I listened to their fears and their complaints. I helped them with their homework. I hugged them and told them that I loved them.

But I no longer knew how this would end. I couldn't catch a breath long enough to work out in what direction I was facing, let alone where I was going. For all I knew, this was it. The long awaited final round.

In desperation, I got down on my knees, non-recreationally, cleared my throat and swallowed my pride.

"Our Father Who Art in Heaven," I murmured, "I beseech you. Hear my prayer."

"New number. Who dis?"

My hackles rose almost immediately.

"My Lord, I humbly submit that you know perfectly well who it is."

"Oh, do I?"

"Well, unless all that talk of omniscience is just the theological equivalent of balled-up socks down the trousers, then yeah."

"You're pretty mouthy for a supplicant, I have to be honest."

"Sorry. I'm really out of practice. And I'm in a lot of pain. Any chance you could you cut me some slack?"

"Oh, of *course*. In pain, are you? Why didn't you say so? Cause I *usually* get last-ditch booty calls from super *happy* atheists."

"Fuck's sake. I knew this was a bad idea."

"Kiss your mother with that mouth?"

"No, actually. Thanks to you."

I might be wrong, but I think I heard the distant sound of a celestial filing cabinet being rifled through.

"Oh, *yeah*. I remember you now. Smart kid. Slightly tapped. Tiniest bit effeminate."

"Wow."

"With a chip on his shoulder."

"This is why we don't talk anymore."

"What do you expect, you little punk? You had an in, don't you remember? You were one of my *chosen*. All set up for everlasting life, world peace and as many pomegranates as you could get down your neck. But, no, that wasn't good enough for you. You wanted *freedom*. You wanted moral ambi-fucking-guity. You wanted to be twenty percent *gay*."

"Aha! I knew it!"

"No, hold on."

"Total homophobe."

"That was a slip of the tongue. Hate the sinner, love the sin, that's my bag. Fuck, no. The other way round."

"Unbelievable."

"Listen, smart arse. I do not have a problem with gay people. Some of my best friends are gay."

"Really? Like who?"

"Umm."

"I'm waiting."

A snap of fingers rumbled like thunder.

"Gabriel. Yeah, good old Gabe. He's a bit light in the loafers, for one."

"Oh. My. You. That is so offensive."

"What? How is that offensive? He's an angel. He's light in everything."

"That's not what you meant and you know it."

"Okay, you got me. I can't keep up with the terminology. The point is, I don't think any less of him because he folds his wings to starboard."

"Can you even hear yourself?"

"Look. *You* called *me*. Do you want my help or not?"

"That depends. Think you can stop being a massive bigot for two seconds?"

"My views on Canadians are due a refresh, I'll tell you that much."

I opened my mouth to answer back, but the last remaining flame had gone out. A sob scuttled out of the shadows and began to crawl up my throat.

"Please," I muttered.

"Sorry, what?"

"*Please*. Forget everything I said. I didn't mean it. Cultural misunderstanding. It happens. I shouldn't have been so rigid. But you have to help me. I can't go through this again. I just can't. I've got kids. I'm no good to them like this. And…"

I choked on the end of the sentence.

"Go on. Say it"

"And I don't know who else to turn to."

"Yep. I get a lot of that."

"I can imagine."

"Okay, fine. Stop snivelling for a second, and we'll see what we can do. The Lord Your God is a forgiving God and all that."

"Thank you, Lord. Thank you so much."

"De nada. Now tell me what troubles you, my son."

I swallowed hard.

"Well, as you know, I have bipolar disorder and…"

"Hold up. Quick question."

"Yes, Lord?"

"Have you tried *not* having it?"

∗∗∗

With divine intervention clearly not forthcoming, things quickly went from bad to oh fuck. I'd struggle through the days, with just enough of the lights switched on to draw my minimum wage. Then I'd head back to the silence of my room and sit, conjuring every worst case scenario, jabbing at every sore spot and carving open jealous wounds, until I'd worked the voices up into a frenzy of angry seagulls.

Then I'd bounce off the walls till I found the door. And then I'd walk the streets.

Looking for anything with which I could torture myself. Any sign that my fever dreams were, in any way, backed up by reality.

If I was going to hurt, then we might as well see just how much I could take.

And so, one night, I went looking.

And the very same night I was seen.

* * *

There is nothing more agonising, when you're mentally ill, than the knowledge that you've scared somebody that you love.

During my first adult breakdown, it was rare for those around me to feel anything other than dread. No one, including me, knew what I might do from one moment to the next, or whether I intended to even make the journey. The remorse for that still lays heavy on my conscience.

In later years, I'd feel it again, on a lesser scale, if I lost my temper with the girls.

But, by this point, I had long ago sworn that I'd never put myself, or anybody else, in that position again.

And now I had. I'd heard the words. I'd seen that look in someone's eyes.

I didn't do anything to anybody. I didn't say anything to anybody. I didn't stalk or harass or become violent in any way. I didn't even find the torture material I was after. I just walked.

In terms of threat level, we were still at DEFCON 5.

But it was clear that my actions and my thoughts were no longer under my control. I was behaving, as the textbooks have it, out of character.

The abyss, from which I thought I'd been running away, was suddenly directly front of me. Every step that I'd taken away from it, I had retraced in my sleep. And now I teetered, the edge crumbling beneath my feet, as the alarm beeped and squawked in the background.

It was time to wake up.

* * *

Two days later, I broke down in a bathroom stall. And, with my last scrap of lucidity, made a phone call to the one person I absolutely did not want to see me like that, but the only one who would see through any attempt on my part to take it back.

It was the smartest decision I'd made in three years.

They came. They always do. And they drove me to the doctor, as I sobbed and shook and babbled.

As we sat in the car, outside of the surgery, Fathead and Baldy strolled up, on their way home from school. Which feels so contrived that it shouldn't

213

have happened in real life, but it absolutely did.

They are a writer's children, after all.

I froze as I saw them cross the street towards the car. Froze further as our eyes met through the glass and I saw the anxiety cross their faces. And was more or less cryogenically-preserved by the time they knocked hesitantly, as though worried they were interrupting some sort of sexual deviancy.

Something was wrong and they knew it. Also, something was happening and they didn't know it, and that would never stand.

The posse of friends with whom they were travelling, stepped to the corner and circled their wagons. Parent stuff. Best not to get involved.

I did my best to compose myself and wound down the window.

"Hi," I said.

"Hi," they said.

They narrowed their eyes and scanned my face.

"Are you okay?" asked Baldy, a nervous smirk tripping over her lips.

I paused. Got as far as "I'm fi-" in my head, before thinking better of it.

"No," I said, "But I will be."

Bi-vouacking

Dear Past Subjective Narrator,

I just wanted to drop you a quick line, because I know you're struggling at the minute.

If this arrives as scheduled, it's been about a month since you went to the doctor and asked—nay, demanded—to be put back on medication. And if I remember correctly, this is also around the time when you're starting to wonder if that was such a bright idea.

I know it hurts. And, I'm sorry, but it's going to hurt for a little while yet. But I promise, though you're going to have to bite down on this thought like a wallet in the meantime, it will, eventually, hurt less.

You feel like someone's in there with you, don't you? Editing your memories with a chainsaw. Or, worse, Final Cut X.

I know that was a pretty niche joke, but don't worry. This is just between us. Did you laugh? I hope so. Cause that will be the first shaft of light you allow into your darkness, and, in time, you'll follow it all the way back to the outside world.

You hoped, I think, that you wouldn't feel anything. That the little Pic 'N' Mix bag full of pills they've given you would make you numb to the world. The way you once worried it would, ironically.

But it isn't quite that, is it? It's more of a cutting away. All the weeds and the overgrowth, everything that was obscuring and distorting the view, is being uprooted and chucked on the fire.

Like waking from a nightmare, but into a different one. No one there to stroke your hair and tell you it was only a dream, just a catalogue of Rip Van Winkle bullshit, where everything has changed for the worse in your absence.

The dog is dead, your house burned down, your girlfriend ran off with your boyfriend and they've discontinued that ice cream flavour you like.

Oh, and it was all your fault.

In fact, you're not going to feel much like yourself at all at first. Which is going to seem especially strange, as it's the closest to being yourself that you've been for a spell.

But like the rest of it, it's temporary. You've just made camp on the road. This doesn't have to be home.

Sorry. I'm telling you things that you already know.

What I really wanted to do was reassure you that it will be okay. I'm not going to lie and say that you're going to get everything that you want, or even that you're going to be happy.

I haven't got that far yet myself.

But the twins are here, and they're absolutely fine. Great, even. You get through this, and even though it doesn't happen the way you imagined it would, you do make a better life for them. You've got a nice house, with plenty of room for them to leave unwashed dishes and damp towels lying around to their heart's content. You've got a job. Yes, a regular one, and no, it's not your dream gig, but it's okay. And that doesn't piss you off in the same way anymore.

Plus, you've got bookshelves again. Many, many bookshelves. And a bunch of *Doctor Who* stuff you could never afford before. (*Lungbarrow*. Mint. I'll say no more.)

What else? Oh, yes. You're still writing. I know that doesn't feel like a priority right now and, no, you aren't going to want to for a year or so, but, I assure you, you will be glad when it comes back.

Right now, you're even working on a book. A real one. For a publisher. This letter is part of it, so you aren't even going to lose your taste for shameless meta references.

I wish I had better news on certain fronts, but try not to think about that right now. The important thing is, you do make it. I know there have been a few nights recently where that hasn't seemed like a foregone conclusion and they won't be the last. But, rest assured, their days are numbered.

You made the right decision. And you were, at your most terrified, incredibly brave. In a couple of years' time, you're going to be writing a letter to your past self and that's finally going to sink in.

When that happens, don't overthink it.

More than anything else, I want you to know that your children are proud of you. And that you and they have some very good days to come.

You just need to hang on long enough.

And you will.

All my love,

Present Subjective Narrator

15: The Beginning of the Mend

"Dad! Get up!"

It was Baldy, banging on the door of my bedroom.

"Put pressure on the wound," I mumbled from beneath the duvet. "I'll be there in a minute."

"What?"

I struggled into a sitting position. If you could call it that. It was kind of lopsided and my head was still lodged between two pillows.

"Sorry, kid. What is it?" is probably what the muffled screaming was meant to suggest.

"I'm hungry!" she shouted through the door.

"Then eat something."

"There *isn't* anything."

"There are several cupboards and a full refrigerator that say otherwise. Take it up with them. Anyway, didn't we just have this conversation?"

"Yes! An hour ago! Get up!"

Fuck, I thought. I'm late. I couldn't quite remember for what, but it was bound to be something important and adult-y. Like work. Or a hip replacement.

With great effort, I rolled myself to the side of the bed and out, hoping the impact with the floor would shake off my now customary torpor.

I'd been back on meds for about a year and one of the biggest adjustments we'd all had to make was dealing with the side effects, especially those of the antipsychotic I'd been prescribed.

Its role on the team, alongside various mood stabilisers and anti-everything-elses was, as advertised, to stave off psychotic symptoms such as delusions and unwanted thoughts, but also to regulate my sleep. At that point, I'd no complaints about the former, other than it had been disconcerting to realise how many of my personality traits and opinions were, in fact, textbook symptoms. Every day, I'd learn that something else I had considered unique to me was actually Bipolar 101 and my response was unvaryingly, "Well, shit."

As for the latter, I couldn't argue with the fact that the two ludicrously small pills I took before bed did, indeed, knock me the fuck out. The problem was, they lacked a counterpoint. I had been provided nothing whatsoever to knock me the fuck back in.

Which meant that every morning was now an agonising journey from the bottom of the well to the top, with only a single piece of floss and four squares of sticky-backed plastic to aid the ascent.

Thankfully, my beautiful daughters provided daily support.

"Dad! Come *on!*"

"Give me a minute."

"We need to *go.*"

"I'm coming. Just hold on."

"You said that half-an-hour ago."

I hadn't really expected that level of role reversal for another forty years or so. Part of me wondered if I could get away with asking for an allowance. I mean, I almost always did my chores. That had to be worth something.

So, yes. Mornings were now not only not my friend, but were laying a decent claim to archnemesis, a position that had opened up since my shadow had been sent down for assault.

That first year on meds was a matchlessly strange one. I still haven't quite got used to the clarity with which I now see the world, but, at first, it felt more like madness than madness had. "I Can't Believe It's Not Madness," I might have said, and laughed, if it wouldn't have made them double my dosages. In much the same way as my illness once caused me to doubt what I saw and felt, so, too, its remission was cause for a certain degree of scepticism.

"Is this how normal people feel all the time?" I found myself asking, on more than one occasion, which is only a single step from, "What is this Earth emotion that you call love?" And when you start saying things like that, you are given different medication. And a long, legally-enforced lie down.

"Yes, Dad," the girls would say slowly, as patiently as teenagers know how, "That's right. Most people do not consider appearing on a reality television programme a capital offence."

"Weird. I don't know how you all manage."

It was a confusing blend of newfound levelheadedness and childlike vulnerability. I was re-learning how to be a person, and it turned out I had a lot less experience of it than I'd imagined.

In some areas, there were immediate improvements. My attention span lengthened. I became more patient and less irritable. I started to plan and to budget and to clean as I though I understood what I was doing. I could suddenly undertake tasks that did not interest me and not come to in the Seychelles, claiming to be King Magnus IV of Sweden. It was a whole new world.

And, most arrestingly, I was no longer angry. I didn't appear to be able to *get* angry.

That would pass. I had children.

I could tell that the girls had their doubts. At least partly because they kept leaving notes around the house that read, "Dad, we have our doubts."

One night, we sat down and talked about it.

Which, of course, they hated. If there's anything that will put a fifteen-year-old's teeth on edge, it's the thought of a serious talk. They prefer to worry in silence and then act out randomly, as God intended.

But I was all hopped up on sanity. I was going to parent properly, whether they liked it or not.

I asked them how they felt about all the changes. Did I seem different? Did they still feel safe? Was it scary?

Was it better? Was it worse?"

Their answers convinced me that we'd be okay.

Fathead, always the more emotionally open of the two, was brutally honest.

"I don't like it that you have to take pills to be okay."

"Okay, thank you for telling me that. And it's perfectly normal to feel that way."

"I know. I'm not stupid."

"I didn't say you were stupid."

"But you think that I'm stupid."

"No, I think you're very clever."

"You have to say that. You're my Dad."

"I wouldn't lie to you, kid. I tell you that you're clever because you are."

"Oh, right. So, you'd just let me walk around being stupid and wouldn't even say anything? Yeah, that's good parenting."

"That doesn't even make sense."

"Told you. You think I'm stupid."

Sigh.

"Baldy, any thoughts?"

"Nope."

"None at all?"

219

"I said no."

"Come on. You must have some questions."

"Okay, then. Are you going to go crazy again?"

"See, that wasn't so hard. And I'm glad you asked. Now, first, I didn't go *crazy* as such…"

Baldy raised an eyebrow, Vulcan-style.

"No, I won't go crazy again. Not if I keep taking my medication."

"We're fine then. Now, can you both hush, I'm trying to watch my show."

I looked over my shoulder to see a Federation starship tracking across camera.

"When did you turn the TV on?"

"When you were busy calling her stupid."

"I didn't call her…"

I took a breath. After all, this is what I wanted. This is what I was supposed to be working towards. Normality. And when you lived in a house with two fifteen-year-olds, this was as close as it got.

I gave them both a hug.

"Cup of tea?"

"Yes, please."

"And a biscuit, please."

When all else failed, remembering they were English could go a long way.

Remembering they were fifteen was harder. It's an odd crossover age, especially if you've been mentally out of the loop for a few years. I'd hear them discussing some film they were planning to see with their friends, and have to fight the automatic desire to remind them they weren't old enough to see it.

Because they *were* old enough to see it.

How were they old enough to see grown-up things? I could still remember when they weren't old enough to see much of anything. You had to get your face right in there, or they'd think you were just another nipple.

I also remember the night, eight or so years before, when they'd fallen asleep with the television on, only to wake up in the middle of a late-night showing of *Jurassic Park*. Within minutes, they had both dived beneath the covers and were shrieking the word "*Inappropriate!*" on repeat until I came and switched the TV off.

Now, Fathead watched *Jurassic Park* movies to lech over Chris Pratt.

I mean, so did I, but that's not the point.

The tenor of our conversations changed as well, and I had more than one opportunity to regret the policy of complete openness that I had encouraged.

"Dad?"

"What?"

"You know anal sex?"

Well, that had just happened.

It had been Fathead who had asked the question, but Baldy had caught the scent of fear from the next room and bolted in to join the fun. And now they were both staring at me. I started to examine, with deep concern, a crack I had just invented in the ceiling.

"Dad!"

"Hmm?"

"Did you hear me?"

"Yes."

"Well?"

Tread carefully there, father of the year.

"I am aware of it, yes."

Well, I couldn't lie, could I? If they ever suspected that they knew more about sex than I did, I'd never live it down. And if I ever suspected that was true, I'd have to go and live in a cave.

"What about it?"

"Why would people even want to do that?"

What I wouldn't have given for a nice, juicy delusion right then. Such as the firm belief that this conversation was not happening.

"I mean," Baldy chucked in, "I get why you'd do it if you were gay, because that's how they love each other..."

So sweet and yet so problematic. What a child.

"Yeah, but you can do other things instead, if you're gay," said Fathead, "Like..."

"Everybody can do..."

"Of course, if you're a gay woman, then it's totally different..."

"Not necessarily," said Baldy, "Sometimes they use a..."

I'm not censoring anything here. I was genuinely blacking out at the end of each sentence, regaining consciousness for the beginning of the next and then sparking out again.

Damn it, I thought, I've done *too* good a job. They had zero hang-ups and they felt comfortable talking to me about literally anything. Whose stupid idea was that?

I realised that I had forgotten to take a number of very important things into account when I'd settled on the candid parenting style of which I was so annoyingly proud.

Firstly, that one day they'd be actually be old enough to make use of it for something other than naming body parts correctly.

Secondly, that while they might not have hang-ups—Go, Team Parent!—I sure as fuck did. I didn't raise me. We all know who raised me.

And, finally, that when you combined conversations like that with my overall lack of emotional availability and the fact that all of their friends now had breasts—put anything on a child and it ruins it forever, which is also why I can't eat mushy peas—I was never going to be able to look at another human in a sexual context ever again.

Along the same lines, whoever taught them that males determine the sex of a baby owes me an expensive lemonade, because in place of the bizarre squeamishness to which some fathers seem to succumb when faced with perfectly ordinary menstrual cycles, I spend a week of every month fetching painkillers and tampons, while they berate me for making them female.

I'd rather be that Dad than a believer in "ladies' things" but I didn't do it on purpose, so they need to lay off.

In the plus column, I've learned more about the experience of being a woman from the twins than from anyone else I've ever known. Because they have a tendency to tell me everything, I've had a running commentary about every thought and development that's cropped up along the way. For my sake, for which I thank them, they've kept the more personal aspects to the hypothetical, but it's been illuminating nonetheless.

I still know next to nothing about the experience of being a man. And the way things are going at the moment, I'm not sure I want to.

Also to my surging pride—and I choose that word with care—Fathead and Baldy don't stop at male and female. They intrinsically understand that gender is more complex than that. That sexuality is more complex. That people are more complex. There isn't a colour in the human rainbow that they haven't encountered and said, "Cool. Tell me more."

In fact, when it comes to anything that matters, there have been times when I've thought, "These kids are *really* well-adjusted. So open-minded. So empathetic. Maybe I wasn't quite as ill as I thought. Cause I appear to have done a bang-up job."

This was especially true that year, because I was in full recovering addict mode. The air smelt fresher, the food tasted better, my brain was a brand new toy, with so many wondrous, unexplored features. Like not snapping in two like a sun-dried twig.

I hadn't found my balance yet. I was coasting on conversion. I still laboured under the vain hope that my disease was gone for good and, from this point onwards, everything was going to be plain sailing.

222

When it came to the girls, I felt such a sense of relief that I hadn't damaged them over the course of my breakdown, that I elevated every positive—genuine gifts, actual traits of which to be proud—to a near messianic level. I was a good Dad. Just look at my kids.

Then, of course, I'd remember that they had other people in their lives, far more skilled than me, with greater emotional intelligence and decidedly better developed personalities—and that I once believed I could take over the world with an alternative country song about a girl I used to know.

And also that their room was still a tip.

I didn't need to pay less attention now that I was on the mend. I needed to pay more. Mends are slippery fuckers. You can't just *be* on them; you have to actively *stay* on them. And children are even slipperier.

Which is why it's important to remind them to wash.

223

Interval Fifteen
Bi the Power of Greyskull

Tomorrow is my birthday. I will be forty-two years old.

How the fuck did that happen?

That's not a rhetorical question, by the way. Well, not entirely. I always intended to die young, so it is possible that I'm just suffering the same sense of ennui that occurs whenever you realise a ship has sailed.

I don't think it's just that though. I keep going over the numbers and I swear that they don't add up.

Yes, I know everyone says that they don't feel their age—or, worse, makes progressively embarrassing attempts to feel someone younger, in order to test the popular theory—but, personally, I think my complaint has unique merits.

All those muddy, murky years. All those gaps. All that time spent being him, instead of me.

Frankly, considering I haven't been shorted on the downsides of ageing, I don't really feel I've had my money's worth of the ups. Most of my twenties are missing, for starters, other than some odd flashes of nudity and a faint taste of rum. I've been told I was almost pretty back then, if you approached me from a certain angle, so it seems a shame that I didn't get much of a go at it.

The first half of my thirties was a bit complicated, although, as far as I recall, it had its moments. The middle started well but then, as you've learned, turned into a long run-up to a short breakdown. And my teenage years? Well, forget about it.

Two quite different men have shared custody of this body over the decades and while, admittedly, they've both done their share of damage, I can't but help but feel that I got screwed in the divorce.

We've covered my lack of physical self-worth already, so I won't spend too much time cataloguing the post-warranty state of the place. It's the usual stuff, anyway—backs and knees and necks and an uncalled for level of anal discomfort. Other than the obvious mental aberrations and the ever-so-frolicsome side effects of treating them, I'm probably no worse off than most people my age.

And, maybe, looking on the bright-ish side, having my youth siphoned off as I did, I had less to lose than most. If you start at the bottom of the hill, it's not the descent you have to worry about. It's the digging.

Still, we have reached the point where the changes are noticeable. And, because it's me, capable of being obsessed over.

My hair started greying shortly after the twins were born, a causal link of which I remind them whenever they suggest that, maybe, just maybe, I might consider dying my roots before their friends come round. And by roots, of course, they mean head.

I do colour in, from time to time—one of the perks of being a performer is that everyone assumes it's for a role—but, increasingly, in an effort to keep it, I try to leave my hair to its own devices. So, for much of the year, it is now a shade that can only be described as mostly brown.

Making our way south, there are patches of my beard that are now whiter than my teeth, which, while still all my own, have taking a slight battering at the hands of British dentists. Who, though I loathe stereotyping, were clearly and collectively hugged insufficiently as children.

As far as I'm concerned, the best word to describe the entire face area is "haggard", although I have been told that I retain a boyish quality. I'm pretty sure that's code for "maybe it's time to lay off the skinny jeans" but I'll take what I can get.

My eyes aren't as blue as they were, but they look like they've seen some shit, and that's as it should be.

Hearing's not great, but that one's not age-connected. For that you can blame one drummer, two children and a series of ear infections that started my first winter in the UK and caused me to pass out in the stockroom of one Harriet Samuel's Jewellery Emporium, where I had taken a temporary Christmas job.

Neck. Something weird going on there. Can't quite put my finger on it, but I don't think it should fold that way.

The shoulders aren't bad. Bit slouchy, but a couple of weeks in the gym and they soon perk up again. You wouldn't think it to look at me, but I am capable of lifting really quite heavy things.

I just don't want to.

Torso. Nope. We're not talking about that. Except to say that if you had lost all sense of perspective, you might argue that one of the most tragic aspects of being forced to take medication for a serious mental health condition is that, despite it being one of your primary depressive triggers, it makes you pile on weight.

Everything between the waist and the ankles is fine, if a bit dusty in places.

Oh, and my feet hurt. Pretty much constantly.

225

All of that taken into account, I am more comfortable in my skin at forty-two than I was at, say, twenty-one. But I would also be more comfortable in a burning building than I was in my skin at twenty-one, so it's not actually saying a lot.

And, before you say anything, no, I'm not wiser. I'm just too tired to act on my stupidity.

The worst thing about ageing, other than physical or mental infirmity, is meant to be the encroaching sense of your own mortality. That thought that drops by unannounced one day, and says, "Hey. Just thought you ought to know—one day you won't exist and everything you've ever thought and felt will disappear into the ether as if it never happened. What's for dinner?"

Entire civilisations have been built up and destroyed over the desire to prove that one wrong.

The most repeated notion is that young people believe they are immortal, which is why they behave as though consequences were optional. I think that's true to an extent. When I was young, I definitely believed I was immortal. It's just that I was hacked off about it.

Even now that I have as much physical and emotional evidence as I could possibly need or want that I am slowly shuffling off this mortal coil—I'd shuffle more quickly, but I've got a dodgy hip—I remain unconcerned about not existing. The idea of being dead does not bother me.

Before you, very kindly, call a hotline on my behalf, I should clarify what I mean by that. Dead is nothing. Literally. I won't know about it, so why worry?

There are only two aspects of taking that long, dirt nap—restful and dirty sounds a brilliant combination—that upset me to contemplate. One is the thought that I will miss things. Won't ever read every book that I'd love. There may—this one keeps me up nights—end up being episodes of *Doctor Who* that I never see. And, slightly more importantly, there will be parts of my daughters' lives that I won't be around for.

Which leads me to the second bad thing about death

Most people's lists are longer, aren't they?

After everything I've put people through in the past, the idea of causing them further pain, especially by doing something as pointless as dying, makes me shudder. In a lot of ways, avoiding that is what keeps me alive now. And will do, so long as it's within my power.

Also, Fathead and Baldy have informed me, quite seriously, that I am not permitted to die. And, if anyone can alter the fabric of existence through willpower alone, it's those two.

So, we'll see.

In the meantime, I'll just keep my fingers crossed that I get better with age. I just might need a hand uncrossing them.

16: And What Do You Get?

What is it about the age of sixteen that has inspired so many poets, so many authors and so many musicians to behave so very creepily? Or, to use the correct verb, to Sedaka? (*i.e.* '*he Sedakad onto the dance floor at the high school prom and was immediately detained by police.*')

Fucked if I know. Even if it weren't skeevy as hell to suggest it, sixteen-year-olds aren't sweet. They're scary.

Let me tell you a story to illustrate my point. It's the last one in the book, so I'll try to make it as epic as possible.

That won't be hard to do.

As mentioned elsewhere, a child's sixteenth year, here in the UK, is pretty much ruined from the get-go by something called a GCSE. If you're from elsewhere, that probably sounds more like a disease than anything scholastic. And that's because it is.

I don't want to sound like I'm ragging on my adopted home. A desire to torture the young is a universal constant, so I'm sure most countries have their own equivalent. Some places still favour the rack, I'm informed. Here in the UK, however, the inquisition takes the form of a series of exams on the results of which, it is repeatedly explained to you, your entire future hangs. And you're forced to take them at sixteen, when you are at your most vulnerable and least organised.

If that doesn't scream for an amendment to the Human Rights Act, I don't know what does.

So, basically, I'd recovered my mind just in time for Fathead and Baldy to lose theirs. If you have children of their age, you will understand my fury at the degree of stress that was foisted upon their hormone-addled brains.

And don't get me started on the new grading system. One to nine. *One to nine.* I don't even have to go into more detail. You only have to look at those three words lying dead there on the page to see they're not right.

228

"Say, Johnny. What did you get on the big exam?"

"Five."

"Out of what?"

Johnny bursts into tears.

"I don't know."

Exactly. Fuck off.

Also, I was the one that had to live with them. I was the one who got screamed at every time I tried to teach them properly and was informed that common sense and actual knowledge had been removed from the curriculum due to budget cuts.

We got through them in the end. But I will say this. If you work in the Department of Education and you had anything to do with this latest attempt to reduce the wonders of learning to a bureaucratic crack dream, you'd better hope these pills keep working, or one night, the last sound you ever hear will be a Canadian goose call, followed by a bottle of maple syrup being swung with great force.

You have been warned.

Look, it was a hard year. I was only just back on my feet mentally, only just beginning, with great trepidation, to consider the likelihood of the possibility of the chance of dipping my toes back into artistic waters.

The girls were stressed to hell. They needed to let off some steam.

They wanted to have a party.

Which was the first sign that we were dealing with people who were not at their best.

The desire of the teenage human to host parties is as old as recorded time. Or it would be, except the teenagers *at* the second party spilled mammoth blood on the cave painting *about* the first party and tried to blame it on the dog.

In our family, we have never had much luck with parties. When I was sixteen, I only ever attended them so that I could sneak upstairs with a guitar and write satirical songs about the idiots cosying up to each other— in that chaste Christian manner that leads to brainwashed young gay men marrying frustrated future alcoholics—on the improvised dancefloor below.

The songs weren't much better.

Anyway, the girls had two strikes against them on the party front. One, we'd tried this before and it had always ended up with some idiot kid—usually some slightly younger tagalong—getting hold of a beer when I wasn't looking and throwing up on something or someone or both.

229

Two, they had seen every single American teen comedy ever made and, so, knew exactly what they were signing up for. Whatever happened next, it was entirely self-inflicted.

However, I have to be fair. They were sixteen-year-old girls at the end of their tethers, wanting to impress their friends and have a good time. I was the moron who, moved by their plight—and tired of being nagged at—gave the go ahead for the blow-out of all blow-outs.

They got me in the end with "don't you trust me?"

Why do we always fall for that? That's not a simple yes or no answer with teenagers. My kids are brilliant and I completely trust, with my life, the people they will be in four or five years. Their sixteen-year-old selves I wouldn't trust with a stuffed rabbit. That's not a judgement, just an acknowledgement of adolescence as a mental illness.

Obviously, said blow-out was not described in such high-flying terms, but as "a few friends coming round. Just to chill out and de-stress."

It sounds like an old-fashioned round of fondue and wife-swapping when you put it like that. Still, as grim as that would be, it would still be preferable to what actually happened.

I was out for the first hour of the party, attending a work event of my own. I can't remember what, as I spent the entire time worrying that the house was on fire.

Don't be silly, I kept telling myself. It's all going to be fine. They're good kids. You trust them, sort of. And even if, God forbid, there was a fire, that kid would probably throw up on it and save the day.

I'd informed their mother and stepmother that the party was happening and asked if they could keep their ears out for trouble, until I returned.

At first, it seemed as if my fears had been unfounded. Their Mum called me on my way home, to report that she'd spoken to them and it didn't sound like anyone was dying or losing their virginity.

I walked through the door. Set down my bag. Took off my shoes. Hung up my coat.

Stepped into my front room.

I believe I'm right in saying that there were seven thousand sixteen-year-olds there that night. And they were all angry.

Not angry at anything in particular, just in a general state of pubescent discontent. It wasn't surprising, and I don't know why I had expected anything else. They were all under enormous pressure and most of them hadn't started having sex yet. I had just stepped into a fireworks factory with a lit cigarette.

The doors to the garden were open, to accommodate the crowd. The music was thumping hard enough to qualify as at least a welterweight in most professional boxing circles.

It was pretty clear what had happened. In accordance with the golden rule of house parties, the thing had snowballed. And if there's one thing you should always avoid, it's a golden snowball.

You know the drill. You invite your friends, they invite their friends, they tell the guy at the bus stop who keeps the dead squirrel in his pocket and he tells his colleagues at the Small Business Association. Before long, your home is full of strangers, all hoping for a bit of a grope and a purloined bottle of Smirnoff Ice.

I spotted Fathead and Baldy pressed up against a far wall, with looks of barely contained panic on their faces. It was clear they'd lost control of the situation and beneath the layers of thick makeup and the currently fashionable Groucho eyebrows, the eyes of two frightened little girls shone out like distress beacons.

I made a quick and easy decision. This was not a job for shouty-father-man, despite my every prediction having come true. This was a job for Dad.

Not "I told you so" but "I tell you what".

I did a quick circuit, so that everyone could see an adult was in play. I checked all the rooms with closed doors to prevent having a series of unwanted children named after me, and then I set to putting out fires.

Metaphorical, thankfully,

Conflagration number one involved separating a young couple who were sat on the twins' bed, their faces inches apart. Not in a romantic way, unless you count shouting at full volume romantic, which I know some people do.

"IF YOU REALLY LOVED ME, YOU'D LOOK AT ME!"

"IF YOU REALLY LOVED ME, YOU WOULDN'T HAVE SAID WE WERE OVER!"

"I SAID THE ARGUMENT WAS OVER!"

"Guys?"

"WHAT?!"

"If you really loved me, you'd chill the fuck out and go downstairs. Thank you."

Conflagration number two involved a pair of girls who, in a dispute over a boy, had forgotten their first language and were now communicating entirely in dolphin.

"Guys?"

"CLICK?"

"WHISTLE?"

231

"He looks like a hedgehog. You're both better off. Sit the fuck down."

Quick side job—work out where the kid had thrown up this time. The alleyway. Ah, well. Could have been worse.

But then came the pièce de résistance. The event that earned this story its place at the climax of ours.

Having sorted out everything on the edges of the party, and herded everyone back to the central corral, I returned to the living room to check on the girls.

To find everyone now screaming, grasping and leaping at each other, like the Battle of Thermopylae as sponsored by Clearasil. The boys were pretending to hold each other back, and the girls were attacking at will.

I moved untouched across the battlefield like the world's worst Florence Nightingale impersonator, took up a central position and drew on all of my voice projection training.

"IT IS TIME," I boomed, like an Old Testament prophet, "FOR YOU ALL TO GO HOME."

Silence fell. The reflex of students when a teacher gets pissed.

But there's always one.

"Dumb bitch," said a voice.

I turned to see a teenage boy, who I didn't recognise, standing against one wall. He had the build of a weasel that had tangled with a fairy godmother. His face looked like the penis he clearly wanted us to measure.

He had directed his comment to one of the girls, and it was obvious that whatever the fight had been about, they were at the epicentre.

There was a beat of silent outrage, and then she leapt through the air like a cat. She'd probably have clawed his beady little eyes out, if her boyfriend hadn't grabbed her by the waist and pulled her back on to the sofa, cursing and scratching.

"IF YOU REALLY LOVED ME, YOU WOULDN'T LEAP THROUGH THE AIR LIKE A CAT!"

I stepped forward, aiming to shut the whole thing down while everyone was still in their separate corners.

Before I could intervene, however, the dick did the worst thing you could possibly do when faced with a pissed-off, pissed-up teenage girl.

He laughed.

It was a short, obnoxious sound—born of testosterone, lager and sexual inadequacy—and it seemed to echo sickeningly from the walls and ceiling.

And suddenly there wasn't a pair of buttocks in the room that couldn't have clasped a pencil.

The boyfriend stood up, snorting steam. The unfortunate side effect of which was that his grip loosened sufficiently for his girlfriend to wriggle free, clamber onto the arm of the sofa and prepare for flight.

In the nick of time, four of her friends leapt across the room and tugged firmly, but gently, at the hem of her skirt. Enough to hold her back, but not enough to damage the clothing, which they knew to be recently purchased. She turned and hissed at them. They wailed back.

Enough was enough.

"Right," I barked, addressing the interloper, "You. Get out of my house."

If I hadn't been the grown-up, the whole crowd would have ooh'd. As it was, they just watched glassy-eyed and swore under their breaths.

Baldy started to cry. Baldy doesn't cry.

Fathead started to laugh nervously. She does that.

And, then, in possibly the greatest moment of my life to date, this scrawny little oik, who looked as if he'd weigh about a hundred pounds if his pockets were full of rocks, stepped forward, and in a misguided effort to impress the friends by which he was flanked, squared up to me.

It was in that moment that I realised how far I'd come. After everything I'd been through, everything I'd suffered, the years of madness and recovery, the tears and the fuck-ups, the confusion and the despair, I finally knew who I was.

I was the father of these two girls and I was going to save the day.

Neck. Scruff. Door. Out.

And don't come fucking back.

All that remained was to arrange seven thousand taxis, negotiate with fourteen thousand parents who fucking well owed me one, then hose down the vomiting wonder and return him to the safety of his own home.

Later that night, as we went off to bed, Baldy hugged me, unprompted, and begged to be grounded. Fathead told me she loved me and thanked me in a tone of voice I don't think she'd ever used before.

I was exhausted and could feel the first flashes of a migraine sparking behind my eyes. But I didn't look at the mess. I didn't think about tomorrow.

It didn't matter.

I had done what needed to be done. I'd taken care of things. I'd been a hero to my daughters.

I'd just had one of the best nights of my life.

Which, if nothing else, was proof that I still could.

And that changes everything.

233

Say Hello, Wave Good Bi

It's eight o'clock on a Monday morning and I'm standing at my kitchen window with a mug of coffee clasped between my hands. The view isn't especially inspiring—the back of the weather-worn fence that separates our garden from the neighbour's—but it doesn't really matter.

I'm not looking at anything in particular.

Upstairs, Fathead and Baldy are stomping and shouting and crashing around, which has always been their preferred way of starting the day.

To the uninitiated, it might seem cacophonous, but to me, each sound has its own unique timbre and thrusts a familiar picture into my head. The relatively quiet scuffle for the mirror as they apply their make-up. The barks of frustration and bursts of profanity as they trade accusations about the current location of each other's belongings. The threat-laden invocations of my name when one of them "accidentally" thumps the other.

There's a sequence to it—a pattern—that, for all of its hormonal fury, I can't help but find comforting. Repetition is no longer the bamboo beneath my fingernails, but a rare and precious sign that all is as it should be.

An inscrutable smile plays over my lips. I cock my head to one side and count silently down.

Five, four, three, two, one.

And there it is, bang on time. The first irregular thump of their wardrobe door, signifying that the process of trying on and discarding every item of clothing in the house, including those I laughably refer to as mine, has begun.

It lasts a little longer than usual this time, but then I imagine it will from now on. Because this isn't an ordinary Monday. Not by a long shot. It's another in what feels, especially lately, like an endless succession of near luminescent red-letter ones.

For, this morning, my daughters—who I swear were only born a few hundred pages ago—are readying themselves for their first day of college. And, as if that weren't pressure enough, they have, in recognition of their new ranks, been released from the uniform requirements that have dictated their sartorial choices for the last eleven years.

Once, I would have celebrated this development. With cake, perhaps, or the life-blood of a consecrated goat. Of the many bees that, in my time, I've imprisoned in my headgear, the subject of enforced dress codes was always amongst the most sting-happy. "Down with educational homogenisation!" I was often heard to bark, before, hand on breast, bellowing out selections from *Another Brick in the Wall (Part 2)*.

Like most of my historic rants, it was wildly over-the-top and unpleasantly steeped in condescension.

I had my reasons, though. Or so I told myself. I was not—am not—overly fond of institutions, for example, and where I came from, school uniforms were worn exclusively by spoilt rich kids, and middle-aged adult performers.

Also, the fucking things were expensive, with the specialist shops that sold them taking full advantage of your lack of options. The week before every new term felt like queuing to placate the Sheriff of Nottingham.

For every obligation, you will find a profiteer.

But now that they're no longer a part of our lives, I finally understand the point of them. And not the much vaunted intention of levelling the social classes, but the incidental effect of giving parents half a chance at levering their children out of the house in the morning. With unlimited outfit choices at their disposal, I'm concerned they may never leave.

In fact, I'm starting to wonder if this is how the concept of gap years started.

A memory trundles unbidden into my mind. Two little girls in identical checked dresses, their first ever school crest embroidered in the corners. Excited to a degree that only five-year-olds seem to be able to manage. You could power the white goods department of a decently-sized department store with their smiles.

It's funny how nostalgic you can become about things you used to hate. How often you ache for what were once your fears.

There was a time, it strikes me, not so very long ago, when I would have stood atop this same section of linoleum, drinking a very similar cup of coffee and eavesdropping on a version of the same teenage machinations, and—instead of beaming like a Buddha, as I am now—been in floods of tears. The day ahead would have seemed like a sentence, my to-do list curling off the page like a curse. They could have used the wall of adolescent noise, as I experienced it then, to drive dictators from their bunkers.

Now, it's all just… life.

It's not perfect. If you look closely, you'll see a slight, but obvious tremble in my hands, the subtle dyskinesia of the medicated man. If you listen very carefully—and can hear anything at all over Fathead cursing out her sister's bathroom etiquette—you'll hear a weak but insistent voice inviting me to fuck it all off and run. And if you are very attentive indeed, you might catch

235

the occasional flick of my eyes to a framed picture on the opposite wall, and find yourself overwhelmed by the impulse to call a loved one, just because.

I am forty-two years old. I am a single father. I have bipolar disorder and a lonesome heart.

This isn't a happy ending.

It isn't an ending at all.

I glance at the clock and briefly think about calling the twins down, then decide to remain in my bubble of calm for a few sips longer.

Steam drifts up from the lip of my mug and I stare into it, as though expecting to glimpse the future in its depths.

Instead, I see today.

Epilogue

So, here we are at last. At the end and the beginning.

The end, of course, for you—unless you're planning to start again at the top to see if makes any more sense the second time round—and the beginning for me, because I'm the idiot who actually has to follow this epistle with the rest of an actual life.

Over the months I've spent writing this, I have attempted, once or twice, to narrow in on some kind of endgame, a philosophy with which to leave you. Something a little more profound than be nice to each other and ask for help when you need it.

Not only would it have tied everything together with a pleasingly lacy bow, but I might have secured a lecture tour or, at worst, a small group of coffee-fetching disciples.

It also, unfortunately, would have been completely inconsistent with everything that came before. And while I'm not usually averse to contradicting myself, or able to prevent it, this does not feel like the time or place.

This was never, for reasons that should be apparent, going to be a tale about getting it right, but rather about getting it done. The point of its existence, if it must have one, has been to share my conviction that survival is not only possible, but desirable. That, even if mental illness has bruised your life, it doesn't have to break it. At least, not permanently.

And it's kept me off the streets.

My particular focus has been on parenting, because that's the experience that altered my perspective. But it's not the only one that can. Whatever it is that piques your curiosity, cling on to it with all your might. It may kill cats, but it can save people.

Likewise, I hope those for whom raising children *is* their primary source of mental disturbance might have found some comfort in the reminder that they too are not alone. And that their children are probably not trying to kill them. It only feels that way.

I hope you laughed. That above all else.

Which leaves only one final question.

Why in the name of holy fuck didn't I call this book "Biography"?

Seems like the obvious choice, on paper, doesn't it? Especially considering the effort—and glee—I've put into the rest of the bi-related puns on offer. I can only apologise and hope the fact that I didn't go down that road hasn't caused you too much distress. I know it might have done me.

I considered it, you can be assured of that. It was written down and scratched out so many times that the girls, fearing I might injure myself, eventually hid my pencils.

But, in the end, I decided against it. On the grounds of rank inaccuracy.

This isn't my memoir. It isn't my life. There are too many people absent, too many thoughts unrecorded, too many convictions uncommuted and far, far too little nudity. Instead, it has been, as the final title suggests, an exploration.

I don't know where it led you, other than the refund counter of your favoured bookseller, but I ended up in a very different place to where I started.

I know myself a little better. I even like myself a little more. And while I've always been grateful for the people that have graced my life, especially but not limited to my children, compressing the last sixteen years between covers has served to remind me how lucky I've been, and in how many ways.

Plus, I finished a fucking book.

And now—not for the first or last time, I hope—so have you.

Acknowledgments

There are a huge number of people who have had an impact on this story, and I'd be heartbroken to think that because their contributions have not been acknowledged in the text—partly for artistic reasons, but primarily to keep our relationships out of the courts—that they are any less important to me.

I hope this section goes some way towards redressing the balance. If not, I shall take comfort in the fact that it will pad out the word count nicely.

***

To my children, whom I adore. The whole bloody book is about you. What more do you want?

Fine.

I could not be more proud of who you are, or who you are becoming. Fathead, you are kind and you are gifted. Baldy, you are wise and you are hilarious. Being your Dad has more than made up for anything bad that's happened in my life. Up to and including the year that you were obsessed with *iCarly*.

I love you.

***

To the woman who believes that she didn't do enough, doesn't do enough and cannot do enough—if you had half as much faith in yourself as I do in you, you'd be unbearable. Suffice it to say, I wouldn't be half of the human or the father I am without your influence, then and now. The rest of it, I hope you know.

***

To the woman who gave me the greatest gift a man could ever receive—it's a little battered now, but it still plays beautifully with a new set of strings on it.

Oh, and the children are alright too, I suppose.

Without your love, your friendship and your support—often undeserved—I would not be here. So, it's at least partly your fault.

***

To Steven Page and Stephen Fry—your respective bodies of work and courage in sharing your experiences with mental illness have, for me, genuinely and repeatedly made the difference between surviving and the other thing. I'll even forgive you for spelling your names differently, which prevented me from composing a far more graceful opening sentence to this paragraph.

***

To a certain rebel Time Lord, who has, since I was a child, transcended (dimensionally) their supposed fictional status to serve as comfort and inspiration in my darkest hours—I'm ready when you are. Just have me back in time to make dinner.

And to Colin Baker, who once lent the above his face—thank you for making a nonsense of the suggestion that you should never meet, let alone work with, your heroes.

***

As for the rest of you, to maintain continuity, I've granted you each a sobriquet of your own, based on our shared experiences. My hope is that you recognise yourself sufficiently not to give me shit about it.

I fully expect that hope to be dashed.

The Seer—You were my first mentor. I'd know nothing of jazz, comics or the Old Ones without you. You are also my longest-serving friend, the weirdest person I know and a stonkingly good writer. We are tied by bonds of background, trauma and religious extremism, but also by a love of words and the magic of which they are capable. In the end, you became a mystic and I became whatever the fuck I am, which I think nods at balance in the universe.

Shifty "Don't Call Me Shifty" McShifty—I miss you, idiot. And you've missed so much. The twins are sixteen now. Two more years and I could have forbidden you to take them drinking.

Also, did you hear? I made a movie, just like we always talked about. It was really hard, and, frankly, I could have done with your help. But I did it and you were in my thoughts the whole time. Pointing and laughing. Wherever you are, I hope you're making a nuisance of yourself. Haunt me if you get into trouble.

The Almighty Beard—You are the loudest man in the world, the only Englishman I know who can wear a trucker cap without irony, and the possessor of the most intriguing mind I have ever encountered. Even if it can't hold on to appointments to save its life.

Big Man—You are my Gaelic brother in both life and art, a man who texts me daily and knows instinctively when I'm off my game, but nonetheless grants me the dignity of calling me a dick whenever it is either deemed necessary and or you consider it funny.

The Hippie—You are the only person I've ever known with whom I have never fallen out. For many reasons, but mostly because you are too kind to attract controversy, too talented not to keep on side and too tall to slap. Also, thank you for the title for Interval Fifteen, which is easily the funniest thing in the book.

Bow-Wow Bunny Rabbit—We've recently reconnected to beautiful effect and you once head-butted me on-stage to see if I'd keep singing. And, if you recall, I did. Friends like that are hard to find. Mostly due to the head trauma.

The Professor—Once upon a time, I met a madman in a bar. An eccentric stargazer, with a long-suffering boyfriend and the kind of sartorial flair that I had previously believed to be the sole province of P.G. Wodehouse protagonists. You are one of a kind. Probably by law.

Dorian Yay—I am clearly the portrait in your attic, but you inspire me daily. I'd have wanted to be you when I grew up, if you hadn't had the unmitigated gall to be younger than me. You are a fantastic actor and director, an even better friend, and when you read Camus to me, I am more than a little aroused.

The Wise Man—You don't like Christmas and you will steal from me. Also, your mum's a Travelodge. In-jokes are fun! You are a fascinating creature and I love to see the world through your unique and caring eyes. When I picture us conversing, we are always wearing smoking jackets and sipping brandy from elaborate receptacles. But that's my problem, not yours.

The Wizard—I come to you for quiet and magic. Far too infrequently, I fear, but never without joy. I have never met a human who wears their talents more lightly, and your existence in this world gives me hope for its future. Also, I'd love to see you dressed as a pirate for some reason.

The Harlequin—Yet another person in my life whose talents outstrip their confidence in them and whose kindness outstrips that which they've received. You're an artist, even when you don't feel like one. Never forget that.

The Actress—Despite your bewildering inability to embrace the genius that is William Shatner and a worrying addiction to Battleships, you are an inspired and faultlessly giving person who deserves everything grand.

The Writer—You are quite ludicrous, in the best possible way. My dearest wish for you, other than receiving the respect you are due for your intelligence and wit, is that you may always ride large stuffed animals in public.

***

Along the way, there have been others who have stood by my side, supported my dreams and shared my life, despite their own being fractured by my chaos. I strongly suspect some of them would not want to be represented here, even obliquely. I shall, as they deserve, respect their wishes, but I hope they know that there is a corner of my heart that will always be theirs.

***

And, finally to **The Chinbeard**, my newest friend.

You asked me, possibly due to a recent brain injury, to write this book. Throughout the process I have been both eternally grateful and desperate for revenge, depending on how well it was going at the time.

You also do a mean Tim Brooke-Taylor and, no, I am not rephrasing that.

Index

À la recherche du temps perdu (book), 33
adoption, shotgun, 66
ageing, 65, 224–26
air pump, battery-operated, *43*
Alarming, Prince. See Narrator, Subjective
alcohol
   excessive consumption of, 2, 44, 45
alligators
   freedom of to fuck right off, 71
alliteration
   vomit-making use of, 38
Andrews, Julie, 7
anemone. See sorry
Angel Gabriel, The, 212
anger
   Baldy's approach to, 21, 46, 67
   effect of mental illness on, 102–5
   Fathead's approach to, 164
   loss of, 219
Another Brick in the Wall (Part 2) (song), 233
Argumenta (bruise), 26
arrogance
   accidental development of, 54
assembly, school, 209–15
asshole, 107, 190
attic
   absence from childhood home of, vi
avocado
   life cycle of, 89

babies
   general dopiness of, 5
Baker, Colin, 239
Bakula, Scott, 201
balaclava, bee-based, 38
Banner, Robert Bruce, 88
Baptist, John the, 141–42
barbarians
   relatively low gate-flanking number of, 89
Barbie Girl (song), 78
Basílica i Temple Expiatori de la Sagrada Família, 68
Battle of Stalingrad, The, 38
Battle of Thermopylae, The, 230
Battleships (game), 242
Bear in the Big Blue House (programme), 67
Beatrice (hypothetical construct), 61
Bedlam, 55
bereavement, 17

Bieber, Justin, 84
Bill and Ted's Excellent Adventure (film), 185
biography
   seemingly obvious, yet unused, title for this book, 236
bipolar disorder, v, vi
   classification of self by, 82
   diagnosis, 2
   effect of religion on, 89–90
   effect on memory, 200–201
   fear of passing on, 46
   generational complications of, 12
   groanworthy puns about, 12, 24, 37, 54, 77, 86, 102, 116, 132, 153, 169, 184, 200, 216, 224, 233, 236
   idiocy surrounding, 15, 40
   impact on relationships of, 24–29
   life-long nature of, 88–89
   misconceptions about, 56
   reclamation of slurs about, 25, 55
   recovery from, 216–17
   secrecy about, 21
   stigma surrounding, 25, 54–64
   survival tips for, 236
   symptoms of, vi, 14, 17, 22, 44, 50, 78–79, 86, 91–93, 102–5, 132–38, 153–58, 169–73, 181–82, 193–94, 209
body image, 132–38
books
   arguably over-the-top addiction to, 20
   children's ambivalence towards, 82
boyfriend
   fictional dead body of, 43
Bragg, Billy, 30
breakdown, 2, 93, 209–15, 209–15
Brooke-Taylor, Tim, 242
Brothers Grimm, The, 163
bullying, 71
business
   none of your fuckingness of, 40
By the End of this Book, You Won't Notice Anymore – Conquering ODC (made-up book, probably), 106
Byron, George Gordon, 45

Callioopsyadaisy (bruise), 27
Camus, Albert, 240
Canadians
   wildly stereotypical proclamations about, 2

Cantankerachore (bruise), 26
cardigan, sturdy, 124
Carroll, Lewis, 44
Cassandra (rhetorical device), 191
Cassidy, Butch, 120
Cat-in-the-Hat, The, 163
Charlie's Angels (film), 83
Chess Records, 57
childhood
    ridiculousness of, 1
    self-righteousness during, 6
children
    abrupt appearances by, 48
    aptitude for darkness of, 71
    awareness of human mortality of, 94
    birth of, 1
    capacity to cause weeping of, 60
    career plans of, 124–29
    changes in, 164–65
    downside to intelligence of, 33
    first words of, 10
    grief at maturation of, 30
    hilarious nicknames for, 3
    mic-dropping proficiency of, 33
    ruthless honesty of, 17
    sarcasticness of, 6
    similarity to comedians of, 18
    threatening phone calls from, 7
    uncanny perceptiveness of, 22
Christ, Jesus, 14
Citizen Kane (film), 127
Clair de Lune (composition), 111
Claus, Santa, 94, 143
clowns
    subconscious infestation of, v
clumsiness, 20
Cold Turkey (song), 7
common sense
    comprehensive lack of, 91
cookies
    long-winded and repeated metaphor regarding,
    19, 71
co-parenting, 160–64
Cosmopolitan
    judgemental questionnaire in, 30
Costello, Elvis, 20
cult
    attitude to holidays of, 141–43
    attitude toward politics of, 184
    membership of, 1, 89–90

Dahl, Roald, 74

day job. See discomfort, anal
Dazed and Confused (song), 209
Dead Poets Society (film), 74
Dean, James, 193
Debussy, Achille-Claude, 111
Deceptinor (bruise), 25
Denny's (restaurant), 56
dentists
    moral turpitude of, 225
Denver, John, 40
Dickens, Charles, 139
disciples
    coffee-procuring duties of, 236
discomfort, anal, 6, 16, 224
Disney Channel, The, 193
Doctor Who (programme)
    nerdy reference to, 4, 164, 226, 239
    super nerdy reference to, 217
Doctor, The, 239
Dorsey, Arnold. See Humperdinck, Englebert
Durex
    suggested revisions to advertisements for, 67
Dylan, Bob, 185
dyskinesia. See medication, side effects of

Eaton-Jones, Barnaby, 242
Ed (lesser deity), 26
Education, Department of
    semi-serious threat of violence to, 228
ego
    male, 6
Einstein, Albert
    erroneous attribution to, 11
Elba, Idris
    muscle tone of, 31
elephants, pink. See alcohol

faeces
    human, 7
father
    mental illness of, 1, 2
feminism. See gender roles
film
    predictable scripted section pertaining to,
    175–80
    that dare not speak its name, v, 174–82, 210
Final Cut X (computer software), 216
Fonda, Jane, 190
fools
    joyless tolerance of, 54
fork, tuning, *43*
Frank (hypothetical construct), 61

Freaky Friday (film), 193
Fry, Stephen, 12, 239

Gatwick Airport, 200
GCSE Examinations
    evilness of, 78, 227–28
gender roles, 116–22
Gibson, Mel, 44
giraffe
    as baby name, 187
    as outerwear, 187
God
    anger management issues of, 1, 2
    children's interest in, 1
    estrangement from, 16, 1
    hearing impairment of, 90
    homophobia of, 212
    pointless conversation with, 213
Grant, Ulysses S
    songwriting tips received from departed spirit
        of, 25
growing up
    rank stupidity of, 65
G-string
    laudable resistance to jokes about, 7
guano, chiropteran, 3

H Samuels (business), 225
HAL 9000, 50
Hallucina (deity), 25
Hamlet (play), 56
Hamm, Jon, 70
Hammerstein, Oscar, 13
Hawking, Stephen, 14
Heartstrings (possibly made-up film), 46
Herod Antipas, 141
Herod, brother of Herod, 141
Herod, father of Herod and Herod, 142
Herodias, wife of Herod and Herod, 141
Him, 28, 38, 44, 59, 88, 89, 93, 107, 122, 169,
    200–208, 219, 224
Hitler, Adolf, 55
Hughes, Ted, 13
Hulk, The, 88
Human Rights Act, The, 227
Humperdinck, Englebert, 200–208

iCarly (programme), 238
Illuminati, The, 88
insomnia, 50
intermission
    unnecessary inclusion of, 123

Interventia (deity), 27

jackassery
    common or garden, 24, 86
    illness-related, 86
Janet and John (children's books), 81
Jefferson Airplane (band), 44
Jeremy the Idiot, 119
jokes, Dad, 153
Juan, Don, 24
Jurassic Park (film), 221

Kafka, Franz, 17
keys.
    mysterious relocation of, 16
Kierkegaard, Søren, 9
kindness, 60
King, Stephen, 65
Knotts, Don, 24
Kraft Dinner, 82, 91
Kurosawa, Akira, 180

Latin
    mutual origin of damn near everything from,
        169
    occasional incantations in, 6
Laurie, Hugh, 20
lawnmower, ride-on, 43
left-handedness, 20
Limbaugh, Rush, 185
Livin' On A Prayer (song), 80
loneliness, 162
Lord of the Rings, The, 40
Lottery
    nightmare about winning, 124
Loudest Drummer in the World, The, 69
    effect on reproductive systems of, 69
love
    romantic, 77
    unconditional, 4
Lucidia (bruise), 27
Lungbarrow (novel), 217
Luxembourg
    percentage of people able to spell, 44

MacGyver (programme), 218
Magnus IV, King of Sweden, 219
Marathon Man (film), 18
Marx Brothers, The, 45
masculinity, toxic. See gender roles
Matilda (film)
    repeated viewings of, 83

McWhackjob, Hippie, 4
medication
  acceptable dishonesty of, 38
  conspiracy theories regarding, 39
  controversy regarding, 37–42
  resistance to taking, 2
  side effects of, 2, 40, 102, 107, 216–17, 218–23,
  224, 225, 234
  unsuitability of potatoes as a substitute for, 37
Men
  What are they good for?. See nothing,
  absolutely
Men are from Mars and Karen is Self-Righteous
  (made-up book, probably), 106
Mental Health Awareness Week, 62
Middle East
  sensible decision to avoid discussion of, 37
Mittens
  purely imaginary but nonetheless stressful
  illness of, vi
Mnemofiend (bruise), 26
moat
  insufficiently explained anecdote regarding, 38
Monobrow (hypothetical grandchild), 84
mother
  mental illness of, 1
motherfucker
  moderately successful attempt not to say, 59
Moustache (hypothetical grandchild), 84
Muppet Show, The (programme), 2
music
  as identity, 79
  obsession with career in, 90–93
mythology, Greek
  pretentious joke about, 9

Nancy (lesser diety), 26
Narrator, Subjective, 159, 165–68, 175–80
  geekiness of, 169
  oblique reference to potential extraterrestial
  origin of, 43
  open letter to, 216–17
  partial homosexuality of, 69, 108, 212
National Express, 139, 200
nature vs nurture, 153–58
Nazi Death Robot, 73
Neglectia (bruise), 26
Nelson, Horatio, 56
Nelson, Willie, 46
New Orleans (city), 116
newspaper columnists, elderly, 34

nicotine
  loveliness of, 6–7, 98
  unsuitability as replacement for medication, 87
night terrors, 47
Nightingale, Florence, 230
Nine Bruises, The, 25
nothing, absolutely, 116
Nottingham, Sheriff of, 234
nudity
  lack of, 237
  vague memories of, 224
nuns
  hot cross, 4

Obama, Barack, 190
obsession, 169–73, See bipolar disorder,
  symptoms of
O'Malley, Rabbi, 41
otter, drawing of
  failure to be shoes of, 68

Page, Steven, 239
painful lives
  avoiding ludicrous bookstore classification as,
  vi
paper
  fear of, v
Paradise by the Dashboard Light (song), 142
Paranoia (deity), 25
Parent Trap, The (film), 193
parenting
  lack of murderous intent of one's children, 236
  single, 3, 17, 24
  smugness about, 7
  worries regarding, 1
parents
  children's relationship to, 153–58
  estrangement from, 8
  mutual antipathy of, 1
passengers, bus
  unpleasant nature of, 8
peas
  digital manipulation of, 164
perambulations, nocturnal. See sleepwalking
Perceptiona (bruise), 25
Petty, Tom, 96
Piña Colada Song, The (song), vi
Plath, Sylvia, 13
polecats
  bereavement-related hygiene neglect of, 15
politics, 184–92

pornography
    free-range, ethically produced variants of, 24
possession
    demonic, 8
post-credits sequence, 252
Pratt, Chris, 221
prejudice, 56

Quantum Leap (programme), 201
quitter
    failure of Mama to raise, 91

racket, tennis
    failure to be shoes of, 68
Rapunzel
    substance abuse issues pertaining to, 45
Rashomon (film), 180
rats, imaginary, 50
raves
    as hypothetically thrown by the Amish, vi
Reefer Madness (film), 142
relationships
    effect of children on, 73
    effect of illness on, 25
    fuck-up to success ratio of, v
    *self-deprecating but hideously true material
    about,* 25
Release Me (song), 200
religion
    clean-living nature of, 6
    collusion with bipolar disorder of, 89–90
    feelings about, 112
    impact on childhood of, 72
    objection to wearing trousers due to, 78
    parents' subscription to, 1
remains
    human, mince-adjacent, 4
Rodgers, Richard, 13
Rogers, Prince Nelson, 127
rompers
    disturbing allusion to adults wearing, 31
Ryder, Winona, 2

Saint Etienne (band), 98
Sainte-Marie, Buffy, 98
Salome, 142
Satan
    statistical unlikeliness of being, 186
Sausage Fingers (hypothetical grandchild), 84
scholarship
    marmot-herding, 13
Schweitzer, Albert, 106

scrounger
    inability of Daily Mail readers to spell, 9
Sedaka, Neil, 227
self-destruction
    extreme predilection for, 10, 16
sexism. See gender roles
sexuality
    bewilderment over, 6, 134
    uncomfortable conversations about, 221–22
Shane (childhood bully), 72–73
Shannon, Del, 96
Shatner, William, 242
shoelaces
    lifelong inability to tie correctly, 20
Showgirls (film), 48
shrimp fork
    as murder weapon, 83
siblings
    ludicrous number of, 1
sleepeating, 50
sleepwalking, 48
smoking
    cessation of. See nicotine, loveliness of
Smurfs
    childhood traumas involving, 13
snowflake, liberal, 59
Solomon, King, 73
sorry
    relative word hardness of, 43
spaghetti
    intoxicated preparation of, 16
Stand by Me (film), 65
Stardust, Ziggy, 22
Starfleet Academy, 65
steel band, Trinidadian, 49
step-parenting, 160–64
Steve (bruise), 27
suicide
    recovery from attempt at, 198
    supposed selfishness of, 58
Sundance Kid, The, 120

teachers
    importance of, 77
teenagers
    parties thrown by, 228–32
    reality of life with, 193–99
    religiously motivated burning of, 12
Ten Ways to Lift Depression – and Strengthen
    Those Inner Thighs (made-up book,
    probably), 106

Thatcher, Denis
    use as derogatory metaphor for mental illness, 25
The Exorcist (film), 67, 96
The Ring (film), 96
The Saturday Boy (song), 30
Thing One. See Fathead
Thing Two. See Baldy
Tigger
    as spirit animal, 13
toilet paper
    unfortunate absence of, 103
tombola, enchanted, 26
Tone-O-Soft, 128
Tormé, Mel, 44
Tour de France, 55
towels
    misconduct surrounding, 4
Treaty of Versailles, The, 39
Tree of Rusty Nails and Gangrene, The, 38
Trevor the Man, 119
triggering
    mixed feelings regarding, 59
Trump, Donald. See asshole
Twain, Mark
    erroneous attribution to, 11
twins
    buggy-related incidents involving, 8
    conversational benefit of being, 69
    differences between, 18
    effect of The Shining on perception of, 5, 18
    surprise existence of, 4
    teamwork of, 32
    telepathic abilities of, 33
    weird-ass bond between, 31–33

Uptown Girl (song), 78

vasectomies
    helpful literature regarding, 9
veal
    soy-based substitute, 88
Verve, The, 39
veterinarians
    sinister cabal of, 25

water
    dryness deficiency of, 39
Waters, Muddy, 57
Watership Down (book), 90
weasels
    obligatory inclusion of, because funny, 56

weight loss, 17
What the fuck was that?. See night terrors
Wheaton, Wil, 65
When Bears Attack (book), 83
When the Levee Breaks (song), 209
White Rabbit
    comparative allusion to song that is not half as clever as it thinks it is, 44
    fictional character, 44
Whitman, Walt, 74
Wilde, Oscar, 72
Wilder, Laura Ingalls, 49
Williams, Robin, 59
Wodehouse, Pelham Grenville, 240
Wonky-Eye (hypothetical grandchild), 84

yacht
    cocktail bar installation on, v
Yellow Submarine (song), 81
yoga
    kitten-related, 15
Your mum
    sarcastic bastardness of, 35
    Travelodge-like qualities of, 241

Post-Script

"Dad? Are you awake?"

"No."

"That means you are."

"No, that means I am *now*. What's the matter?"

"Nothing. Fathead fell asleep and I got bored."

"Oh, right. Do you want to hang out with me for a while?"

"Okay."

"Cool. Is it okay if rest my eyes for a bit though? I was up late finishing the book."

"That's fine. I'll just watch TV."

"Thank you."

"Dad?"

"Yes, honey?"

"You know how movies sometimes have an extra bit at the end? After the credits?"

"Uh huh."

"Do books have that as well?"

"No. Not usually."

"Well, they should."

"Yes, dear."

About the Author

Kenton Hall is a Canadian author, actor, musician and director. Most importantly, however, he is a cautionary tale about the importance of having something to fall back on.

He was born in Estevan, Saskatchewan – the sunshine capital of his home country – but now lives and works in the United Kingdom, where his disposition makes more sense.

Everything in between is a bit of a blur.

If you care to find him, though we can't imagine why you'd put yourself through such a thing, he is usually pontificating in one or more of the following places:

Twitter: @**KentonHall**

Facebook: **kentonhallauthor**

Blog: **kentonhall.wordpress.com**

By the Same Human

Film

A Dozen Summers

Theatre

The Public Interest

Music

Idiopath

(with *ist*)

Toothpick Bridge
King Martha
Freudian Corduroy
I am Jesus (And You're Not)

People

Fathead and Baldy

Lightning Source UK Ltd.
Milton Keynes UK
UKHW041835190421
382278UK00001B/34